Undaunted

ALSO BY SPENCER DUNMORE

FICTION

Bomb Run (1971)

Tower of Strength (1973)

Collision (1974)

Final Approach (1976)

Means of Escape (1978)

Ace (1981)

The Sound of Wings (1984)

No Holds Barred (1987)

Squadron (1991)

NON-FICTION

Reap the Whirlwind:
The Untold Story of 6 Group, Canada's Bomber
Force of World War II (with William Carter) (1991)

Wings for Victory:
The Remarkable Story of the British Commonwealth
Air Training Plan in Canada (1994)

Above and Beyond:
The Canadians' War in the Air, 1939-45 (1996)

In Great Waters:
The Epic Story of the Battle of the Atlantic, 1939-45 (1999)

Undaunted

LONG-DISTANCE
FLYERS IN THE
GOLDEN AGE
OF AVIATION

SPENCER DUNMORE

M&S

Library and Archives Canada Cataloguing in Publication

Dunmore, Spencer, 1928–
    Undaunted : long-distance flyers in the golden age of aviation / Spencer Dunmore.

Includes index.
ISBN 0-7710-2937-3

    1. Air pilots – Biography.   2. Endurance flights – History.   3. Aeronautics – Flights – History.   I. Title.

TL539.D85 2004   629.13'0092'2   C2004-904845-7

We acknowledge the financial support of the Government of Canada through the Book Publishing Industry Development Program and that of the Government of Ontario through the Ontario Media Development Corporation's Ontario Book Initiative. We further acknowledge the support of the Canada Council for the Arts and the Ontario Arts Council for our publishing program.

Typeset in Bembo by M&S, Toronto
Printed and bound in Canada

This book is printed on acid-free paper that is 100% recycled ancient forest friendly (100% post-consumer recycled)

McClelland & Stewart Ltd.
The Canadian Publishers
481 University Avenue
Toronto, Ontario
M5G 2E9
www.mcclelland.com

1 2 3 4 5   08 07 06 05 04

CONTENTS

Acknowledgements   vii

Introduction   I

ONE: The Earliest Birds   3

TWO: Bigger Challenges   25

THREE: Triumph Down Under   54

FOUR: Girdling the Globe   63

FIVE: Atlantic Antics   74

SIX: Promoting Pineapples   109

SEVEN: Enter the Ladies   119

EIGHT: "Impenetrable Mediocrity"   146

NINE: Distant Destinations   162

TEN: Amy, Wonderful Amy   194

ELEVEN: The Mollisons   211

TWELVE: Bill and Chubbie   220

THIRTEEN: A Costly Contest   233

FOURTEEN: Pacific Tragedy   241

FIFTEEN: Breaking More Records   254

SIXTEEN: Incredible Journey   285

Epilogue   297

Switches Off   299

Bibliography   307

Notes   310

Index   315

ACKNOWLEDGEMENTS

The author is most grateful for the generous assistance of the Smithsonian Institution, particularly Bob Breesen, Melissa Keiser, and Kate Igoe. In Canada, Fiona Smith-Hale of the Canadian Aviation Museum was consistently helpful. In addition, the ladies of the Burlington Public Library worked their usual magic to find obscure volumes. Thank you.

INTRODUCTION

In 1903, the longest flight of a powered airplane stood at precisely fifty-nine seconds. It was a world record, achieved by the redoubtable Wilbur and Orville Wright in the Flyer, an aircraft of their own design. A year later, an improved Flyer stayed aloft for more than five minutes. No one took much notice. Most people didn't really believe it was happening. But during the next few years, names like Blériot, Farman, Roe, Quimby, and Rodgers began to register with a public looking for sensation. It was the beginning of an astonishing era in which long-distance flights became a major sporting event, with millions following the fortunes of the men and women who donned leather and goggles and entrusted their lives to aircraft of varying degrees of efficiency and reliability. They quickly became the heroes and heroines of the day, celebrities *par excellence*. A breathless public studied their every move. Photographs of them were printed in newspapers all over the world. Crowds lined the street when they drove by. Admired, adored, they were the crown princes and princesses of the techno-logical age. When Charles Lindbergh landed in Paris in May 1927, he was instantly transformed from unknown young airman to the most admired celebrity in the world. Others shared in the glory. Alcock and Brown, Amelia Earhart, Amy Johnson, Howard Hughes. To make a record-breaking flight in the so-called Golden Age of aviation was to gain immediate fame and, with any luck, fortune too. It was a dangerous game; few of the pioneers lived to enjoy old age. They accepted the risks. They were colourful, those early birds, willing to stake everything on the swing of a propeller. This is their story.

| *The Earliest Birds*

*H*e looked like everyone's plump favourite uncle with his flowing white moustache and his natty yachting caps. But he was no ordinary uncle; he was the celebrated Count Ferdinand von Zeppelin, who had created the amazing dirigibles that criss-crossed the sky with the assurance of railway trains. The Count had thrilled everyone with a glimpse into the world of tomorrow, when travel by air would be commonplace. No wonder he was revered throughout Germany. In August 1908, when he was seventy years old, the rotund Count announced that his dirigible LZ4 would embark on a twenty-four-hour flight. It was unprecedented, everyone said, a milestone for mankind! An entire *day* in the air! Although flights of such length had already been made, few Germans knew about them, just as few knew of the achievements of the Wright brothers in America. As far as most Germans were concerned, Zeppelin was the world's leading aeronaut.

For Zeppelin, much depended on the flight. If it was successful, the government promised to purchase the dirigible, plus an
earlier model, for a princely 2.15 million marks. Zeppelin would
be financially secure and able to proceed with the development
work he had been planning since he built his first airship ten years
before – a passion sparked by a jaunt in a balloon during the
American Civil War.

The huge crowds sang patriotic songs and buzzed with excitement as the 446-foot-long airship eased herself from her floating
shed at Manzell on the Bodensee, in the southernmost part of
Germany. She was colossal; the sight of her in the sky defied logic;
some onlookers found the experience as troubling as it was fasci-
nating. Nothing that vast could possibly be up *there*, unsupported.
Heaven only knew what dark events it all implied. With the Count
in command, LZ4 purred along the Rhine Valley on its way to Basel
and Mainz. Below, the entire population seemed to have come out
to cheer and wave flags at the incredible machine passing overhead,
the immense yet graceful form, slim and purposeful, a cogent
symbol of a new and exciting age. All Germany thrilled to the
spectacle and prayed for the Count's success. He was the hero of
the hour. Soon his airships would be travelling everywhere, not
only over Germany but throughout the world, crossing oceans as if
stepping over streams, dazzling every foreign land with the bril-
liance of German engineering.

But aboard the LZ4, everything was not well. One of its two
engines wheezed into silence. The problem was simple: lack of
fuel. Neither engine was connected to the fuel supply, so cans had
to be carried along the narrow walkways flanked by massive,
hydrogen-filled gasbags that pulsed and sighed like living organ-
isms. At the same time, the summer sun was industriously warming
the airship's hydrogen. The result was that the dirigible became

progressively lighter. LZ4 soared heavenward. At 2,700 feet, automatic valves began releasing hydrogen — a safety precaution to prevent an explosion of the gasbags.

The airship lost altitude. Hastily, the crew dumped ballast. For what seemed an eternity, the action had no effect. Then, ponderously, almost reluctantly, the descent slowed. Relieved, the Count watched the ground keep its distance. Equilibrium had been restored. The journey resumed. An hour later, the rear engine needed fuel. The whole tedious business had to be repeated; crewmen hurried along the narrow walkways laden with cans of fuel, lining up to pour them into the thirsty engines. To add to the Count's woes, a fan belt on the forward engine snapped. Quickly, the engine began to overheat. Then it failed. The crew worked feverishly but to no avail. Now insufficient power combined with cooler temperatures to force LZ4 down to ever lower altitudes. She made a safe landing near Mainz. The Count breathed again. He set the crew working on the recalcitrant engine, and soon after ten that night the huge ship eased off the ground once more — minus two crewmen and some items of equipment, because the Count had prudently decided to save a little weight.

With the engine repaired, LZ4 flew on to Mainz and, as planned, turned around and began the return journey. But the brisk wind that had helped the dirigible on the first leg was now blowing directly into the line of flight. It grew stronger. Soon an engine began to overheat. It had to be shut down. But with barely adequate power, LZ4's forward speed was pitiable — and when the remaining engine needed refuelling, the strengthening wind blew the ship backwards for a few humiliating minutes. Near Stuttgart, Zeppelin decided to land and have the troublesome engine serviced at the nearby Daimler works. The landing was smooth; the huge airship settling on a large field like some Brobdingnagian

creature in repose. Police and soldiers – and countless eager young-
sters – helped to secure her. The Count went for a nap at a local
hostelry while troops helped control the masses of people – small
fry in lederhosen, solid citizens in their Sunday best suits, and their
wives in frilly hats and white gloves – who swarmed around the
fantastic machine that had actually flown – *flown* – into their midst.

Zeppelin confidently declared that the flight would resume
shortly, once the Daimler mechanics had attended to the recalcitrant motor. But the weather turned treacherous. The winds freshened; soon they became gusty. LZ4 bucked at her moorings like a
netted elephant. The soldiers did their best, clinging to the ropes,
trying to secure her. It was impossible. While the crowd gazed,
dumbfounded, LZ4 abruptly took to the air with two crewmen and
a soldier still aboard. One of the crew gallantly made his precarious way to the forward gondola and opened the gas valve. It hissed
angrily – and at last the nose angled down toward the ground. The
ship settled back to earth. The emergency was over. Or was it? LZ4
hit a clump of trees. A rip appeared in the outer cover, and gas
began to leak. No one knew how, but a spark must have been
introduced into the equation. A tongue of flame appeared – a terrifying sight to anyone with any experience of dirigibles. The three
men hastily abandoned the enormous craft and ran for their lives.

The shattering explosion sent onlookers scattering in alarm.
Huge, hungry flames consumed the ship in a matter of minutes,
the metal framework twisting as if in agony, while burning fragments of fabric danced in the updraft. Zeppelin returned to the field
where the fire still raged. He stared, aghast. He could hardly believe
the evidence of his eyes. He was ruined. All the hopes of a lifetime
lay in the twisted, charred framework before him. It was all over: his
life's work. Everything lost. Every dream. Every hope. The crowd,
so boisterous a few minutes earlier, was silent now, respectful of

Zeppelin's tragic loss, the men doffing their hats as the count made his lonely way through the throng. (Later it was determined that the rubberized cloth of the gas cells generated static electricity when it rubbed on itself, thus producing the fatal spark.)

Zeppelin returned to his home, trying to grapple with the enormity of the disaster, resigned now to the failure of his company and the end of his dreams of dirigible travel all over the world. But something extraordinary happened, something almost magical. Fellow citizens saw his tragedy as their own, a national disaster, something involving everyone. A British politician (soon to be prime minister), David Lloyd George, happened to be visiting Stuttgart at the time and wrote, "Disappointment was a totally inadequate word for the agony of grief and dismay which swept over the massed Germans who witnessed the catastrophe. The crowd swung into the chanting of 'Deutschland über Alles,' in a fanatic fervour of patriotism." To the count's amazement, contributions and gifts, including wines and food, flooded into his home. The Kaiser himself contributed to this *largesse*. Within a matter of days, the count had more than enough money to rebuild the lz4 and fabricate others. Disaster had turned to triumph.

▌▌▌▌

Zeppelin was the first airman to capture the imagination of an entire nation. He was not the last. In France, a burly thirty-seven-year-old man with a walrus moustache and a short temper had for some years made a handsome living producing automobile accessories; it didn't satisfy him. Louis Blériot was interested in the business only as a source of funds for his real passion: designing, building, and flying airplanes. He began his aeronautical work at about the same time as the Wright brothers' first venture at Kitty

Hawk, North Carolina. Blériot's creations were nothing if not original. The first was a model omithopter – that is, with flapping wings. It did its stuff with considerable élan but steadfastly refused to leave the ground. The second Blériot aircraft was a float-mounted glider biplane which had all the instincts of a submarine when it was tested on the Seine, disappearing from view with barely a splash. Undeterred, Blériot went on to devise a float plane with ellipsoidal wings. It caught everyone's eye but never became airborne. If Blériot was discouraged, he didn't show it. He plunged into the development of a canard (tail-first) aircraft which in 1907 made a few feverish hops before smashing itself into kindling. Blériot escaped with cuts and bruises.

The Blériot VI had tandem-mounted cantilever wings with pivoting tips. It was in this aircraft that Blériot flew for the first time – without the benefit of any instruction. Blériot taught himself, no easy task for a man of impatient temperament lacking good coordination of hand, foot, and eye. The learning process cost him many broken bones, but he did succeed in mastering the controls of his aircraft, at least to a degree. It was enough for him. Fortunately, such bureaucratic impedimenta as pilots' licences weren't necessary in those first days of the twentieth century. If you wanted to fly, you simply climbed into (or onto) your aircraft, took off, and good luck to you. While Blériot may have lacked some of the characteristics of the perfect pilot, he certainly didn't lack courage. He bounced back from crash after crash, to the distress of his long-suffering wife, Alice. It was usually easy to spot him at aviation meets; he was the one on crutches with bandages adorning various parts of his anatomy.

In the early morning hours of July 25, 1909, Blériot hobbled to his monoplane, having suffered burns to his foot in a minor mishap a few days earlier. In spite of impassioned entreaties by his wife, he was about to embark on his most hazardous flight to date: an attempt to fly the English Channel.

He had competition. Another pilot of means, a jaunty young English-educated Frenchman named Hubert Latham, also wished fervently to be the first across the Channel – and to collect the one-thousand-pound prize (then worth some $5,000) offered by the London *Daily Mail*. Six days earlier, Latham had taken off from the Calais area in his Antoinette monoplane – only to end up in the water when his engine failed. He exhibited the expected degree of sang-froid: "I swung my feet onto a cross-bar to prevent them from getting wet. Then I took out my cigarette case, lit a cigarette, and waited." He was rescued unharmed, whereupon he set off for Paris and ordered a new Antoinette.

Blériot was also flying from near Calais, in an aircraft of his own design, a monoplane known as the Model X1, a frail contraption of steel tubing, ash, and bamboo covered with rubberized and water-proofed fabric. It was powered by a twenty-five-horsepower, three-cylinder engine built by Alessandro Anzani. Like all engines of the period it was crude and messy – and only intermittently reliable. The continued functioning of the motor was uppermost in Blériot's mind as he readied himself for his big test. He had nearly forty kilometres of sea to cross, a body of water notorious for its unpredictability. Blériot had installed an inflatable air bag in the rear fuselage – which was uncovered – to assist in flotation should the flight terminate in the Channel. He had been up since 2 a.m. He was cold and irritable. If it weren't for Latham, damn him, everybody could be snug in their warm beds instead of sitting on the cliffs waiting for the dawn. He had been tempted to return to his hotel but the thought of his rival stealing an aerial march on him had driven him out into the pre-dawn chill. The wind wasn't strong but it was enough to stir the aircraft; the taut fabric of the wings shivering as if in apprehension. Blériot gazed sourly about him. There was plenty to be apprehensive about. And these idiotic spectators didn't help matters. Didn't they have anything better to do with their time than stand around in the middle of the night and get in the way? Earlier, a stray dog had run into Blériot's propeller during warm-up. The unfortunate little creature had been killed instantly – a bad omen, murmured the spectators, shaking their empty heads. Blériot refused to countenance such thoughts, for they had a nasty habit of eating away at a man's confidence. He looked up at the sky, beginning to lighten now with the approach of dawn. In a few minutes it would be light enough for him to depart. The *avion* was in perfect condition. He took it for a brief test flight around Calais, a distance of about nine miles. Now he was ready for whatever the day might have in store.

At 4:41 a.m. it was time to go. The peculiarly colourless dawn light gave the scene the quality of an underdeveloped black-and-white photograph. Blériot's navigational procedures were basic; as he clambered aboard his monoplane he asked an assistant to point in the direction of Dover, invisible in the misty conditions ahead. Blériot, who had no compass, made a mental note of his approximate course. Now the ground crew took their positions, prepared to hang on to the aircraft when Blériot gave the engine full power, for there were no brakes to restrain it. Blériot advanced the throttle. The engine clattered, blasting the ground crew still clinging to the aircraft, flattening the grass around them.

At a signal from Blériot they let go. As if eager to be away, the diminutive monoplane leapt forward, the engine burbling merrily, the structure rattling, seventeen gallons of fuel sloshing about in the brass tank. The tail rose at once, borne on the moving air. Blériot worked the rudder, doing his best to keep the aircraft pointed in the right direction. The thumping of the landing gear ceased. The sand dunes slipped beneath the wings. The French ship *Escopette* came into view a moment later. Blériot's wife was on board, anticipating disaster no doubt, poor woman.

Blériot had to maintain constant forward pressure on the controls because the airborne craft had a tendency to pitch up. The all-important speed was forever tending to slip away. A few minutes of inattention and one could end up – or rather down – in the Channel.

Cloud and mist made it impossible to see far ahead. The English shoreline, supposedly dead ahead, was invisible in the haze. "I am alone," he later wrote, recalling those moments, "I can see nothing at all. For ten minutes I am lost. It is a strange position, to be alone, unguided, without compass, in the air over the middle of the Channel."

There was nothing to do but wait and see. Blériot settled back in his tiny seat, his crutch beside him. Now that the big adventure had begun, a certain calm overcame him. "I went on and on, peacefully, without any feeling, any impression of anything. . . . And the engine, what a marvel! Ah, that fine Anzani of mine, it didn't miss a turn."

Suddenly, shockingly, it did. A cough. A splutter. The aircraft shuddered. Blériot's heart missed a beat. *Sacré bleu!* The cursed abortion of an engine was overheating. In a few moments it would seize up. And he would be down. Like Latham.

Below him, the sea was a vast expanse of pewter framed by dirty cotton wool. Is that where it would all end? All his hopes? All his ambitions? A minute later . . . a miracle! According to legend, a rain shower chose that moment to put in an appearance. It was a light shower – but enough to cool the engine. It clattered on, sending a fine spray of oil into Blériot's face. The minutes ticked by. No vessel to be seen, nothing to tell him where he was. A nasty, nagging thought kept tugging at him, telling him he might have strayed to the east and was heading into the immense spaces of the North Sea. No, he refused to permit such treacherous, courage-destroying ideas. He flew on, still without seeing the horizon or any vessel. Then, another miracle: a wonderful vista. To his intense delight, he saw "a grey line in the west separating itself from the sea and getting bigger as I looked."

It was the English coast. A splendid sight. But just *where?* He studied the shoreline. It told him nothing. He had only the vaguest idea where he was. The winds had freshened since his takeoff, probably blowing him off course. The question was, how far? Ah, but here was a clue! Three ships hove into view. Were they heading for Dover? Blériot bet on it and followed them. He was low enough to see sailors lining the railing, cheering, waving their arms. More important, he could see the cliffs beyond. "Suddenly," he later wrote, "at the edge of an opening that appeared in the cliff, I saw a man desperately waving a tricolor flag."

Instantly, Blériot knew where he was. The man with the flag was a journalist named Fontaine from the Paris paper *Le Matin*. He had been positioned on the cliff to guide Blériot to his destination. Everything had worked out as planned! The flight was over – except for the tiresome business of getting the aircraft and occupant down in one piece.

Landings were Blériot's *bête noir*. The wind had picked up. Blériot could feel it nudging the aircraft as if trying to upset its equilibrium. The cliffs came for him, massive, craggy. He had to clear them, then it would be plain sailing. Fontaine and his flag slipped below. A brace of English soldiers pointed up at him, open-mouthed.

Now that he was over solid ground, Blériot reached to his left and switched off the ignition. The big mahogany propeller jerked to a halt. The air was loud now, sighing past him as if in regret that the flight was over. For his part, Blériot was overjoyed. Never had earth looked so appealing. The grass beneath him blurred into a soft sea of green. But it wasn't soft when he touched down. A thud and a bang and a splitting of timbers. The landing gear collapsed; the propeller splintered. Blériot clung on to the side of his cockpit. He was shaken but unhurt. In a moment it was all over. By Blériot's standards it was a moderately successful landing. After the clattering of the engine and the commotion of touching down, the stillness was delicious – a *symphonie* of silence. It was broken by the sound of running feet. Fontaine, the journalist, came panting to the aircraft, still clutching the flag – which he threw around Blériot's shoulders before kissing him resoundingly on both cheeks. Behind him, the two British soldiers in khaki approached cautiously, hands gripping rifles, as if fearing that all this was the beginning of an invasion. And behind them, a motley assembly of citizens. Blériot soon learnt that he had landed on Northfall Meadow, near Dover Castle.

It was 5:18 a.m. Thirty-seven minutes had elapsed since the takeoff. Not a long flight, but a highly significant one. For the first time, an aircraft had flown the English Channel. Great Britain was no longer an island.

Blériot was the man of the moment. Vast crowds mobbed him in London. More than a hundred thousand Londoners came to gape at his monoplane, on exhibition in Selfridge's department store on Oxford Street as of 9:00 o'clock the morning after the flight. Wherever he went, Blériot was cheered as a hero, although the *Daily News* hinted at the "sinister significance" of his flight. (In France, *Le Figaro* declared darkly that because of Blériot's exploit "within the foreseeable future, the condition of human life will be profoundly changed.") There were dinners and receptions, speeches and presentations. Blériot understood practically none of it, for he spoke no English. But as long as the speakers kept smiling, he reasoned that all was probably well. When he returned to Paris, the welcome was even more boisterous. Peddlers hawked photographs of him, and street musicians sang songs praising his skill and daring. His monoplane was on show for several days outside the *Le Matin*'s offices. The correspondent, Charles Fontaine, accompanied the Blériots as they toured the city in triumph. The tricolour flag that he had used as a signal on the English cliffs went along for the ride, flapping proudly at the head of the procession. Newspapers lionized him; every politician wanted to shake his hand. He knew how Napoleon must have felt. In fact, one newspaper cartoon depicted the ghost of Napoleon gazing at Blériot's airplane and lamenting, "Why not a hundred years earlier?"

Blériot found it all rather "wonderful" yet "frightening." He prospered from his cross-Channel flight, taking orders for more than a hundred monoplanes by mid-September. Three months later he crashed again, this time in Turkey, running into strong winds during an air show and colliding with a house. His aircraft was demolished but Blériot survived with only minor injuries. His luck still held.

||||

Aviation technology was advancing at a remarkable pace. Almost daily, it seemed, new records were established. In June 1910, Charles Royce (of Rolls-Royce fame) completed the first non-stop *double* crossing of the English Channel. The same year, Robert Loraine flew a Farman biplane across the Irish Sea, and a Peruvian pilot, George Chavez, managed to cross the Alps in his Blériot biplane – a feat which cost him his life.

Aerial exploits quickly became big news, and inevitably they attracted the attention of that most flamboyant of newspaper publishers, William Randolph Hearst. He had little interest in aviation, but he was intensely interested in any idea that would add to the lustre of his newspapers. Noting the public enthusiasm for the newfangled flying contraptions, he announced a fabulous prize of fifty thousand dollars for the first pilot who could fly from coast to coast across the United States in thirty days or less. His advisers had probably assured him that his money was safe. There wasn't an aircraft in existence capable of making the trip. Nevertheless, several aviators were captivated by the mere thought of it. *A fortune! A king's ransom!* Three pilots who had learned to fly at the Wright brothers' school at Simms Station, Ohio, immediately tossed their helmets into the ring. Harry Atwood, then the holder of the world's aerial distance record – 1,265 miles, with many stops along the way – journeyed more than a thousand miles from St. Louis to New York but couldn't raise the money to attempt the coast-to-coast flight. Robert Fowler flew from Los Angeles to Jacksonville, but the trip took him 112 days, putting him out of contention. Third among the hopefuls was lanky Calbraith Perry Rodgers. Brimming with confidence and good cheer, the six-foot-four-inch, two-hundred-pound Rodgers came from a family notable for its military and naval heroes. His father lost his life fighting Indians in Arizona; his grandfather was Commodore Matthew Calbraith Perry, who had established trading rights with Japan in 1854. His grand uncle, Commodore Oliver Hazard Perry, had won the Battle of Lake Erie, uttering the immortal words "We have met the enemy and they are ours." Cal himself had once entertained thoughts of a military career, but a bout of scarlet fever had left him hard of hearing. Fate had put another impediment in Cal's path to aeronautical glory: he couldn't fly a plane. But as far as Cal was concerned, that was a minor detail. He lost no time enrolling at the Wright school, where he proved himself an apt pupil, soloing after a mere ninety minutes of instruction. He invested five thousand dollars in a Wright EX – an open-cockpit "pusher," with one engine in the rear – and considered himself good and ready to take on the North American continent. He had a stroke of luck at an air show in Grant Park, Chicago, when he met the president of Armour, the meat-packing company. As it happened, Armour was about to introduce a new soft drink called Vin Fiz. To promote the concoction, Armour offered to pay Cal a generous five dollars per mile if he would advertise the product name on his airplane, for everyone to see, as he flew across the country. Delighted, Cal suggested that the underside of his wings be used as an advertising banner, the Vin Fiz name being displayed from tip to tip. The Armour people thought that a bully idea.

Confident, splendidly undaunted by his inexperience and by the total lack of airfields along his route, Cal prepared for his trip. He was eager to be away. He had calculated that he had to average two hundred miles a day to win the glittering Hearst pot. He said he could do it. And he kept on saying it. Armour was providing a train to follow Cal's airplane. His wife, Mabel, would travel in the observation car in company with various Vin Fiz executives; a baggage car was to be packed to the roof with spare parts.

At 4:24 p.m. on September 17, 1911, Rodgers took off from a racetrack near Sheepshead Bay, Brooklyn, New York, a cigar clenched firmly in his teeth. Waving to the crowds gathered below, he circled Coney Island, dropping leaflets advertising Vin Fiz before turning west. Umpteen New Yorkers gaped in wonder as he clattered over Manhattan and the Hudson River. In less than two hours he reached his first stop, Middletown, New York. The next morning, sitting in the totally exposed wicker seat, cigar jutting out at a suitably defiant angle, cap turned back to front so that the speeding air would not take the peak and whip the headgear away, he waved confidently and advanced the throttle, eager to resume his odyssey. With a roar and a rattle, the Vin Fiz headed purposefully along the grass strip — but before it could take to the air, it clipped a tree, skidded wildly, and ended up in a chicken coop. Cal suffered a few scratches and a bruise or two, nothing serious, but the Vin Fiz had need of a goodly number of spare parts from the baggage car. Four days later, his head bandaged but his cigar unbowed, Cal was in the air again, as confident as ever. Near Buffalo, a minor collision with a barbed wire fence necessitated more repairs. Cal was undeterred. In all, it took him eleven days to traverse New York State. He was making good time in Pennsylvania when he discovered to his mortification that he was painstakingly following the wrong railway track. Precious time slipped away as he consulted his charts, such as they were, while struggling to tame their frantic flapping. Over Indiana, he ran into a violent thunderstorm and had to cover the magneto with his hand to keep the engine running. Coming in for a landing at Huntingdon, Indiana, he swerved to avoid wandering spectators, and the Vin Fiz took another beating. So did Cal. The mechanics hurried to the cache of spare parts and patched up the battered Wright pusher. To raise a few dollars along the way, Mabel came up with the idea of selling postcards — with the added attraction that for twenty-five cents Cal would transport your card, "officially" rubber-stamped and bearing the proud legend: *Carried by Rodgers Aeroplane Vin Fiz*, on to the next stop along the interminable way. On October 8, Cal and his entourage arrived in Chicago to an enthusiastic welcome, then it was off to Joliet and a few turns over the penitentiary to the delight of the prisoners in the yard. In Missouri, Cal's appearance was the biggest event of the year. Schools and offices were closed so that everyone could witness the extraordinary scene. The people cheered and waved. It was a glorious moment. But Cal had problems. The odyssey with its many mishaps had taken longer than he had calculated. Hearst's deadline was drawing near. Would Mr. Hearst extend the deadline? A wire soon arrived declaring that Mr. Hearst would not extend the deadline. Cal shrugged off his disappointment. He still had the Vin Fiz contract. He would fly on and complete the cross-country trip, no matter what.

The public seemed to sense this. The crowds grew larger, the cheers louder. At Kansas City, he landed at Swope Park to an accompanying chorus of packing-house whistles. Cal gave the city "an aerial thrill the like of which it had never experienced before" in the breathless words of a local reporter. After Kansas City, Cal flew 189 miles to Vinita, Oklahoma, the best day's flying of the entire trip – and the only time he came anywhere near the goal of two hundred miles per day he had set for himself. At the Texas State Fair he stunted for a crowd estimated at seventy-five thousand. On October 18, engine trouble brought him down at Kyle, northeast of San Antonio, Texas. On October 24, he made it to Spofford, a hundred and fifty miles to the west. A splintered propeller held him up for a day there. The first of November saw him arrive at Tucson, Arizona. The end of the journey was almost in sight.

But an unkind fate had not yet finished with Calbraith Perry Rodgers. A few miles beyond Imperial, California, an engine cylinder exploded, peppering his arm with small but painful fragments of metal. Oil spattered his goggles, blinding him. He was lucky to get down without killing himself. A local doctor attended to Cal's injuries while the faithful mechanics laboured for two days in the searing heat to make a serviceable engine from the parts of two wrecks. The result was only partially successful. When he resumed his journey, Cal found the plugs working loose, followed by the failure of a connecting rod. He pulled off a successful dead-stick landing near Banning, California. On November 5, he was off again, and made it to the jam-packed Pasadena racecourse. He reported his accomplishment to the Associated Press; flower-bedecked, he was driven around the course for all to see. He had survived fifteen crashes in his forty-nine-day journey. The crowds cheered. As far as the Vin Fiz people were concerned, the trip was over. It had cost them some $180,000, and had apparently done little to popularize the purple pop. It was soon just a sticky-sweet memory, quickly forgotten. As for Cal, he had flown 4,231 miles at an average speed of 51.5 mph. He had spent a total of eighty-two hours and twenty-four minutes in the Wright's seat, exposed to everything the elements threw his way. But he hadn't completed the trip. The Pacific coast was still twenty miles away and the city of Long Beach was offering him a purse to fly there. He was glad to accept; he needed the money, desperately. The Vin Fiz subsidy had long since gone on repairs and parts. On Sunday, November 12, he took off for the last leg. True to form, he soon came thumping down again, crashing in a ploughed field, suffering a concussion, a broken ankle, and burns. Nearly a month passed before he was well enough to fly to Long Beach. On Sunday, December 10, broke but still cheerful, the usual cigar clamped between his teeth, he hobbled to his bedraggled aircraft, clambered onto his seat, tucking his crutches beside him, and took off for the final lap. It had taken him eighty-four days. He had survived five major crashes and numerous minor incidents. Most of the original components of the airplane had been replaced. The rest were in sad shape. So were Cal's finances. Since he had taken more than the prescribed thirty days on the trip, he earned fame but little cash. Hearst, one of America's richest men, seemed to feel no compulsion to pay Cal even a fraction of the fifty-thousand-dollar prize. He had come up short, therefore he got nothing.

‖‖

By now the Channel had been crossed and recrossed. What was left to prove over that narrow strip of turbulent sea? A striking green-eyed brunette named Harriet Quimby knew. A *woman* had to fly it! And she was the one to accomplish the feat. At the time, Harriet Quimby was the drama critic for *Leslie's Weekly*, an intelligent, successful woman who had carved a career for herself in a field dominated by men. She had learned to fly at the Moisant Aviation School at Hempstead, Long Island, becoming the first licensed woman pilot in the United States. (The first in the world was Elise Deroche of France, who earned her licence in 1910.) The standard fee for instruction was five thousand dollars but it seems probable that Harriet arranged for at least part of the fee to be paid in publicity, for she wrote extensively on her aerial adventures. Once qualified, Harriet joined Moisant International Aviators, one of a number of teams of flyers that performed at the air shows of the day. The attractive Harriet Quimby was a big draw, being known as the "Dresden China Aviatrix." Keenly aware of the importance of publicity, she had a purple flying suit made for herself – becoming instantly recognizable even in the air, since most of the aircraft of the day had only partially covered fuselages. In the fall of 1911, she electrified a crowd estimated at twenty thousand with a moonlit flight over Staten Island. She was the author of innumerable articles for *Leslie's* discussing aviation for women – how to learn, how to avoid dangers, how to make a living from aviation. "Driving an aeroplane is more a matter of personality than of sex, since it requires so little physical exertion. . . . It is easier than walking, driving, automobiling; easier than golf or tennis. . . . I never mount my machine until every wire and screw has been tested. I have never had an accident in the air."[1] She foresaw the day when airlines would regularly fly distances of "50 to 60 miles" between cities – with women pilots at the controls. It seems likely that the idea of becoming the first woman in the world to fly the Channel occurred to her late in 1911. It captivated her. It was her golden opportunity. Her name would be spoken along with M. Blériot's. She would be famous all over the world, providing a huge boost for both her careers – journalism and aviation.

She sailed for England in March 1912 on the Hamburg–America liner *Amerika*. On arrival, she went to see the editor of the *Daily Mirror*, who offered her "a handsome inducement" to make the flight as the *Mirror*'s representative. She then crossed to France to see Louis Blériot to arrange for the loan of one of his monoplanes – similar to the craft that had carried him across the Channel in 1909, but with a more powerful engine. She had never flown the Blériot, but that didn't deter her. She would have plenty of time back in England to learn its intricacies before the flight.

As it happened, the frightful English weather left her very little time at all. Rain and high winds plagued her day after day. Gustav Hamel, a noted British aviator, did his best to instruct her in the handling of the aircraft and the workings of the compass, which she had never used. Hamel was frankly dubious about her chances and even offered to fly the Channel dressed in her purple costume to bamboozle the public. Hamel was particularly concerned about her ability to find France unless the visibility improved greatly. His concern was valid; an error of a few degrees could send her out into the lonely seas far from solid ground.

On the misty morning of April 16 she donned "two pairs of silk combinations" under her flying suit, plus a hot water bottle which, she said, Gustav Hamel insisted "on tying to my waist like an enormous locket." At 5:30 a.m., she set off, plunging into walls of mist that enveloped her small airplane, chilling her to the bone. Unable to see more than a few feet in any direction, she kept her eyes glued to the compass, its quivering needle her only visual link with the outside world. She flew on, through mass after endless mass of haze and fog. The grey blanket cleared momentarily. "Far beneath me I saw the *Mirror's* tug, with its stream of black smoke. It was trying to keep ahead of me but I passed it in a jiffy. Then the thickening fog obscured my view. Calais was out of sight. I could not see ahead of me at all nor could I see the water below. There was only one thing for me to do and that was to keep my eyes fixed on the compass. My hands were covered with long, Scotch woollen gloves, which gave me good protection from the cold and fog; but the machine was wet and my face was so covered with dampness that I had to push my goggles up on my forehead. I could not see through them."[2]

Could the compass be deceiving her? The same doubts that had haunted Blériot came to nag at her. The strip of water that had looked so insignificant on the map seemed never-ending now, a vast ocean invisible beneath curtains of mist that kept parting – only to reveal more mist.

Then, like a signal from heaven, "Sunlight struck upon my face and my eyes lit upon the white and sandy shore of France." She had done it! Her original destination had been Calais, but no matter . . . a beach lay before her, white and inviting. Without delay she reduced power and descended. Below her, the smooth expanse of sand stretched ahead, a perfect place to land!

She touched down at a place called Hardelot, a tiny fishing village some twenty-five miles south of Calais. Within minutes, excited crowds surrounded her. Harriet spoke no French, but the villagers soon knew that they had in their midst the first woman in the world to fly the English Channel. They gave her a hero's welcome, hoisting her on their shoulders and carrying her in triumph along the beach. One woman provided her with a very welcome cup of hot tea and a cheese sandwich.

Sadly, Harriet Quimby didn't win the global fame she expected. On the day of her flight, the world's newspapers had little space to devote to anything as trivial as a cross-Channel hop. A far bigger story had captured the headlines: the sinking of the liner *Titanic* after colliding with an iceberg. Events had outmanoeuvred Harriet in a particularly unfortunate way. At another time, her flight would have been headline news; but on that day, she rated only a few lines in the back pages.

Another aviatrix, a young American named Ruth Law, installed extra fuel tanks on her aging Curtiss pusher and set off to fly from Chicago to New York. A man, Victor Carlstrom by name, had attempted the same flight in November 1916; a broken fuel pipe had brought him down at Erie, Pennsylvania. Ruth Law possessed both courage and imagination. Facing a chilly trip to New York in her open-cockpit aircraft, she had an aluminum windshield installed to protect her legs and feet. What's more, she cut her maps into strips and glued them onto thin cloth and made a camera-like mechanism so that she might roll the maps during the trip – which lasted nearly six hours in cool, blustery fall weather. She could turn her map with one hand while she flew with the other. She made her way east, landing at Homell, New York, after flying a record 590 miles non-stop. She received a tumultuous welcome from the President and Mrs. Wilson and such luminaries as Admiral Robert E. Peary.

Other flyers were just as anxious to make their mark in the long-distance stakes. André Beaumont became the first pilot to fly from Paris to Rome, Jules Vedrines flew from Paris to Cairo; Roland Garros managed – just – to cross the Mediterranean. What an amazing age! Soon, declared the pundits, airplanes would strike out across the world's oceans, challenging the vast expanses and the treacherous weather. But first came the Great War.

CHAPTER TWO | *Bigger Challenges*

If William Randolph Hearst had a rival, it was surely the shamelessly jingoistic Alfred, Lord Northcliffe, proprietor of the London *Daily Mail*. In 1910 he had galvanized the entire aviation community with the most exciting challenge yet: a whopping ten thousand pounds (then worth some fifty thousand dollars) for the pilot who completed the 186-mile flight from London to Manchester within twenty-four hours. A Frenchman, Louis Paulhan, won it after a difficult trip in cold, blustery conditions. Among the spectators who watched Paulhan's arrival at Manchester was a young apprentice engineer at Vickers named John Alcock. Three years later, Northcliffe would capture headlines with the offer of a similar prize for the first flight across the Atlantic – and Alcock would be one of the flyers to go after it. The *Daily Mail* prize was offered for the first crossing "in an aeroplane in flight from any point in the United States, Canada, or Newfoundland, to any point in Great Britain or Ireland in 72 consecutive hours." Any "intermediate stoppages" could be made on the water. Towing was not prohibited, provided the pilot resumed the flight from the point where he landed. The rules stated that the flight could be made from land or water.

The Great War intervened – which was probably just as well, considering the state of aeronautical science at the time. Alcock joined the Royal Naval Air Service. He was a good pilot, shooting down seven German aircraft; but engine trouble succeeded where the enemy had failed, bringing him down in the Sea of Marmara, Turkey. He spent several months in a prisoner of war camp, where thoughts of flying the Atlantic and winning Northcliffe's colossal prize were seldom far from his mind. At the time, Alcock must have been one of the most experienced pilots in the world. He had learned to fly in 1910 – by the unusual method of sitting behind a French pilot named Maurice Ducrocq and following his movements during takeoff, turning, and landing. A quick study, Alcock had two hours of this form of dual instruction before embarking on solo flight. He took part in some of the first aerial races in Britain, coming third in the London–Manchester–London race held just before the outbreak in 1914 of war. He also raced cars and motorcycles with some success. After the Armistice, the twenty-six-year-old Alcock returned to England and lost no time going to Vickers to look for a job. His timing was impeccable. The company had decided to go after the *Daily Mail* prize using a modified version of their new Vimy bomber – and was just then recruiting a crew. Alcock was hired as pilot.

Typical of many large aircraft of the day, the Vimy (named after the celebrated Canadian victory of 1917) was an angular creation, a heavily braced biplane held together by a forest of struts and wires, hard work to fly but powered by two excellent Rolls-Royce Eagle engines. The Vimy had been designed as what would later be known as a strategic bomber; it was capable of reaching and bombing Berlin, but the war ended before it saw service. Despite its many shortcomings, it was an efficient aircraft for its day. Although the Vickers engineers calculated that the Vimy would be about one thousand pounds overweight on takeoff, they believed her capable of crossing the Atlantic, cruising at a steady one hundred miles per hour all the way. Alcock liked the aircraft and had no hesitation in signing on.

A few days later, a young man in RAF uniform came to Vickers looking for a job. His name was Arthur Whitten Brown. Born in England of American parents, he had, like Alcock, been brought up in Manchester. On the outbreak of war in 1914, he joined the British army, later transferring to the Royal Flying Corps. He was shot down and captured during a bombing raid, seriously injuring his leg, and thereafter used a walking stick. During the dreary months of imprisonment, he studied navigation from books supplied by the Red Cross. He became an expert.

Originally intended to accommodate a crew of three, the Vimy was modified to become a two-seat aircraft for the transatlantic flight. The aircraft's fuel capacity was increased to over eight hundred gallons, giving her a range of some 2,500 miles, sufficient for the journey from Newfoundland, providing the weather co-operated – which was a question mark, since it would be years before any system of Atlantic weather reporting was introduced. The best Alcock and Brown could hope for was a local report, and a great deal of luck. The Vimy's wingspan was just over sixty-eight feet and her weight in transatlantic form was thirteen thousand pounds.

Alcock and Brown hit it off at once. They were an interesting study in opposites. Alcock, the ebullient pilot, supremely confident and apparently indifferent to danger. Brown, the quieter, more introspective individual, engrossed in his sums and his reading, painstakingly studying Atlantic weather patterns and weighing factors like a scientist. Brown told Alcock that he had recently become engaged but had yet to explain to his fiancée, Kathleen Kennedy, that the marriage must wait until he had flown all the way across the Atlantic. He was not looking forward to the task.

Alcock and Brown sailed to Halifax, Nova Scotia, aboard the liner *Mauretania*, completing the journey to Newfoundland by rail and ferry. They arrived to find a rugged, rocky island inhabited by good-natured people speaking an odd *patois*, a curious combination of English, Irish, and Scottish, with a touch of American/ Canadian thrown in for good measure. The young men discovered that they were not the only aviators in Newfoundland with transatlantic aspirations. Several others had set out to become the first across the dangerous ocean and lay claim to Lord Northcliffe's ten thousand pounds. There was the ruddy-faced extrovert Australian Harry Hawker and his British navigator, Mackenzie Grieve, in their Sopwith Atlantic, a big single-engine biplane; Frederick Raynham and C.F.W. Morgan with their Martinsyde; Admiral Kerr, Major Brackley, and Major Gran in their massive Handley Page V1500 with its four Rolls-Royce Eagle engines. Like Alcock and Brown's Vimy, the V1500 had been designed for war but hadn't been completed in time.

All these flyers had to create their own airfields, for Newfoundland possessed not one in all its more than 150,000 square miles of rocky, hilly territory. The early arrivals had already struck deals for the few reasonably level sites. Raynham and Morgan had a meadow near Quidi Vidi Lake, half a mile from St. John's. Hawker and Grieve had taken possession of an L-shaped field near Mount Pearl, six miles from the city. Admiral Kerr — a doughty old salt of fifty-five who had served in the last of the Royal Navy's wooden frigates, HMS *Newcastle*, and had won his pilot's wings at the age of forty-nine – went further afield, selecting a site near Harbour Grace, some sixty miles away. A great deal of work had to be done to ready it for use, including the demolition of several farm buildings and walls and the levelling of the uneven ground. When Alcock approached Kerr about using the strip, the admiral agreed – but only if the Vimy team picked up half the cost of the preparatory work, and only if Alcock agreed not to take-off until the Handley Page had departed. Alcock turned the offer down. He and Brown explored the island in an elderly Buick, looking for suitable sites, eventually settling for a meadow with a swamp at one end. It wasn't ideal, but, with a modicum of luck, it would do.

While the airmen prepared for their flights, they lived in a state of perpetual tension, every man tormented by the thought that one of the other crews might get away first. For the locals, the influx of Atlantic hopefuls and their aircraft was the most exciting event in years – although few expected any of the flyers to be successful. They were nice enough young fellers but no match for the Atlantic; it was too big, too unpredictable. In fact, two aspirants had already failed. A Swede, Hugo Sunstedt, lost his aircraft when it crashed into the sea off Bayonne, New Jersey, with another pilot at the controls. He survived. A British competitor, Major J.C.P. Wood, took off from Eastchurch, England, but ditched in the sea near Holyhead, Wales, with engine trouble.

||||

While the Atlantic hopefuls were readying themselves and their aircraft in Newfoundland, the United States Navy caught most of them by surprise by announcing its intention of flying the big ocean. Not with one airplane. With a *formation*. The other competitors thought the Americans more than a little unfair. They had an entire navy behind them, complete with an armada of ships and heaven knows how many people. Not for them the lonely flight of a single aircraft; neither did they intend to conquer the ocean in one hop. In what seemed more like a naval pageant than a long-distance flight, a formation of big (126-foot span) Navy-Curtiss, or NC, flying boats was about to tackle the "pond" by stages. Four of the big "Nancies," as they were popularly known, had been under construction at the time of the Armistice. The Navy had intended to fly them to the war zone, but the war had ended before the plan could be put into action. The Navy wanted to demonstrate that, in the event of war, a thousand seaplanes might be *flown* to the war zone if needed.[1] Every phase of the operation appeared to have been organized by a committee charged with the responsibility of ensuring success, no matter what the cost. The goal of the flight was Portugal, with a refuelling stop in the Azores. And to assist the flyers on their journey, the way was to be marked by a line of destroyers, forty-one in all. The ships were ordered to signal to the Nancies as they passed, making smoke so that the airborne navigators could check on wind speed and direction. At night, the ships were to "torch" their funnels and fire rockets to make themselves visible to the aircraft above.

The Nancies were cumbersome contraptions with boat-like hulls to which were attached wings and tails by means of forests of booms and struts – a collection of spare parts flying in close formation, someone called them. One of the aircraft, NC-2, had been damaged in a dock fire; she was dismantled for spares. The Navy declared that their aircraft were not competing for the *Daily Mail* prize; the flight was being undertaken purely for "scientific purposes."

Commander John Towers led the expedition, having selected NC-3 as his flagship. Towers was a short, assertive individual, determined to succeed in his mission come what may. He assigned NC-1 to Lieutenant Commander P.N.L. (Pat) Bellinger, and NC-4 to Lieutenant Commander Albert C. (Putty) Read.

On May 8, 1919, the three Nancies took off from Jamaica Bay, New York, capturing the biggest headlines since the Armistice. With NC-3 in the van, they formed a neat "V" as they headed for Newfoundland. Each aircraft carried a crew of four, wearing fur-lined flying suits over their naval uniforms, silk socks under woollen ones, and fur-lined boots and helmets. At the same time, a Navy dirigible, C-5, slipped her moorings at Cape May, New Jersey. Although Navy spokesmen stoutly denied it, the rumour began to gain momentum that C-5 might also attempt an Atlantic crossing. After all, it was common knowledge that the British were preparing their dirigible, R-34, for a shot at it.

The Nancies droned on in perfect formation. Walter Hinton, pilot of NC-4, later wrote, "The stars came out cheerily. We put the NC-4 up to 1,000 feet. Ahead and so far below that she looked like a toy on a lake in the park, we saw a destroyer brilliantly lighted and sending star shells up to signal her position. We checked her off the chart. The destroyers were passed as regularly as railway stations. The moon seemed to appear as if by magic, and its rays brightened the edges of the wings and glinted off the helmets of the men in the open cockpits, as one after another we went off watch and below, inside the hull, where there were sandwiches and hot coffee."

Near Cape Cod, NC-4 reported by radio that she was experiencing trouble with her Liberty engines. First one, then a second gave out. The big boat came down one hundred miles off Cape Cod to effect repairs. Two of the four Nancies were now out. The Navy ordered NC-1 and NC-3 to continue to Trepassey Bay in Newfoundland and complete the Atlantic flight as soon as weather permitted.

But when would that be? At Trepassey Bay, the winds became stronger with every passing day. The crews could do little but keep their aircraft ready for flight at short notice. Interest in the venture intensified. A contingent of reporters arrived and set up house in a press car, which soon became known as Nancy 5. The local children had never had it so good, with dazzling quantities of candies coming from the airmen. The excitement intensified as the cruiser *Chicago* nosed into St. John's harbour to serve as the base ship for the blimp, C-5. It looked as if those early rumours had been accurate: the Americans were determined to conquer the Atlantic with lighter-than-air as well as heavier-than-air machines.

Yet another in an apparently endless series of gales swept in on May 15 while the C-5 was moored. The blimp bucked and bounced like a maddened beast. A hundred sailors from the *Chicago* couldn't tame her. Bravely, Lieutenant Charles G. Little clambered up to deflate her. But when he yanked the rope to vent some gas, it snapped. Little, and two sailors, had to jump more than twenty feet; they escaped in the nick of time, but a couple of boys in the crowd were injured slightly by the backlash of a broken line. The bulbous blimp shot skyward. Although a destroyer attempted to give chase and shoot it down, the C-5 went bounding out to sea, never to be seen again.

Later that same day the weather improved. Towers decided to set off on the transatlantic trip, even though NC-4 was still on her way from Cape Cod. He said he hated the thought of starting without Read, but a break in the weather was too important to miss.

Towers soon found that getting airborne was easier said than done. A vigorous crosswind had developed – a common phenomenon in Newfoundland. Twice the big flying boats thundered across Trepassey Bay, creating impressive wakes but failing absolutely to get into the air. Twice they had to admit defeat and return to their moorings. During the second attempt, a speck appeared in the sky, growing larger by the minute. It was the NC-4, back in the air after diligent work by mechanics. Towers's formation of three surviving aircraft was complete again.

The next day, late in the afternoon, Towers ordered his crews to ready themselves for departure. The usual onlookers gathered on shore to watch the preparations: the harsh buzzing of the engines, the endless swarming of the maintenance crews over every inch of the lumbering aircraft swaying at their moorings, the testing and retesting of every control, the curt, matter-of-fact farewells, the bursts of power as the boats taxied to their takeoff positions . . . then, a ragged cheer as the Nancies bellowed over the water, and rose. Airborne at last!

They headed in the direction of the Azores, following the line of assembled destroyers. While the presence of the ships was undoubtedly good for the flyers' morale, it almost precipitated disaster. Because of dense cloud, the formation of Nancies had climbed, levelling off at 4,500 feet. The destroyers were ordered to adjust their star shells to burst at 4,000 feet. But something went wrong. Towers's aircraft, NC-3, was nearly brought down when a star shell exploded directly beneath one wing. The idea of flying in formation across the ocean also created problems. Several hours into the flight, as the visibility deteriorated, NC-1 and NC-3 came frighteningly close to colliding, missing each other by a matter of inches.

The weather worsened. Soon the wispy mist became thick fog. The pilots had to fly blind on the planes' primitive instruments. Read almost lost NC-4 in cloud but got control again when the sun peeped through the murk and provided a fleeting visual reference. The science of blind flying was little more than theory in 1919. An airman's competence tended to be measured by how well he could fly "by the seat of his pants." Few pilots understood how dangerous it was to trust his own instincts in poor visibility.

The formation became scattered. Pat Bellinger in NC-1 was experiencing the worst problems, flying at less than one hundred feet above the heaving sea. Something was seriously wrong with the controls, and the combined strength of both pilots was required to keep her on track. (Bellinger's pilot was Marc Mitscher, who would become a renowned admiral in the Pacific during the Second World War.) Bellinger, having lost sight of the other aircraft, was becoming increasingly concerned about his position. One thing he did know: the volcanic island of Pico couldn't be far away. He imagined it, thrusting more than seven thousand feet out of the ocean near the Azores. In these misty conditions he might easily fly straight into it. He decided to land and take stock, but the sea proved far rougher than he had anticipated. Bellinger touched down, and immediately lost part of his tail unit to a violent wave. The crew had to bail the seawater out of the pitching hull to stay afloat.

At least the radio still worked, and a series of urgent SOSes brought a Greek freighter to the scene. The airmen quickly boarded her, thankful to be alive.

The American plan to keep the aircraft in constant touch by radio proved impractical. Intense vibration and the crackle of static from forty-eight spark plugs per aircraft made intelligible reception impossible. The weather worsened at dawn. Driving rain was followed by fog. Soon, inevitably, visual references were lost. Instinct took over, deceptive as ever. Putty Read in NC-4 suddenly became aware that one wing was angled down. The compass needle was revolving like the hands of a clock gone mad. He was navigating at the time and he had no intercom. He had to signal to the pilot, who didn't appear to comprehend – until a tiny break in the fog gave him the visual references he needed to pull the aircraft into straight and level flight. Read breathed again. Another moment or two and the plane would have spun into the ocean.

Towers was low on fuel. He made the same decision as had Bellinger. It was time to put down and review the situation. He didn't know it, but his radio had stopped transmitting hours before. No one knew where he was. He descended cautiously, passing through layer after miasmic layer, the visibility worsening, the aircraft lurching uneasily. Suddenly the murk cleared. The ocean was mere feet below. No room to pull out. The Nancy hit the waves with a violent, cracking blow that sounded like a gunshot. Towers would not have been surprised had the flying boat disintegrated around him. But it stayed in one piece. And it floated. A little water was finding its way into the hull. Not a lot, but enough, he calculated, to prevent him taking to the air again.

Read in NC-4 was no more certain of his position than were any of the others. But he was luckier – and in the business of long-distance flying, luck counted for a great deal. The clouds of fog parted, revealing a most glorious sight: the small island of Corvo, in the Azores, bathed in sunlight. Now Read knew where he was. He flew on to Horta and landed in the sheltered harbour. Two days later he flew the short trip to Ponta Delgada, at the eastern end of the collection of islands, anticipating a departure for Lisbon in a day, two at the most. The Atlantic had other ideas. Capricious as always, it abruptly decided to become stormy again.

The other two Nancies out at sea had their share of bad luck and good. Bellinger, Mitscher, and their crew had been rescued, but their NC-1 had been sunk by a shot from a destroyer after repeated and unsuccessful attempts to take it in tow. And what of NC-3? The usual declarations of confidence among the others gradually gave way to resignation. The Atlantic was tough; everyone knew it; everyone had accepted the risks.

Then, the unexpected happened. Again. Word arrived from a U.S. Marine battery stationed in the hills west of Ponta Delgada that the missing Nancy was at this very moment taxiing into port. Despite the bad weather the crew had managed to keep the flying boat from sinking while the elements did their utmost to tear it to pieces. At one point, crewmen had to stand on a wing tip to balance the craft. Fortunately the wind abruptly shifted, helping to push the boat toward the Azores.

Amazingly, the crippled Nancy had drifted and taxied for more than two hundred miles. A U.S. Navy destroyer offered to take the aircraft in tow. Towers said no. He was determined that NC-3 should make her own way to port. And she did.

On May 27, Read and his crew aboard NC-4 flew from Horta, Azores, to Lisbon in a nine-hour, forty-three-minute trip. On arrival, Read radioed base: "We are safely on the other side of the pond. The job is finished."

||||

While the Nancies were still making their uncertain way to Portugal, Harry Hawker and Mackenzie Grieve lifted their Sopwith Atlantic off the rough turf of Glendenning's Farm, half a dozen miles from St. John's, Newfoundland. As they passed over Quidi Vidi, they saw Raynham and Morgan preparing for their own departure. The airmen waved a friendly greeting. Raynham and Morgan seemed unconcerned by their rivals' departure. They knew that their Martinsyde was faster than the Sopwith and would soon overtake the other aircraft. A crowd of two thousand had gathered to watch the takeoff, much as the Roman crowds gathered to watch chariot races, readying themselves for the mayhem to come. Something was sure to go wrong.

Hawker was pleased at the way the Sopwith was performing with its back-breaking load of fuel. The coast of Newfoundland slipped beneath the wings. A tug on a lever in the cockpit released the landing gear, adding seven miles per hour to the aircraft's speed but promising a bumpy landing on skids at the end of the journey. Relieved of the extra weight, the Sopwith climbed through the mist that seemed to be a permanent feature of this part of the world. The broad Atlantic lay ahead, a vast expanse of water, totally unpredictable, brutally unforgiving. It was, declared the *New York Times*, "the start of the most perilous airplane flight in history." The aircraft seemed absurdly insignificant, a noisy little insect cheekily buzzing its way into a frightening unknown. The airmen were glad of the electrical heating that had been provided for their Burberry flying suits. Another modification was a tiny boat built into the aft fuselage, easily detachable and reasonably seaworthy. If the worst came to the worst, it might support them long enough for a ship to come and rescue them. The land had dissolved into the mist behind, back where the ground was solid and the sea a thing of beauty in the safe and secure distance. Ahead, the sky was dark with the approach of night. The weather began to deteriorate. Turbulence tossed the biplane about like a leaf.

Engine running well, on course, thirty minutes elapsed. Speed, a steady 105 miles per hour. Nothing to see but cloud and glimpses of pewter-coloured water, an endless expanse of it. The clouds thickened. The aircraft bounced as turbulence battered her. Soon the sky darkened; the ocean vanished beneath a curtain of cloud. Night cloaked the scene. The two airmen snuggled down in their cockpits, warm enough in their thick flying gear, their entire world pulsating with the engine.

The radio failed. The airmen weren't surprised; radios were always failing.

They had travelled some six hundred miles when Hawker noticed that the reading on the water-circulation thermometer was high. He opened the shutters over the radiator. It didn't help. Indeed, it seemed to make it worse. The thermometer was acting up? No, the temperature had risen from 168 to 176 degrees Fahrenheit even though he was giving the radiator maximum ventilation. Hawker cursed his luck. After all the planning, all the hoping, to be brought down by something as *paltry* as rotten little bits of rust and solder in the radiator blocking the filter, for that's what he was sure was the trouble. Steam was already issuing from the radiator, wisps of it streaking back toward the cockpits. Hawker shook his helmeted head in frustration. The damned thing was only a few feet away, yet totally out of reach. What to do? He stopped the engine, and the sound of rushing air was suddenly deafening. Hawker was trying an old trick: stop the engine and dive so that the accumulation would spread itself and the filter could clear it.

Down, down, down, from twelve thousand feet to nine thousand feet, the wires whining, the structure quivering. He levelled out. Restarted the engine. Waited. Relieved, he saw the temperature remaining steady. He grinned. They were going to defeat those bits of metal after all.

Or were they? After a few minutes the temperature needle began to climb again. Impatient raps on the glass of the instrument accomplished nothing. The needle kept rising. Heart heavy with the thought of failure, Hawker switched off the engine and glided down almost to sea level before starting the engine again. The engine temperature had dwindled satisfactorily. But not for long. Soon the needle began its inexorable climb while Hawker gazed at the dials with the intensity of a surgeon monitoring a desperately ill patient. Steam spouted out of the engine, condensing and freezing on the fuselage and on the upper wing. The engine cut out. Hawker yelled to Grieve to pump fuel into the carburetor. Down through the clouds sank the biplane. The wind sang a disconsolate song through the Sopwith's wires as the biplane emerged from the cloud. The angry sea lay directly below, no more than ten feet away, a vague but awful presence in the darkness. Hawker called to Grieve to prepare for ditching.

But at that moment, the engine came back to life with a clattering roar. The relieved airmen took the aircraft up to ten thousand feet – whereupon the engine immediately began to overheat yet again. Hawker wearily resigned himself to the inevitable. The engine was methodically committing suicide. It couldn't possibly keep going much longer and soon he was going to land in that heaving sea. He had no choice. Thank goodness he had jettisoned the landing gear. It would make the water landing a little easier – he hoped.

Hawker and Grieve decided on a course of action. They would look for a ship and ditch beside her. It seemed the best plan. In fact, the only plan.

||||

Within an hour of Hawker and Grieve's departure, the Martinsyde team of Raynham and Morgan clambered aboard their aircraft. Dubbed the *Raymor* after the names of the crew, it was faster than the Sopwith. But would it get off the ground? Raynham did his best to dismiss any doubts on the matter as he ran up the motor. The engine sounded healthy. But the enormous weight of fuel would undoubtedly make the biplane a handful to control on the ground. As to its behaviour in the air, well, time enough to worry about that. Much later. Raynham noted the brisk crosswind. He had coped with gusty crosswinds umpteen times before. The trick was to take command from the start. Never let the aircraft have the initiative.

Time to go. A not-a-care-in-the-world wave to the onlookers. Someone doffed a trilby in formal response. The big biplane began to roll. Slowly, methodically, she picked up speed. And with speed came trouble. Never had Raynham had to contend with such a grossly overburdened machine. The smallest adjustment of the controls set off violent swings. The Martinsyde careered one way, then the other, its undercarriage groaning under the awful strain. Raynham corrected as the plane swung to one side. It swung the other way. Again, Raynham corrected, and frantically re-corrected, the overloaded aircraft. Engine roaring at full throttle, the biplane dashed across the field in a wild zigzag. Raynham knew that the strain on the undercarriage was critical, probably insupportable. The question was whether the aircraft could be coaxed into the air before the gear collapsed. Engine bellowing, she dashed over the rough Newfoundland turf, vibrating, trembling as if eager to take to the air. But it was all too much for the wood and metal taking the load. As the end of the strip loomed large, the landing gear collapsed with a sort of weary groan like a man abandoning an unequal burden. The Martinsyde skidded to a stop in a cloud of dust. Luckily, there was no fire. Raynham scrambled from his cockpit unhurt, but Morgan received a nasty blow to the head. The *Raymor* was out of the running.

Meanwhile, what of Hawker and Grieve? Nothing had been heard from the aircraft – and no one on the ground knew that the radio was out of action. The same calculations obsessed countless people: so much fuel, so many hours. By now, the Sopwith should have been spotted approaching solid ground. Its fuel supply could last no more than twenty-two hours. Had the Sopwith crashed? Were the airmen dead? Harry Hawker's wife refused to believe it.

No matter that flags in Newfoundland were already flying at half-mast, Harry, she told anyone who would listen, was alive. There were dutiful nods of agreement. Harry was all right. So was Mac. They would soon be home. No doubt about it.

But as the days crept by, hopes dimmed. Someone at Buckingham Palace sent Hawker's wife a telegram, and there was little comfort in the words: "The King, fearing the worst must now be realized regarding the fate of your husband, wishes to express his deep sympathy and that of the Queen in your sudden and tragic sorrow. His Majesty feels that the nation has lost one of its most able and daring pilots, who sacrificed his life for the fame and honour of British flying."

But even kings can be confounded. On May 25, a Sunday, an astonishing thing happened. A cable arrived in Newfoundland. Incredibly, it declared that Hawker and Grieve were safe. The details soon emerged. Nursing their ailing motor, Hawker and Grieve had spotted a ship through sheets of rain. They dived and fired three Very light distress flares. At first the flares seemed to have no effect, but then the crew of the small Danish ship *Mary* began to emerge on deck to see what the commotion was about.

The sea was rough, but Hawker managed to put the Sopwith down in a trough between the powerful waves. Only his skill prevented the aircraft breaking up and sinking immediately. The two airmen scrambled into their emergency lifeboat and detached it from the Sopwith as they had practised so many times. The angry sea didn't make it any easier, tossing the downed aircraft around like so much jetsam. Conditions were so bad, it took some ninety minutes for the boat to reach the downed flyers. Clinging to the wreckage of the Sopwith, Hawker and Grieve were cold, wet, and uncomfortable, but alive. Gratefully, they clambered aboard the small tramp steamer – to discover that she carried no radio. Thus the amazing news of the mid-Atlantic rescue remained a secret until the *Mary* transferred her passengers to a British destroyer off the Scottish coast.

An enthusiastic welcome awaited the airmen in London; indeed, their reception could hardly have been better had they succeeded in crossing the ocean. Hawker and Grieve were the heroes of the hour, and the *Daily Mail* awarded them a consolation prize of five thousand pounds.

Interestingly, the wrecked Sopwith stayed afloat for several days and was picked up by a passing ship and brought back to England. The sad remains were exhibited at Selfridge's department store on Oxford Street, where, ten years earlier, Blériot's monoplane had been on display. Later, there appeared to be some evidence that the aircraft's radiator may have been assembled incorrectly. When the cooling louvres were pushed open, they in fact closed, *increasing* the temperature of the engine. Hawker and Grieve had been doomed to failure before they took off.

▋▋▋▋

Alcock was supremely confident. "All we have to do is keep the engines going and we'll be home for tea," he declared, never admitting to a single doubt about the Atlantic flight. Brown was less sanguine, all too aware of the array of difficulties that would face them over the world's most violent ocean.

In England, the Vimy had been dismantled and packed into four large crates – one for the fuselage, two for the wings, and one for the engines – and sent off to Newfoundland by freighter. Although the teams of Hawker and Grieve and Raynham and Morgan were no longer in the running, the formidable Handley Page V1500 and its crew still represented a threat. With a wingspan of 126 feet and four Rolls-Royce Eagle engines, the V1500 had a crew of five with two pilots, Admiral Mark Kerr and Major H.G. Brackley. The smart money was said to be on Admiral Kerr's crew, if for no other reason than that they had the best field in Newfoundland.

The crates containing the Vimy and her engines arrived on May 26. Vickers had sent a team of mechanics to assemble the plane on the bleak shore of Quidi Vidi Lake. A local drayman named Lester said he knew of a field that might be suitable for getting the Vimy into the air. The two flyers drove out to see it. It was only three hundred yards long, but a further two hundred yards of more-or-less-open land lay beyond it. A few trees would have to be felled and some boulders moved, but it definitely had possibilities. A disadvantage was the slight incline. It meant that the takeoff run would be uphill. Not ideal. But as long as the wind was blowing in the right direction, it would probably be all right, they hoped. Alcock dubbed it Lester's Field, "The first transatlantic aerodrome."

As the work of assembling the Vimy and preparing the landing field proceeded, the impatient flyers called daily at the naval station at Mount Pearl to ask about the weather over the Atlantic. The response was not encouraging. All that could be said for certain was that there was no improvement. Mist and rain. Day after day. There was a good deal of time to ruminate, to keep weighing the chances of success. "Rather amusingly," said Brown, "the numeral '13' figured a great deal in the preliminaries. It dogged our steps. Erection of the bomber was started February 13. There were 13 men in our party. The machine was the thirteenth of its class. When Alcock and I, with seven mechanics, landed in advance of the rest, the date was May 13. And it just occurred to me last night that the air voyage across the Atlantic was made in the year which was the four hundred and twenty-seventh anniversary of Columbus's discovery. Add the numerals 4-2-7, and you have thirteen!"[2]

Early in June, the flyers were dismayed to see Admiral Kerr's Handley Page droning overhead. Had the crafty blighter beaten them to the takeoff? No, the big biplane turned and headed back toward Harbour Grace. A test flight, that was all. Everyone breathed again.

On Monday, June 9, Alcock took the Vimy up. The test went well, except that the radio failed and the fuel supply was found to be contaminated by a gummy residue. Vickers had had the foresight to provide a fresh supply of fuel, a mixture of gasoline and benzol that was supposed to be easier on the engines' valves than gasoline alone. The crew poured it into the Vimy's tanks, a canful at a time.

It was a tense time for the two teams. They lived in an agony of suspense, and dreaded hearing the news that the competition had got away ahead of them. What Alcock and Brown didn't know was that the Admiral Kerr team had encountered technical trouble with their cooling system. The big Handley Page was out of commission while parts for the troublesome radiators made the long journey from England to Newfoundland.

It was a totally unexpected break. As day succeeded day, Alcock and Brown watched as Kerr's head start dwindled and disappeared. It was neck and neck.

On Friday, June 13, Jack Alcock ordered the Vimy refuelled. They would leave early the next day, June 14. But the weather wrecked those plans. A boisterous wind was blowing directly across the strip. Any attempt to take off in those conditions would have ended in disaster.

Alcock decided to wait for better weather. By afternoon, after a meal eaten under the Vimy's broad wing, he decided they would go. There was fog around, as well as drizzle and rain, but in this part of the world, conditions would probably not improve all that much, no matter how long they waited. The two airmen clambered aboard and took their seats, pilot and navigator side by side in the large cockpit. The wind was blowing at about forty miles per hour, but at least it was in the right direction now. The Vimy's overall weight had risen to over five tons. Provisions for the crew included sandwiches, chocolate, Horlicks malted milk tablets, and hot Oxo in a vacuum flask.

At 4:13 p.m. local time, Alcock waved the chocks away and advanced the throttles. The engines roared, and the Vimy began reluctantly to move up the incline. The onlookers held their breath. The big plane was trundling along like a cart. Puffing. Toiling. It would never get up enough speed to take to the air. Another take-off disaster was in the offing. You could see it starting to take place, like a bloody Greek tragedy. Bumping and swaying over the rough ground, the Vimy gobbled up the available takeoff run. Alcock's face was streaming with sweat as he worked to control the Vimy's run. Then, with a kind of noisy dignity, the biplane rose, clearing a fence, startling the onlookers by apparently sinking into the ground, an illusion created by the hilly terrain.

They were off. Delighted, Alcock climbed to one thousand feet, passing over St. John's and Cabot Hill. At twenty-eight minutes past the hour the Vimy was over the sea, on a course of 124 degrees magnetic.

Brown tapped out a brief message for the Mount Pearl Naval Station: "All well and started." Having sent this message, the radio transmitter failed.

The sun shone. Briefly. Then the fog moved in again. Soon the journey became a matter of finding a passage between the upper limits of the fog and the lower level of thick cloud. For seven hours, the airmen glimpsed neither sky nor sea. When they came to a relatively clear patch, Brown fixed their position from the Pole Star, Vega, and the moon. For half an hour the sky became clear overhead. But not for long. Thick fog soon moved in again, enveloping the aircraft.

Rain and sleet battered the Vimy and her crew. The airmen had a primitive form of intercom, but Alcock found the earpieces uncomfortable and discarded them. From then on, they communicated by means of gestures and scribbled notes.

Just after six in the evening, they were startled by a clattering sound, not unlike the noise of a machine gun. Anxious glances at the engines soon revealed the source. A section of exhaust pipe had broken away. The rest of the pipe, quivering feverishly in the intense wind, was becoming red-hot, then white. The exhaust from six of the engine's twelve cylinders now played directly onto the bracing wires between the wings. They glowed. Heaven knows how long they would last.

Although the radio transmitter had failed, the receiver was still working, and Brown kept listening for messages. The only one he picked up was someone calling "BMK." Brown never did learn what the message meant, but the communication cheered him. It provided the strangely comforting knowledge that the universe outside the Vimy's cockpit did still exist.

In London, there was no mention of the flight in the newspapers. Kathleen Kennedy, Brown's fiancée, was enjoying a sunny Saturday afternoon at the family home in Ealing, taking tea in the garden with her mother and sister Eileen. Other Londoners were looking forward to the evening's entertainment. The West End theatres offered *Chu Chin Chow* at His Majesty's, *The Maid of the Mountains* at Daly's, *Cyrano* at Drury Lane. If they preferred something a little more lowbrow, there was the incomparable Chaplin in his movie *Shoulder Arms*, or the ever-popular Mary Pickford in *Less than Dust*.

That afternoon Lord Northcliffe, the man directly responsible for the Atlantic prize, lay in a nursing home waiting to undergo a minor operation on his throat. A piano had been installed in his bedroom, and as he listened to a pianist play his favourite Mendelssohn, his thoughts may have turned to Alcock and Brown. The choice of a Saturday for their takeoff was most unfortunate for the *Daily Mail*. With no Sunday edition, only a skeleton staff was on duty in Carmelite House. If the flight was successful, and Alcock and Brown landed early enough on Sunday morning, the story would be scooped by special editions of the Sunday papers, and Northcliffe's paper would be left with only a detailed follow-up on Monday.

Over in Ireland, the three reporters who had been assigned to cover the landing of the flyers, idled away their time. They had made their preparations, bribed the coastguards to warn them of the first sighting of an aeroplane, hired cars to stand by, engaged local photographers with their cameras; it was just a question of when and where the landing would take place. . . .

Far to the west, the Vimy clattered on. The ocean below was a deep blue-grey, occasionally dotted with brilliant white floes, fragments of pack ice carried down from the Arctic by ocean currents. Over their cockpit windscreen, Alcock and Brown could see ahead where the ice had drifted into a thick belt across the horizon, with the telltale shape of bergs casting long shadows. The sky was broken overhead, dirty white cumulus clouds alternated with patches of clear blue sky through which the sun shone strongly. Both men were relaxed and at ease, like partners of long-standing, yet this was only their fourth flight together.[3]

Shortly after 9:00 p.m. Brown scribbled a note to Alcock, informing him that the Vimy's ground speed was 140 knots. Half an hour later, he asked Alcock to climb so that he could get a fix by means of the stars. By now, daylight had faded, and it was necessary to use the electric lamp to take readings from the instruments. Brown had a standard naval sextant with extra-deep engravings so that he could decipher them in a vibrating cockpit. The sextant had a crude artificial horizon. Using a slide rule and navigation tables, he could convert the sextant readings into positions on the chart opened out on his knees. The moon appeared. "The moon was not much good for navigation purposes," Brown later wrote, "but I wish I had the words to describe the beautiful effect of the clouds lighted by the moon. The cloud edges became iridescent, like a luminous rainbow, tinted with delicate colours. I identified Vega and the Pole Star and made some observations."[4]

The weather cleared. Half the journey was done. There could be no turning back now. At four thousand feet the Vimy skimmed the top of the clouds. "An aura of unreality seemed to surround us," Brown wrote, "as we flew onward towards the dawn and Ireland." He became almost poetic as he revelled in the totally new experience. "The fantastic surroundings impinged on my alert consciousness as something extravagantly abnormal – the distorted ball of a moon, the weird half-light, the monstrous cloud shapes, the fog below and around us, the misty indefiniteness of space, the changeless drone, drone, drone of the motors."[5]

A moment later, the airspeed indicator failed. Turbulence rocked the Vimy. In spite of his wide experience as an aviator, Alcock didn't know how to fly on instruments – and his aircraft didn't have any blind-flying equipment anyway. In the roiling fog, his senses deceived him. He thought he was descending. He was wrong. The aircraft stalled and whirled into a spin. Down through the endless layers of mist they fell. The world had turned into a grey soup. Alcock tried desperately to see something – *anything* – that would provide him with some visual reference.

Abruptly, the fog parted, like some nightmare curtain. He saw the ocean, dull and threatening, churning before him, terrifyingly close. He had just enough time to drag the big bomber out of its plunge. The ocean sped below. Gasping with relief, Alcock climbed to seven thousand feet. A near thing. Far too near.

They had anticipated improving weather. Instead, it got worse. Heavy rain battered the bomber, followed by snow and hail. The snow began to accumulate, caking the space between the wings and tail and the ailerons, elevators, and rudders which controlled the heavy plane. They were out of reach; Alcock could only work the controls to keep them free. Then another problem: sleet obscured the overflow gauge on the centre-section struts. At the same time it began to plug up the pitot head. Moreover, the accumulation of slush was partially blocking the air intakes, resulting in disconcerting backfiring from the engines.

To make matters worse, the electrical heating in their flying suits failed. The numbing cold quickly took over, seizing their limbs like some deadly paralysis.

The engines had to be seen to. And since Alcock dared not let go of the controls for even a moment, the responsibility fell to Brown. Putting his charts and instruments aside, he managed, despite his injured leg, to heave himself out of his seat. He succeeded in standing up in the cockpit, wincing as the icy slipstream assailed him, and while clutching the edge of the cockpit with one hand, he wiped away snow and ice with the other. It was a ghastly experience, but he made little of it. "The change from the sheltered warmth of the cockpit to the biting icy cold outside was startlingly unpleasant," he would write, in his understated way, adding that there was "scarcely any danger in kneeling on the fuselage, as long as Alcock kept the machine level."

The job took only a few moments. When it was done, Brown slumped thankfully back in his seat and revelled in the comparative warmth and comfort. But not for long. The snow and hail were soon causing trouble again. And again Brown had to clamber up on his seat and clear the accumulation. The dreadful business had to be repeated no less than six times until the Vimy flew into drier air.

At a chilly altitude of more than eleven thousand feet, Brown caught a glimpse of the sun. At last he could take a sun shot and find out precisely where they were! To their delight, the two airmen found that they were now only some eighty miles from Ireland. At that moment, the starboard engine emitted a peculiar popping sound. Alcock throttled back. The popping sound faded; the brief rest seemed to have cured the engine's ills. They descended to one thousand feet. Cloud still enveloped them. Down lower still, cautiously, for there was a danger of flying straight into the ocean before they could see it.

There it was! Grey, restless, thoroughly uninviting. Brown gave Alcock a sandwich. The pilot took it with a nod, his eyes never straying from the view ahead. His right hand had been firm on the control wheel since takeoff.

Brown had a bite of food and a drink, too. He was returning what was left of the provisions to the tiny locker behind the seat when Alcock grabbed his shoulder and pointed, grinning. He shouted something, but the wind whisked his words from his mouth and flung them back into the miles of endless ocean. It didn't matter. Brown could see for himself. Land. Solid land. They had done it!

Brown checked the time. The Vimy crossed the coast of Ireland at 8:25 a.m. on June 15. Ahead loomed lofty wireless masts.

Clifden! Mindful of the low cloud, Alcock decided to land at the military radio base. A smooth green meadow lay invitingly before them. A handful of men waved at the Vimy as it approached to land. Brown waved back.

The Vimy's wheels made contact. The flight had lasted sixteen hours and twenty-eight minutes.

The adventure wasn't over, however. Fate had one more trick up its sleeve. A dirty trick. Too late, the airmen realized the truth. They had made a perfect landing on a bog. The wheels dug into the soft moist earth. With an ugly squelch, the Vimy tipped up, threatening to turn completely over onto her back. The nose skid that Alcock had eliminated to save weight might have prevented the tip-up, and they were lucky they weren't trapped beneath her. With more gurgles and groans, the Vimy settled herself into the bog. Alcock and Brown scrambled out of the aircraft onto the soft earth. Alcock had braced himself against the rudder bar, which had acquired the shape of a horseshoe. Brown fired two Very flares. A small group of officers and men appeared, looking with interest at the upended Vimy.

"Anybody hurt?"

"No."

"Where are you from?"

"America."

Someone chuckled, thinking it was a joke. It took time for the truth to take hold; Brown had to show the mailbag they had brought from Newfoundland. Only then was the amazing story accepted. There were handshakes and vigorous slaps of congratulation. Everyone was talking, and the airmen had difficulty responding, for they were partially deaf, their ears ringing after listening to the throaty Rolls-Royce engines for so many hours. Besides, intense fatigue was overcoming them. As they trudged stiffly toward the officers' mess, they yearned for sleep, but their excited hosts had a thousand questions.

There were endless receptions for the two airmen – Galway, Dublin, then over to England and a gala affair arranged by Northcliffe, with poached eggs à la Alcock, sole à la Brown, and spring chicken à la Vickers Vimy. When Alcock was asked how he enjoyed the trip, he responded,

> We have had a terrible journey. The wonder is we are here at all. We scarcely saw the sun or the moon or the stars. For hours we saw none of them. The fog was very dense and at times we had to descend to within three hundred feet of the sea. For four hours the machine was covered in a sheet of ice carried by frozen sleet; at another time the fog was so dense that my speed indicator did not work, and for a few seconds it was very alarming. We looped the loop, I do believe, and did a very steep spiral. We did some very comic "stunts," for I had no sense of horizon. The winds were very favourable all the way: north-west and at times south-west. We said in Newfoundland we would do the trip in sixteen hours, but we never thought we should. An hour and a half before we saw land we had no certain idea where we were, but we believed we were at Galway or thereabouts. Our delight in seeing Eashal Island and Turbot Island [five miles west of Clifden] was great. People did not know who we were when we landed, and thought we were scouts on the lookout for the Vimy. . . . We drank coffee and ale and ate sandwiches and chocolate. The flight has shown that the Atlantic flight is practicable, but I think it should be done not with an aeroplane or seaplane, but with a flying boat.[6]

Winston Churchill handed them the winners' cheque, declaring that he did not know what to admire most – the flyers' audacity, their determination, their skill, their science, their Rolls-Royce engines, or their good fortunes. The days of speeches and barrages of congratulations were climaxed by a visit to Windsor and the knighting of both men by King George V.

And what of the big Handley Page V1500 left behind in Newfoundland? After the successful flight of Alcock and Brown, Handley Page instructed Kerr to fly the aircraft to New York before returning to England. On the way, a mishap wrecked the big biplane's landing gear. The transatlantic flight was abandoned. Instead, the V1500 became a sort of aerial salesman, journeying around America loaded with British goods, mainly dresses, suits, and furs. The aircraft was eventually broken up in the United States.

CHAPTER THREE | *Triumph Down Under*

*L*ater in that first full year of peace, another long-distance flight took place that is still rated as one of the most remarkable of the era. The goal was Australia – Down Under, the Antipodes, the other side of the world – a huge land of more than three million square miles, most of them arid and inhospitable, wherein five million people made their homes, the vast majority of them squeezed into the continent's southeast corner. To get there from Britain you had to fly over some of the worst territory in existence, with an almost total lack of airfields or other facilities along the way. But there was an attractive reward for the airmen who could do it within thirty days: *ten thousand pounds*, the same glittering prize awarded to Alcock and Brown for their Atlantic flight. And you had to be an Aussie to enter. No wide-open, everyone-welcome spirit here.

The whole idea was to foster air links between Britain and Australia and assorted stops in between, particularly if they happened to be in the British Commonwealth. The idea originated with the Australian prime minister, Welsh-born William Morris Hughes. During the Paris Peace Conference of 1919, Hughes had visited wounded Australian airmen. These men faced journeys of two months or more to get home, and Hughes thought how splendid it would be if they could fly there. Of course, no such service existed; in fact, Europe's nascent airlines were only just beginning to organize flights from London to Paris, and from Brussels to Amsterdam. Airline travel to Australia was the stuff of futuristic adventure stories. But seeing those airmen set Hughes to thinking. Why not sponsor a flight to Australia to show the world that it could be done? Hadn't Northcliffe done precisely that for the Atlantic? It seemed certain that at some point in the future, passengers would be transported by air across distances far greater than the Atlantic. With the triumphal transatlantic flight still making news, Hughes cabled his cabinet in Melbourne (then the capital of Australia) to suggest a ten-thousand-pound prize for the first flight from England to Down Under. It was Chief of the General Staff General Legge who suggested that entrants should be limited to Australians. Hughes agreed. By any measure, it was a prodigious challenge for the era's aircraft and airmen, but Australian public opinion was by no means unanimous about the enormous outlay (probably equivalent to a million pounds today) for what many described as a mere circus. Couldn't the money be put to better use? Hughes didn't think so. His proposal was approved.

One of the first to enter was an exceptional flyer, the most decorated airman in the Australian Flying Corps (and T.E. Lawrence's pilot at one time), twenty-six-year-old Ross Macpherson Smith. The son of the manager of a sheep station near Broken Hill, New South Wales, Smith had joined the Third Light Horse Regiment on the outbreak of war. He had fought in the disastrous Gallipoli

campaign and in Palestine. In 1916 he joined No. 1 Squadron of
the Australian Flying Corps (AFC), serving first as an observer, then
as a pilot. He was awarded two Military Crosses and three
Distinguished Flying Crosses – and was wounded, four times.
Vickers agreed to make a Vimy available for the long trip. Ross's
elder brother, Keith, joined the team as co-pilot and navigator. Two
experienced mechanics, Sergeants Wally Shiers and Jim Bennett,
completed the crew.

Since this was an Australians-only endeavour, it surprised
everyone when a French pilot, Etienne Poulet, was the first one to
depart, piloting a Caudron G4. He was not eligible for the prize,
yet his motivation deserves mention. He was attempting to raise
money to help the family of a close friend, Jules Vedrines, killed in
a crash a few months earlier. Engine trouble eventually forced him
to retire. An Australian pilot, Bert Hinkler (who would later
become one of the nation's best-known aviators), was scheduled to
fly a Sopwith Dove, a civil version of the wartime Pup powered by
an eighty-horsepower Le Rhone rotary engine. Hinkler couldn't
interest anyone in sponsoring him, and he had to drop out because
of lack of funds. The Sopwith company then entered the Wallaby,
a hefty single-engined biplane, piloted by Captain G.C. Matthews,
a former Light Horseman like Ross Smith, with Sergeant T.D. Kay
in the mechanic's seat. They departed from London on October 21,
flew to Cologne on the first leg of their lengthy journey – and
damaged the aircraft on landing. After repairs, they took off again,
only to be forced down several times by bad weather and mechanical troubles. They would eventually reach Java, but by then the
great race was over.

Other competitors encountered even more serious problems.
On November 13, Captain R.M. Douglas took off from London
in an Alliance P.2 Seabird biplane with a crew of three. He had

engine trouble over London and spun into the ground, killing all aboard. At the coroner's inquest, Douglas's fiancée stood up and declared the tragedy was the fault of the aircraft manufacturer; at the time many airmen agreed with her, for in that era of open cockpits, the enclosed cabin of the Seabird was thought to be dangerous, liable to play tricks with a pilot's visibility and sense of balance in the air.

Yet another hopeful team left London on December 4, flying a Martinsyde Type "A" biplane. Captain C.E. Howell, a wartime ace, was in command. His mechanic and navigator, Sergeant G.H. Fraser, had the distinction of being, at forty, the oldest man in the race. Encountering bad weather, the Martinsyde crashed into the sea near Corfu, killing both men. Howell's father compounded the tragedy by declaring that his son had been murdered for the money he was carrying – although no evidence to that effect was ever forthcoming. A few days later, the angular Blackburn Kangaroo departed with a four-man crew commanded by Captain Hubert Wilkins, later knighted for his Arctic and Antarctic explorations. The team got as far as Crete before abandoning the attempt. The last team to leave was that of lieutenants Ray Parer and J.C. McIntosh in an Airco de Havilland 9.

Ross Smith took off from Hounslow aerodrome (later named Heathrow) on a snowy morning in November 1919. The crew had nearly fifteen thousand miles to fly, most of it over wild country offering absolutely nothing in the way of facilities for passing airplanes – or *aeroplanes*, as they were then called. Adelaide was the goal. And it had to be attained before January 1, 1920, in order to claim the prize.

The Smiths' Vimy had extra tanks, equipping it to carry more than five hundred gallons of fuel, forty gallons of oil, and ten of water. Keenly aware that they could expect little in the way of

technical assistance en route, the crew carried no less than eight
hundred pounds of spares and tools. The aircraft had no radio,
partly because of the weight – radios, in 1919, were big and heavy
– and partly because radio stations were scarce anyway east of
Central Europe. Better to carry a few extra gallons of fuel. To ease
the strain on the pilot's shoulders, a shock absorber had been built
into the Vimy's control column, enabling the pilot to fly hands-off
for brief periods.

The newly introduced system of aircraft registrations had
decreed that the Vimy should carry the identification G-EAOU.
Some wag solemnly declared that it stood for "God 'Elp All Of Us."

Snow continued to fall as the Vimy climbed away from
Hounslow – uncommonly wintry weather for the London area in
November. The unpleasantness continued as the Vimy made its
ponderous way across the Channel into France. The crew's goggles
iced up; their flying suits became caked with ice; snow accumulated in the open cockpits. The airmen spent the first night at Lyon,
then took off for Pisa and Rome. The temperature rose a little, but
the visibility remained poor. The Mediterranean was the colour of
putty as Crete appeared in the distance. At Cairo and Damascus,
the Vimy encountered vigorous winds and rain. One particularly
strenuous blow almost swept the plane from its landing ground;
repairs took all the following morning. Then the heat moved in,
welcome at first, then increasingly sticky and enervating. It grew
more intense as they flew into India then on to Burma (now
Myanmar). At Rangoon (now Yangon) they were astonished to
find an enormous crowd of about forty thousand to greet them –
the Vimy was the first aircraft ever to land there. The next morning,
during takeoff, they ran into some kite hawks, sizable birds. One
smashed into a propeller, another into a wing, but Smith continued, missing a line of trees, he said later, by no more than a foot.

The crew could do little but hope that the hawks had done no serious damage to the aircraft. They were lucky. The sturdy Vimy remained in one piece.

Rain battered the aircraft as it climbed to eleven thousand feet to clear the mountains between Calcutta and Rangoon. The crew could see nothing of the ground. They descended with caution, unsure of their precise position, hoping against hope that they had left the main mountain range behind. Life was reduced to elemental proportions. If they hit a mountain, they had got it wrong. If they didn't, they had got it right. Their luck held. The weather cleared as if in celebration, and they had a smooth trip to the Siamese Air Force base at Don Muang.

Ross Smith had reckoned on covering 600 miles a day; but bad weather and various other factors brought his average down to 450 miles. Considering the state of many of the landing fields, he did well to maintain that figure. Coming down at Singora, Thailand, he broke the Vimy's tailskid; a local junk shop provided a steel shaft which they laboriously machined overnight using an ancient, muscle-powered lathe in a rice mill. Primitive it may have been, but it provided an acceptable replacement. While the work was going on, a veritable tidal wave of rain lashed the area, some ten inches in all. The crew spent most of the night trying to protect the Vimy against the ferocious elements. The morning found them exhausted, but they had to push on to Singapore.

Ross had been warned about the inadequate length of the landing field at Singapore; it was in fact the local racecourse. To get the aircraft firmly on the ground as quickly as possible, Sergeant Bennett made his precarious way along the top of the fuselage until he reached the tail. There he clung while the Vimy bumped its way in the turbulent air to a landing. Ross brought the Vimy down as smoothly as he could. The big aircraft's wheels kissed the grass.

Bennett's weight forced the tail down, the skid made contact with the grass, dragging the big biplane to a halt. Limp with relief, the wind-pummelled Bennett scrambled off the fuselage; terra firma had never felt better.

Two thousand five hundred miles to go. With eight days remaining. The next 650 miles took them to Batavia, now Jakarta. A good nine-hour trip with no mechanical problems. Things were looking up. Or were they? Landing at Sourabaya, the Vimy encountered a situation similar to that faced by Alcock and Brown in Ireland. What appeared to be a firm surface proved to be a bog in disguise. The Vimy sank with a despairing gurgle to squat on her broad wings, while locals swarmed about the field, busily making bad conditions worse. The airmen were lucky, however. No damage had been done to the Vimy apart from a thorough soaking in mud. She could be dug out – but how could they get the plane back in the air? The frustrated airmen gazed at the dismal scene, mouthing obscenities. Was it the end of all their hopes? How could fate be so cruel? But maybe all hadn't been lost. A resourceful Dutch engineer had an idea: bamboo mats, hundreds of them, common enough in that part of the world. Spread over the takeoff area, they would create a reasonably firm surface. It would work, the airmen were sure of it. A lifesaver! That night, the two sergeants worked on the weary engines while the Smith brothers filled the fuel tanks, a lengthy, tedious process. Not only did they have to manhandle every one of the gallon-cans, but the gasoline had to be filtered through chamois leather to remove the many and varied impurities which so often found their way into fuel in those days. It took some six hours to load the Vimy with sufficient fuel for the next leg of the trip. At the same time, hundreds of bamboo mats appeared, forming a rough and ready runway.

In the morning, the bleary-eyed airmen clambered aboard the Vimy, started up the engines – then found the precious mats were being blown away like so many autumn leaves. Still muttering, they switched off. And waited while more mats were obtained from the helpful and generous locals. Then there was more waiting while every one of the newly acquired mats was pegged securely into the ground. Eventually a 1,500-foot strip took form, two rows of mats, one for each pair of main wheels. Smith poured on the power. The Vimy heaved herself into reluctant motion, her big wheels crunching on the bamboo mats. Some were whipped away in the hurricane churned by the twin Rolls-Royces, but most held. The Vimy clattered along, gathering speed, finally lifting into the warm, damp air. Next stop: Sumbawa, where the Dutch Air Force provided fuel and oil and maintenance assistance. Only the length of the field could be criticized. The takeoff was a frighteningly near thing, the Vimy's undercarriage brushing the palm trees.

Now the last stage of the journey lay ahead. The Timor Sea. Five hundred miles of the loneliest flying in the world to reach the almost uninhabited north coast of Australia. Not a trip to be treated lightly. But the presence of the Australian cruiser *Sydney* at the halfway point buoyed the flyers' spirits. Cheering sailors greeted the weary airmen, cramped and numbed by noise. Australia was almost at hand! Just there, over that hazy horizon. The engines – those magnificent Rolls-Royces – didn't falter. Their roar became part of the airmen's being, pulsating like a heartbeat.

At last, at 3 p.m. on December 10, twenty-seven days and twenty hours after leaving Hounslow, Ross Smith brought the Vimy down at Darwin, having flown over eleven thousand miles, a world record. The flight was over, although the full celebrations did not begin until the Vimy went south, to Melbourne. There, the crowds went wild, a foretaste of the enthusiasm that would greet future long-distance flyers. Every Australian, it seemed, came to cheer their heroes. Their exploit had electrified the country. The Smiths were knighted; Bennett and Shiers were commissioned in the Australian Army Reserve. The Vimy went on permanent display in Adelaide, the Smiths' hometown.

CHAPTER FOUR | *Girdling the Globe*

*E*arly in 1922, two wartime comrades met in London. One was
Norman Macmillan, a leading British test pilot and winner
of several air races; the second was Major W.T. Blake, who had
ambitious plans for a flight around the world. Blake invited
Macmillan to join the expedition. The plan was to follow a route
largely over colonies and dominions of the British Crown; indeed
the whole enterprise took on the flavour of a national undertaking, although there was nothing official about it. Four aircraft were
to be used, two de Havilland DH9s, a Fairey 111C floatplane, and a
twin-engine Felixstowe flying boat for the various over-water legs,
all aircraft being supplied from wartime stocks.

On May 24 – Empire Day – the airmen set off, with a third
crew member, Lieutenant-Colonel L.E. Broome, and various
items of film equipment occupying the extra cockpit that had been
cut into the DH9's fuselage. The plan was to make a movie of the
entire trip, and thus help to defray costs by sending home footage

for exhibition as the flight proceeded. Things didn't work out as planned. The DH9 got only as far as the south of France before engine trouble – the DH9's bugbear – brought it down on a race-track near Marseille. Whereupon Colonel Broome wisely opted to travel ahead and organize the Vancouver-to-Tokyo segment of the trip. His place was taken by Geoffrey Malins, an experienced filmmaker.

The second DH9 was immediately despatched to France and the odyssey continued. The aviators recorded the first non-stop flight over the eastern Mediterranean from Greece to Egypt, but it was an insignificant hop for men with round-the-world ambitions. Engine trouble continued to plague them. When they ran into intense heat, they had to fashion an addition to the aircraft's radiator. Then white ants decided to take up residence in the wooden propeller, eating the inside away until it became a hollow shell, brittle and useless. Torrential rains assaulted the team in India. Blake fell ill and was ordered by a doctor not to fly on to Calcutta; later, an operation relieved him of his appendix.

At Calcutta, the weary DH9 was auctioned off, her fabric bearing the signatures of hundreds of people who had greeted the flyers on their innumerable stops. The plan now was to transfer to the Fairey floatplane. As arranged, the aircraft was waiting. But it was in no condition to fly. Tropical heat and humidity had done their worst with the pontoons, which leaked like sieves. No replacements were available locally, so repairs had to be made with pitch, tar, and caulking.

Macmillan took off, heading for Burma. Over the Ganges, the engine cut out because of an airlock – a rare failure for a Rolls-Royce Eagle. Macmillan got the seaplane down successfully, coming to rest on a mud shoal. The Fairey remained there for three frustrating days, with the crew trying in vain to induce the few locals who came near in their boats to provide some assistance. Those worthies gave the stranded aircraft cautious glances and promptly went on their way. Eventually, Macmillan got the aircraft free and took off yet again, intending to reach Chittagong. But once more the conditions proved too much for the engine. Down came the Fairey to land heavily in a choppy sea. Macmillan got the engine going again, but a takeoff was impossible in these conditions. Frustrated and impatient, Macmillan decided to taxi the twenty miles to Chittagong, but the sea soon put paid to that idea. The propeller shattered and the tail pontoon flooded. The flight was over.

The two occupants fired Very lights without result. A native windjammer came close, but after the crew got a close look at the downed seaplane, they turned around and sailed away. By now the situation was becoming desperate. The Fairey was breaking up, and the aviators could do little but watch the sharks endlessly circling, waiting.

Macmillan and Malins spent two unpleasant days on the sagging, disintegrating wreck. They had almost resigned themselves to a watery end when a steam launch under the command of the harbour master of Chittagong put in a welcome appearance and rescued them.

Undeterred by their harrowing adventures, Macmillan and Malins soon recuperated and were full of plans for another attempt in 1923. They returned to England and obtained sponsorship from an organization called the Legion of Frontiersmen. The Legion had been formed to "undertake adventures for the public service"; an all-British round-the-world flight was just the right sort of venture for this organization consisting largely of retired army and naval officers. Plans were developed for the production of a special aircraft for the job – an amphibian, capable of operation from land or water. Meanwhile, a yacht, *Frontiersman*, manned by thirty-nine adventurous young men, set out to establish supply depots for the forthcoming flight. That was when the plans started to unravel.

While taking on cargo at San Pedro, California, the *Frontiersman* received a visit from U.S. Treasury agents. It was the era of Prohibition, and relations between the U.S. and England had become strained due to disagreements over the use of liquor on foreign ships in American waters. The Treasury agents confiscated sixty-five gallons of Scotch whisky and attached the ship. To compound the indignity, a federal marshal slapped another attachment on the vessel on behalf of a Los Angeles dry-dock. The claim was for a mere $250 – an indication of the expedition's miserably inadequate financing. Soon members of the crew were to be found taking odd jobs at dockside to provide a few dollars for essentials. The Macmillan-Malins flight was abandoned.

Although the actions of the U.S. officials may have been justified in their eyes, many British citizens saw the episode as a thoroughly dirty trick. The U.S. Army Air Service had recently announced its intention of undertaking its own round-the-world flight. Indeed, while the *Frontiersman* was being impounded, American teams were busy establishing supply dumps along the proposed route. At the same time, another British attempt was being organized to fly in the opposite direction over much the same route. This time the leader was an RAF officer, a navigator, Squadron Leader A. Stuart MacLaren, with Flying Officer J. Plenderleith, pilot, and Sergeant R. Andrews, mechanic. The team had selected a Vickers Vulture, a biplane amphibian powered by a single Napier Lion engine beneath the upper wing; the aircraft was a variant of the unsuccessful Viking. A second Vulture was to be sent ahead in readiness for the Pacific leg.

On March 25, 1924, the MacLaren aircraft slipped into the water at Calshot on England's south coast. Heavily laden, the amphibian took an inordinately long time to gain flying speed – so long, in fact, that someone suggested that MacLaren intended to *taxi* around the world. MacLaren was not amused. Eventually he succeeded in getting airborne, dragging the overloaded Vulture into a cautious circuit before heading for France – where it narrowly missed a cliff in poor visibility. The aviators got only as far as Corfu before engine trouble brought them down, where they had to wait sixteen days for a new engine. The British lead had vanished like a puff of exhaust smoke.

Meanwhile, in California, fledgling airplane builder Donald Douglas was putting the finishing touches to the four aircraft he had built for the U.S. Air Service. Called World Cruisers, they were fifty-foot-span biplanes powered by four-hundred-horsepower Liberty engines and named *Seattle*, *Chicago*, *Boston*, and *New Orleans*. Each was manned by a crew of two, a pilot and co-pilot/mechanic.

Again, the Americans hedged their bets by sending several aircraft together instead of just one. Few blamed them. There were twenty-six thousand miles to be flown, and the problems that would be encountered along the way could only be guessed at. In those days of Prohibition, the christening of the World Cruisers was done with water from Lake Washington, Lake Michigan, Boston harbour, and the Mississippi. The aircraft took off from Clover Field, Santa Monica, watched by hundreds of local townspeople, and flew to Seattle, Washington, the official starting point.

On April 6, the World Cruisers began their odyssey, journeying up the Pacific coast to Alaska. One of the aircraft, the leader, *Seattle*, came down with engine trouble. *Seattle*'s crew, Major Martin and Sergeant Alva Harvey, fired distress rockets into the cold night sky until they attracted a U.S. Navy destroyer. A new engine was to be dispatched immediately by Coast Guard cutter. Martin ordered the rest of the flyers to continue, making for Dutch Harbor, in the

Aleutian Islands. Lieutenant Lowell Smith was to take command.

The replacement engine duly arrived, but Martin and Harvey didn't make it to Dutch Harbor. They and their plane were missing for ten days and feared lost, until they materialized at Port Moller, having crashed into a hill, miraculously without killing themselves. The three surviving Cruisers took off from Attu in the Aleutians, braving hideous weather to reach Paramashiru, in the Kuriles, completing the first crossing of the Pacific, albeit only a tiny section of it.

In Tokyo, the American airmen met British Colonel Broome, who had been involved in the original flight of Blake and Macmillan two years earlier. Despite strained diplomatic relations between their two nations, the flyers got along well. By odd coincidence, they were breakfasting when Broome received a telegram: *MacLaren crashed at Akyab. Plane completely wrecked. Continuance of flight doubtful.*

MacLaren's backup aircraft was at Hakodate, Japan, some 450 miles to the north. The Americans at once organized the dispatch of a USN destroyer to Hakodate, loaded the crated Vulture and rushed it to MacLaren in Burma – while the Royal Navy was apologizing for not lending a hand, explaining that no suitable vessel was available. It was not the Senior Service's finest hour.

The three remaining World Cruisers droned on, their crews enjoying enthusiastic welcomes in Paris and London. They flew to Yorkshire and exchanged their wheeled undercarriages for pontoons, then headed to the Orkneys to prepare for the final leg, the westward crossing of the Atlantic. First stop on the Atlantic trip was Iceland. Two of the aircraft made it successfully, but *Boston* experienced a loss of oil pressure and came down in the sea. The USS *Richmond*, one of the ships sent to shepherd the World Cruisers across the oceans, came to the aircraft's aid. The crew, Lieutenant

Leigh Wade and Sergeant Henry M. Ogden, were rescued, but their World Cruiser sank, a sad fate after completing nineteen thousand miles.

At the same time, the British team of MacLaren, Plenderleith, and Andrews, still attempting to reach the Aleutians, smashed their wings and tail in a heavy landing in Soviet territory. Disappointed and frustrated, the British flyers gave up, leaving the Americans without rivals – although the Americans did have a travelling companion for the last leg of their long journey. Lieutenant Antonio Locatelli of the Italian Air Service had been scheduled to fly to the North Pole with Roald Amundsen, the renowned Norwegian explorer. But Amundsen ran out of money and the plans fell through. The expedition's three Dornier Wal flying boats were taken over by Italy. Lieutenant Locatelli had the bright idea of using one for an attempt at a round-the-world flight. He followed the Americans to Iceland. There, Lowell Smith invited him to join the team to fly the rest of the way; he accepted, and the two World Cruisers and the Wal took off from Reykjavik on August 21. The Dornier was faster than the Douglas biplanes and surged ahead of them, resulting in some negative comments in the press, though not from the American flyers. Smith was of the opinion that Locatelli did the right thing. But it didn't get him to North America any faster. He encountered engine trouble a little more than a hundred miles from the Labrador coast, landing on the sea in thick fog. He and his crew were lucky to be found by the USS *Richmond*, one of several American ships on patrol in the area.

The World Cruisers arrived back on North American soil at the colourfully named Icy Tickle, Labrador. Later they headed to Boston, New York, and Washington, where the normally lugubrious features of President Calvin Coolidge broke into a reasonable imitation of a smile – despite the fact that he had been kept waiting three hours in a downpour. Similarly warm welcomes awaited the aviators wherever they appeared. They were America's heroes. "Magellans of the Air," one paper called them. They arrived back at Seattle on September 28, five months and twenty-two days after their departure.

Other nations were quick to establish their own record-breaking flights. Portugal was so keen to be the first to fly the south Atlantic that the naval air service was prepared to lose most of its seaplane fleet in the attempt. In 1922, two Portuguese naval officers, captains Sacadura Cabral and Gago Coutinho, set out to fly from Lisbon to Rio in a Fairey 111c seaplane named *Lusitania* (the ancient name of the Iberian Peninsula). The Portuguese navy stationed ships at various spots along the proposed route to supply fuel and render whatever assistance might be required by the flyers. The flight began on March 30, 1922, with the two captains heading first for the Canaries, then on to the Cape Verde Islands, where bad weather held them up for a few days. Resuming their journey, they made for St. Paul Rock, on the Brazilian mainland, where one of the ships was stationed. Unfortunately, gusty weather and a choppy sea resulted in serious damage to the Fairey during the landing, although the airmen were uninjured. The navy picked the two men up and took them to Fernando de Noronha, some two hundred miles off the east coast of Brazil, where another Fairey 111C was to be delivered. The airmen decided to return to St. Paul Rock, however, so that they could resume their flight where it had been interrupted. But when the ship carrying the Fairey arrived there, the aircraft could not be unloaded, and the vessel had to sail to Fernando de Noronha as originally intended. Still determined to travel the full route by air, Cabral flew the plane back to St. Paul Rock. Circling, he lost his engine – and the second Fairey quickly became a tangled mess floating on the ocean. The crew was unhurt, and still game. Fortunately, a British steamer came along, picked them up, and returned them yet again to Noronha. Lisbon dispatched yet another Fairey, landing at Pernambuco. Brazilians were delighted. Four years later, a group of Spaniards challenged the South Atlantic, with Christopher Columbus as a kind of silent partner in the enterprise. The chief pilot, Ramon Franco, was known as the "Columbus of the air." The flyers – Franco plus three crew members – used Palos, the Atlantic port from which Columbus sailed on August 3, 1492. Their aircraft was a Dornier Wal flying boat named *Plus Ultra*. In it, Franco and his crew achieved the first totally successful crossing of the equatorial Atlantic.

||||

Alan Cobham became one of the best known British flyers in the twenties and thirties, a pilot who combined great skill with a keen entrepreneurial instinct. After service with the Royal Flying Corps, he made a precarious living barnstorming around the British Isles, taking passengers for brief aerial hops in an Avro 504 (and described in an advertisement as "the pilot who has carried more passengers than any other living man"). Soon he was involved in an air-taxi tour business that generated some publicity, but not much money. After a spell with the aircraft manufacturer Airco, he joined Geoffrey de Havilland, formerly Airco's chief designer, becoming the chief pilot of the de Havilland Aeroplane Hire Service, whose slogan was *Fly Anyone – Anywhere*. Cobham was an exceptionally hard worker, a desirable quality in any employee during those difficult post-war days when no one knew what, if anything, the future held for commercial aviation. In 1921,

Cobham flew a well-heeled American, Lucien Sharpe, on a chartered tour of Europe and the Middle East, probably the longest charter flight to that date – although engine trouble ended the trip prematurely.

Two years later, de Havilland sold a number of light aircraft called the Humming Bird to the air force. The company wanted to exhibit the aircraft at the 1923 Aero and Automobile Exhibition in Brussels. Cobham volunteered to fly a Humming Bird there. But could the tiny monoplane – powered by a 750-cc motorcycle engine – make it across the Channel and all the way to Brussels? The technical staff at de Havilland said yes, but insisted that an extra fuel tank be fitted for the trip. Containing precisely two gallons of fuel, this modestly proportioned tank was fastened to the fuselage immediately behind Cobham's head. It had a rubber tube into which he had to blow vigorously to establish pressure feed. Cobham commented, "This is the maddest thing I have ever done. No wonder they named it the Humming Bird – this little propeller is revolving at 3,000 rpm! One magneto! And then an ordinary motorcycle engine revving as it has never revved before!"[1]

The flight took place in wintry weather on Saturday, December 8. Cobham arrived safely at Brussels but the weather deteriorated and he had to return to England by ship.

Soon Cobham was involved in flying of a more political nature. In 1924, he flew the monocled director of civil aviation, Sefton Brancker, to India and Burma to assess the setting up of airship routes to the Far East – although the perspicacious Brancker was soon of the opinion that it would be the airplane, not airships, that would dominate the Empire's air routes. Cobham, determined to impress an indifferent government with the possibilities of air travel, flew from Rochester, England, to London – via Australia. His spectacular finale was to land the float-equipped DH50 on the

Thames beside the Houses of Parliament, an event witnessed by an estimated one million people packed along the river and on the bridges. Particularly impressive was the fact that Cobham arrived precisely on time – all part of his desire to convince the public at large that aviation was a safe, reliable means of travel.

CHAPTER FIVE | *Atlantic Antics*

R aymond Orteig had done well in America. He had arrived in New York from his native France as a mere lad of twelve years. Bright and personable, he soon had a job in a New York hotel shining shoes. He made rapid progress, becoming in turn a busboy, a waiter, manager, eventually an owner. He acquired two New York hotels, the Brevoort and the Lafayette, both of which became renowned for their comfort, cuisine, and delightful French *ambiance*. In 1919, Orteig, now a wealthy man, wrote to the Aero Club of America offering a prize of twenty-five thousand dollars to the first aviator – "of any Allied country" – to cross the Atlantic in one flight, from Paris to New York or New York to Paris.

For several years no one attempted to win the attractive prize. The reason was simple: there wasn't an aircraft in existence capable of the flight. Alcock and Brown's trip from Newfoundland to Ireland had involved only about half the distance of a New York to Paris journey. For several years it seemed that no one might ever claim Orteig's prize. But at last, a contender appeared, a major star in the aeronautical firmament: no less than Rene Fonck, the leading Allied fighter pilot of the Great War. Fonck had seventy-five aerial victories to his name, was a brilliant pilot, but remote, rather haughty, respected but not regarded warmly by the aviation fraternity.

Fonck sailed for the United States in 1925, under the auspices of an American syndicate called Argonauts Inc. with their collective gaze firmly focused on the Orteig prize. Fonck intended to take advantage of the prevailing winds, flying from New York to Paris in a large biplane, the S-35, built by Igor Sikorsky, a Russian designer who had fled the Revolution in 1917.

Sikorsky had become famous in pre-war Russia for his large, multi-engine aircraft, but he was little known in the United States. Financially strapped, he had invested heavily in the S-35, reasoning that a successful flight would make him and his products world-famous. (A contributor to the project was the renowned pianist and composer Sergei Rachmaninoff, a fellow exile.) Originally designed for two engines, the S-35 was modified to take three – French Gnome-Rhone Jupiters. The legend *"New York – Paris"* adorned the biplane's metal flanks. The aircraft's interior was luxurious, finished in red, gold, and silver, equipped with wicker chairs and a divan. Costing over a hundred thousand dollars, the S-35 was reputed to be the most expensive airplane in the world.

Underlining the French-American character of the enterprise, Captain Homer M. Berry of the U.S. Air Service Reserve was chosen as Fonck's co-pilot – and he was not pleased; he had been under the impression he would be named pilot-in-command. Lieutenant George O. Noville became the flight engineer. Another American, John R. Irwin, was hired as radio man.

As the flight date neared, nerves tautened; squabbles among the crew flared up. Noville quit over an argument about the type of lubricating oil to be used in the Jupiter engines. Fonck, as frosty as ever, then informed co-pilot Berry that he had been replaced by another American, Allan Snody. Berry promptly threatened legal action. Then Irwin backed out. Snody came down with a bad case of bronchitis and was replaced by a U.S. Navy pilot, Lawrence Curtin. Within hours of the planned takeoff, Fonck added Clavier, a French radio man, plus Jacob Islamov, a mechanic and fellow emigré.

Fonck announced that he would leave at daybreak on September 21 from Roosevelt Field, Long Island. The weather experts promised a short spell of reasonably fair conditions, about the best the airmen could expect at that time of year. Sikorsky spent the night before the takeoff going over every inch of the S-35. Before dawn, crowds began to gather, buzzing in a festive way, as if they were going to see the Yankees play. Everyone seemed confident that Fonck and the S-35 would succeed. Why wouldn't they? Such a magnificent airplane and such a brilliant pilot in control. Success was certain . . . wasn't it? What few people knew was that the aircraft was now some ten thousand pounds over-weight. Sikorsky had added a small auxiliary undercarriage to help take care of the extra load. The plan was to jettison it after takeoff.

The crew arrived, led by Fonck in a handsome blue uniform. Clavier, the radio man, had an armful of gifts for his wife; he told onlookers that he was looking forward to dinner in Paris on Wednesday night, two days hence (at a time when it was consid-ered a triumph to do the trip by sea in less than five days). The engines burst into noisy life. A gentle breeze began to blow, but it was on the aircraft's tail; it would be of no help during takeoff. Nevertheless, the big craft stirred, its wheels rolling, slowly, delib-erately; a forest of arms rose to wish the flyers Godspeed. The his-toric flight was about to take place . . . but only if the plane could pick up more speed . . . *much* more speed. The Sikorsky lurched across a service road, clattering on the unpaved surface, picking up speed, but, oh, so slowly. The onlookers gasped when part of the auxiliary gear broke away. A piece of the mechanism flew back and hit the rudder. Spectators expected Fonck to abandon the takeoff. He didn't. The big aircraft, travelling rapidly now, but still unable to become airborne, bounded up the hillock that marked the end of Roosevelt Field and the beginning of the adjacent Curtiss Field. A gully lay between them. For an agonizing moment the S-35, engines howling, hung almost motionless as if permitting everyone to admire her one last time.

Then she thudded into the gully. And erupted in flame as the fifteen thousand pounds of fuel and oil exploded in a ghastly fireball. A column of black, oily smoke shot into the air. Spectators screamed, instinctively backing away from the conflagration. Sikorsky ran the length of the field, horror distorting his features. Reaching the raging fire, he found the two pilots, Fonck and Curtin, alive. They had scrambled out of the cockpit in the nick of time. Clavier and Islamov weren't so lucky. Both died in the flames, the first fatalities of the Orteig stakes. For Sikorsky, it was also a financial disaster, for the S-35 had not been insured. His debt-plagued company had sunk even deeper into the mire. True to form, Fonck shrugged off the incident. Such happenings were the inevitable price of aeronautical progress, he declared. When criticized for not aborting the takeoff immediately after the failure of the landing gear, he replied coldly that he could not have slammed the throttles shut without throwing the aircraft completely out of control. The aircraft would probably have skidded into the crowd with heaven knows what consequences. A coroner's inquest agreed, absolving Fonck of any blame, ruling the crash "an unfortunate accident."

The French aviator declared that he would set off on another transatlantic flight the following year, 1927. Sikorsky would build the aircraft; Mrs. Robert L. Dodge of Oyster Bay would be the principal backer. Sikorsky was soon busy with the new machine, the twin-engine S-37. At the same time, several other flyers had transatlantic stars in their eyes. Lieutenant Commander Noel Davis, USN, had ordered a three-motor biplane from the Keystone Corporation, to be completed in April. The American Legion was putting up most of the money; as it happened, the Legion was to hold a major convention in Paris, and Davis planned to dazzle everyone there by arriving in the Keystone. His plane was named in their honour. He would do it with the help of Stanton Wooster, co-pilot and navigator. In late April 1927, they took the aircraft to Virginia for a series of tests at full load. On taking off from Langley Field, the aircraft seemed sluggish. Approaching a line of trees, Davis veered sharply. The *American Legion* lost flying speed. Davis tried to bring the aircraft down for a landing, but, like many flyers before him, he mistook marsh for solid ground. The Keystone stood on her nose. The occupants weren't as fortunate as Alcock and Brown. Both Davis and Wooster died in the smashed cockpit. One of the engines crushed Davis's head; Wooster suffered a broken neck.

Another French war ace appeared to claim Orteig's prize. The handsome but badly battered Charles Nungesser had shot down forty-four enemy aircraft during the conflict, suffering a grisly series of injuries in the process. He numbered among his many prosthetics a silver ankle and jaw. In the latter stages of the war he was in constant pain and had to be carried to and from his aircraft. But he refused to give in to his injuries. Nungesser had good reason for going after the Orteig prize. He needed the money. After the war he had married New York heiress Consuelo

Hatmaker. The marriage failed and left Nungesser with a mountain of debt. If he won the Orteig prize, he could pay off his creditors; all his problems would be solved. He originally planned to
make the flight alone, from Paris to New York. Later, he changed
his mind and took on François Coli, a navigator who had lost an
eye during the war. The pair had a powerful Levasseur PL8 biplane,
a handsome aircraft painted white, with a watertight fuselage made
of sealed plywood. Like Hawker in 1919, Nungesser employed a
jettisonable landing gear; he intended to cross the ocean *sans le train
d'atterrissage* and to alight in New York harbour. The aircraft, christened *L'Oiseau Blanc*, was powered by a twelve-cylinder water-
cooled Lorraine-Dietrich engine that could generate an impressive
450 horsepower. Nearly nine hundred gallons of fuel would be
pumped into three tanks – but Nungesser refused to test his aircraft
at full weight. He preferred to stake everything on the big day. If it
went well, *bon!* If not, it would be quickly over for both occupants.
In the meantime, the two airmen trained with barbells and medi-
cine balls and practised going without sleep. Coli claimed he could
stay awake for sixty hours at a time.

Poor weather delayed Nungesser's departure until early May.
On the seventh, the weather office on Avenue Rapp reported with
some excitement that an east wind was developing – an uncom-
mon occurrence, and one that would help *L'Oiseau Blanc* on her
way. In fact, the predictions were that the tailwind would blow for
about half the journey.

Nungesser and Coli announced that they would depart at
dawn. The news made for an exciting night at Le Bourget Field
near Paris. President Gaston Doumergue arrived; so did the boxer
Georges Carpentier and a huge crowd, many of them in evening
dress. They were still there as the night sky paled with the approach
of dawn. The flyers clambered aboard their aircraft. At 5:17 a.m.,

Nungesser raised an arm in farewell. The engine roared. *L'Oiseau Blanc* began her takeoff roll, slowly at first. Gradually she picked up speed. The tail rose; the aircraft took to the air. A moment later she sagged back to the earth. The crowd gasped. Were they about to witness another horror like the one that had overtaken Fonck? No, again the heavily laden biplane eased herself into the air, hesitantly, it seemed, as if testing the strength of the air. Could the wings – slender, delicate-looking things – support such a weight? Watchers winced, every one of them feeling the burden as if it were on their shoulders. They breathed again. *L'Oiseau Blanc* cleared the field, climbing gently. Near Cherbourg, Nungesser jettisoned the landing gear. The white biplane headed out over the ocean.

It was Joan of Arc Day. All over France, candles were lit and prayers said. If sheer intensity of emotion could do the trick, the two aviators would have flown the ocean with never a hitch. But they vanished. One Paris newspaper, determined to sell copies no matter what, printed a detailed account of the landing of *L'Oiseau Blanc* in New York harbour close to the Statue of Liberty. The news sent Parisians flocking into the streets with bottles of champagne and balloons. Not since Armistice Day had the city seen such a celebration. It was short-lived. The truth soon emerged. For weeks, reports kept surfacing of all-white biplanes being seen in Newfoundland, Labrador, and elsewhere. Naval vessels searched in vain. A benefit show at New York's Roxy Theater generated thirty-five thousand dollars for the lost flyers' families.

In New York, three other aircraft were being readied. The well-known polar explorer Richard Evelyn Byrd had acquired a Fokker trimotor the previous year, financed by department-store mogul Rodman Wanamaker. Impressed by the Fokker's performance in the Far North, Byrd decided to use the type for a transatlantic flight –

although he was careful not to associate himself with the Orteig prize. His flight was to be for scientific purposes, he declared, "to point the way for the transatlantic plane of the future, to the practical way of crossing the Atlantic commercially."

Wanamaker and Byrd leased Roosevelt Field for their exclusive use and built a ramp to help the aircraft get away: it was a wooden hill down which the big monoplane would trundle, a way of gaining extra speed for the all-important takeoff run. Tony Fokker, the personable and intensely ambitious head of the firm, came to Roosevelt to take the tri-motor up for a test flight. Byrd, his pilot Floyd Bennett, and flight engineer George O. Noville, formerly Rene Fonck's flight engineer, decided to tag along. All four squeezed themselves into the cabin, which had become uncomfortably tiny because much of its space was occupied by an extra fuel tank installed for the Atlantic trip. The result was a nose-heavy aircraft – a condition that could not be improved by moving the passengers aft; there simply wasn't room for them to get into the rear fuselage. The flight went well, but on touchdown, onlookers gasped as the big machine nosed over, somersaulting onto its back, slithering to an untidy halt, and suffering considerable damage. Fortunately, there was no fire, but Byrd had a broken arm, Noville was in agony with internal injuries, and Bennett had fractured a leg and punctured a lung.

Byrd immediately set about repairing the damaged aircraft. He replaced Bennett with an outstanding Norwegian pilot, Bernt Balchen. Wanamaker insisted on an all-American crew, so the young man applied for citizenship. With Byrd's influential connections, the process didn't take long (although Balchen's application for citizenship later ran into difficulties when it was discovered that his mandatory five years of residence in the U.S. had been interrupted while he was a member of Byrd's Antarctic expedition in the famous Little America camp. A special act of Congress was needed to solve the problem).

At College Point, Long Island, Igor Sikorsky was testing Rene Fonck's S-37, bearing the proud name *Ville de Paris*. In far-off San Diego, California, the Ryan Company was busy on another aircraft, a trim high-wing monoplane, a modified Ryan Brougham. Originally equipped with five seats, the aircraft now had only one. The rest of the available space was taken up by fuel tanks, the largest of which was directly in front of the pilot's seat, completely obscuring the view ahead. The young man who had ordered the aircraft didn't care. He reasoned that he could see enough out of his side windows and through his small periscope to manage the takeoff. After that, he would be unlikely to encounter any other traffic until he reached Europe. The young pilot's name was Charles Augustus Lindbergh. He was twenty-three years old. A skilled pilot and uncommonly clear thinker, he approached the task of flying the Atlantic with the attitude of a minimalist and the fortitude of a Spartan. Not for him the lavish accommodations of Fonck's Sikorsky, or the services of another crew member in the form of a navigator, or the weight (some ninety pounds) of a radio set. He even decided against installing fuel gauges; his considerable experience as an Army pilot and barnstormer told him that they were heavy and usually inaccurate anyway. He intended to check on fuel consumption with a tachometer – which recorded engine speed – and a watch. The work would help to occupy him during the long flight. So would the task of maintaining his course. He had no illusions about his skill as a navigator; he laboriously plotted a great arc of a route, which would necessitate small changes of heading throughout the trip. Another task to help keep his mind occupied.

Aware of the danger of vibration and its effects on the lines of copper tubing that were the aircraft's vital arteries, he ordered the lines broken every eighteen inches and reconnected with rubber hose. Thus any vibration would be effectively tamed. His aircraft was equipped with one of the great engines of that era, the Wright Whirlwind, a nine-cylinder radial, designed by a stocky musta-chioed engineer and amateur watercolour painter named Charles L. Lawrance and manufactured by the Wright Corporation (with which Orville, the surviving Wright brother, had long since severed all connections). The Whirlwind powered most of the era's successful long-distance flights, acquiring an illustrious reputation for reliability. Lindbergh had the deepest respect for it:

When the Whirlwind engine arrives from Paterson, we gather around the wooden crate as though some statue were to be unveiled. It's like a huge jewel, lying there set in its wrappings. We marvel at the quality of cosmoline-painted parts. Here is the ultimate in lightness of weight and power – two hundred and twenty-three horses compressed into nine delicate, fin-covered cylinders of aluminum and steel. On this intricate perfection I'm to trust my life across the Atlantic Ocean. . . . The inner organs of this engine – its connecting rods, cams, gears, and bearings – will be turning over many hundred times each minute – sparks jumping, teeth meshing, pistons stopping and reversing at incompre-hensible speeds. And I'm demanding that this procedure continue for forty hours if need be, for all the 3,610 miles between New York and Paris![1]

By late April, Lindbergh's aircraft was completed. The work had taken Ryan two months. The name *Spirit of St. Louis* was resplendent

on the Ryan's burnished engine cowling. Lindbergh tested the aircraft, recording a top speed of 128 mph. His modifications had
resulted in an unstable aircraft, but Lindbergh didn't care. The fact
that he would have to control it all the way to Paris was, in his
estimation, a positive thing. He knew that one of the main hazards
would be his need for sleep. Thus, the more essential tasks to
occupy his mind, the better.

On May 10, while Nungesser and Coli were still believed to be
airborne, Lindbergh departed for New York, with a stopover in St.
Louis to show the aircraft off to his backers, a group of businessmen from that city. The trip provided a few tense moments over
Arizona. His engine began to miss, vibrating, shaking the entire
structure. Alarmed, Lindbergh eased back on the throttle and
mixture controls. "I stare at the earth. There's not a single light on
its surface, not a ranch-house window to break this desperate soli-
tude of night."[2]

The only positive was that the Whirlwind was still putting out
some power. Lindbergh, now convinced that the problem was due
to the intense cold at altitude, made a mental note to install a carburetor heater in New York before attempting the ocean crossing.

He touched down at 6:20 California time, some fourteen and a
half hours after takeoff. He had done the cross-country trip in
record time. Half a dozen invitations to dinners awaited him; he
disregarded them. The newspaper reporters swarmed around
Lindbergh. He was the new star attraction, the "kid flyer" who had
leapt onto centre stage with a spectacular flight from California.
The papers were uniformly incorrect about his background, one
declaring him to be from Michigan (he was from Minnesota),
another saying he learned to fly in Texas (he learned in Nebraska),
a third revealing that his nickname was "Lucky" (in fact, it was
"Slim"). He loathed the photographers, who kept popping up and

demanding "just one more" picture. "I'm tired of shaking hands, and writing my name on slips of paper, and being poked and stared at. I want to spend a normal hour for a change."[3]

Lindbergh had originally wanted a Bellanca WB2 for his transatlantic flight, but although the company was perfectly willing to sell him one, it insisted on selecting the pilot to fly it. No, Lindbergh told them, *he* was going to fly the plane. Negotiations ceased forthwith. A Bellanca was, however, among the aircraft being prepared for a flight across the Atlantic. It was at nearby Curtiss Field, and it had been named *Columbia*. Her owner was a dynamic, intensely argumentative individual named Charles A. Levine. He had made a fortune in his early thirties with astute dealings in scrap metal and automobiles. He should have been content with his lot in life; he was wealthy, had a beautiful family – had everything, except aeronautical glory. And although he barely knew how to fly an airplane, that was what he wanted. Levine decided to undertake a sensational flight – such as crossing the Atlantic – only, someone else would do the flying. He would travel as a passenger. There were plenty of pilots around for hire. After lengthy negotiations with former Army pilot Leigh Wade and a highly experienced but distinctly spirited airman named Bert Acosta (who had a reputation of being able to fly as well, if not better, with a drink or two under his belt), he chose Clarence Chamberlin, a highly regarded flyer who had done much of the test flying of the Bellanca. The handsome fee offered by Levine sounded good to Chamberlin, a slim, quiet-spoken man of modest demeanour. He signed on.

At Curtiss Field, *Columbia* was literally torn apart by an army of mechanics and technicians. Extra fuel tanks were installed in the sturdy yellow monoplane. Her engine was a Whirlwind, the same engine that powered Lindbergh's *Spirit of St. Louis*. Levine had the latest instruments installed, including three chronometers, an octant, a drift indicator, a turn indicator, and an earth inductor compass. Soon he would be world-famous. He could hardly wait.

Late in April, Levine announced that Lloyd Bertaud had been selected as navigator for the *Columbia*. Taught to fly by the famous pioneer Lincoln Beachey, thirty-one-year-old Bertaud was a good navigator and a congenial companion. On the twenty-fifth, a bright, sunny day, Levine's nine-year-old daughter, Eloise, christened the *Columbia* with a beribboned bottle of ginger ale, after which she and a young friend, Grace Jonas, daughter of the president of the Brooklyn Chamber of Commerce, climbed aboard and took off with Chamberlin at the controls. Unfortunately, a pin on the left undercarriage leg fractured during the takeoff run, leaving the left wheel dangling uselessly. Spectators on the ground stared in horror. They couldn't contact Chamberlin; the aircraft had no radio. Chamberlin had no knowledge of the catastrophe taking shape. He proceeded to fly his young passengers on their joyride.

A pilot named Dean Smith took off in his Curtiss Robin with a mechanic who held a spare wheel and pointed to it as they flew alongside the *Columbia*. The girls, already a little pale from Chamberlin's manoeuvres, now lapsed into tense silence. At last the situation became unpleasantly clear to Chamberlin. He quickly decided to head for nearby Mitchell Field, where the Army had excellent fire and rescue facilities. He didn't need them. Exhibiting his customary skill, he put the Bellanca down on its good wheel and tail skid, coming to a halt in a cloud of dust with no harm done to anyone. The papers made much of the incident, but Chamberlin dismissed the fervid stories as so much hot air. Typical newspaper hype.

At this point Bertaud, the recently appointed navigator, declared himself in favour of flying over the shipping lanes. Although the route was a little longer, it increased the chances of rescue should the aircraft come down at sea. Moreover, he opted for a radio to be installed. Chamberlin and Bellanca, the designer of the aircraft, disagreed. Not only were radios heavy, they represented a fire hazard, because they periodically emitted sparks. Levine was on Bertaud's side; he had a contract with the American Newspaper Alliance for an exclusive on the flight. He looked forward to telling the world, via his radio, of *Columbia*'s progress – with suitable references to one Charles Levine. On his orders, the radio was installed; Chamberlin ordered it removed; Levine demanded that it be reinstalled; Chamberlin insisted that it be removed a second time. To add to Levine's irritation, technicians charged him seventy-five dollars every time they had to adjust the compasses to compensate for the radio. By the end of April, three new radios were waiting in the *Columbia*'s hangar, each to be tested in flight pending the final decision. Technicians continued to examine every part of the Bellanca, while Chamberlin spent his days checking out the aircraft's performance, taking it up for endless tests – all of which were watched open-mouthed by the crowds of spectators around the field. They grew day by day. The reporters and cameramen never seemed to leave the field, clutching their notebooks and asking fatuous questions of anyone who looked as if he knew anything. In fact, no one really knew anything, largely because of Levine. The former scrap-metal mogul possessed a Machiavellian mind. Not for him the simple business of making a deal and sticking to it. There was no fun in that. He liked to work and rework every detail of every contract until no one was sure what the original agreement had been. It was a strategy that had served him well for years, making him a millionaire while still in his twenties. On May 15, a conference took place at the nearby Garden City Hotel. Chamberlin and Bertaud were both represented by legal counsel.

One point to be discussed was the airmen's need for financial security for their families. Richard Byrd's crew had negotiated insurance policies that would pay substantial sums to their families in the event of their deaths. Chamberlin and Bertaud wanted similar coverage. Another point of contention was brought up by Bertaud. He objected to the provision calling for a splitting of the prize money between Levine's company, Columbia Aircraft, and the crew. Finally, he saw no reason why he should agree to a clause in the contract insisting that he work for Columbia for a year after a successful flight.

The arguments were eventually settled one by one. At least that's what everyone thought. The terms stipulated that the wives were to be paid $50,000 each should their husbands not come back. But when the new contracts were produced, the insurance turned out to be for only $12,500 for Chamberlin and just $5,000 for Bertaud. Levine never stopped trying.

The two airmen refused to sign. A lawyer then issued an injunction, preventing the *Columbia* from flying the Atlantic without Bertaud aboard. Levine shrugged off the problems. He was enjoying himself; life was fun again, an exciting mélange of arguments and angles, schemes and counter-schemes. He loved it. He also loved accompanying Chamberlin on his test flights, sitting contentedly in the co-pilot's seat, smiling his enigmatic smile at the crowds of onlookers who kept wondering if this was the day the *Columbia* was finally getting away. But the Bellanca kept taking off, vanishing over the horizon, then returning to disgorge once again Chamberlin and the exuberant Levine. Levine told anyone who would listen that he would soon start the world's first transatlantic airline. When asked what aircraft would be used, Levine replied that it was currently being designed. At the Garden City Hotel, meeting followed meeting. At one point it seemed that the

The conqueror of the English Channel, Louise Bleriot (in cockpit), a few days before taking off on that famous flight. The aircraft was one of Bleriot's own designs, the Type XI, a frail contraption yet surprisingly successful. Like the Wright Flyer, it had no ailerons, relying on wing-warping for lateral control. *(Smithsonian photo 78-14972)*

FROM NEW YORK TO LONG BEACH
AVIATOR RODGERS LANDING ~ 191

The irrepressible flyer Cal Rodgers (at left, with cigar and crutches) at Long Beach, California, during his coast-to-coast flight. It was an eventful forty-nine-day trip, with frequent mishaps necessitating a virtual rebuilding of the Wright EX. William Randolph Hearst sponsored the flight but in the end refused to pay Cal anything; he had taken longer than the thirty days specified. *(Smithsonian photo 2002-13915)*

Harriet Quimby was a leading aviatrix of the pre-World War One era and became the first woman to cross the English Channel by air, flying a Bleriot XI monoplane. She was killed in July 1912 when she fell out of her aircraft, which had no safety belts. *(Smithsonian photo A-44401-C)*

A pioneer aviatrix, Ruth Law was a regular performer at air meets all over the United States. In 1918, she earned a place in the record books with a 512-mile nonstop flight from Chicago to Hornell, New York. She protected herself against the elements by adding an aluminum fairing to the front of her Curtiss biplane. *(Canadian Aviation Museum)*

The first to fly the Atlantic nonstop: John Alcock (left) and Arthur Whitten Brown beside their modified Vickers Vimy bomber. Alcock was the pilot, and Brown the navigator. Both men were knighted and shared a ten-thousand-pound prize awarded by the London *Daily Mail*. Alcock was killed in an air crash less than a year later. *(Smithsonian photo 2003-22802)*

Alcock and Brown's Vimy taking off from Newfoundland at the start of the crossing. *(Canadian Aviation Museum)*

In May 1919, the U.S. Navy set out to conquer the Atlantic with three Navy-Curtiss flying boats shepherded by sixty-eight destroyers. Only one, NC-4, completed the voyage – twenty-three days later. Here, NC-3 at lies damaged at Ponta Delgada, the Azores, after taxiing for two days in heavy seas. *(Canadian Aviation Museum)*

The NC-4 arrives at Lisbon, May 27, 1919. *(Canadian Aviation Museum)*

Harry Hawker (right) and his navigator, naval commander K. Mackenzie-Grieve, wearing ill-fitting borrowed suits after being rescued at sea by the small steamer *Mary* in May 1919 following their attempt to fly the Atlantic nonstop. The ship had no radio, and thus the news of the airmen's remarkable survival couldn't be told for several days. *(Canadian Aviation Museum)*

The Sopwith Atlantic in which Hawker and Mackenzie-Grieve made their attempt. Engine trouble brought them down in the ocean after flying for some fourteen hours. *(Canadian Aviation Museum)*

The remains of the Sopwith Atlantic salvaged by the U.S. steamer *Lake Charlotteville* after floating in the Atlantic for nearly a week. The wreckage was later exhibited in London, at Selfridges in Oxford Street, attracting huge crowds. *(Canadian Aviation Museum)*

The *New Orleans*, one of the Douglas World Cruisers used by the U.S. Army Air Service to circumnavigate the world in 1924. Four of the modified torpedo bombers set out from Seattle, Washington, on April 6; two completed the journey in 175 days, a flying time of 371 hours, 11 minutes. *(Canadian Aviation Museum)*

The world-famous Lindberghs, Charles and his wife, Anne, at Baker Lake, NWT, with admirers. The couple had embarked on a round-the-world trip, leaving New Haven, Maine, in late July 1931 in a single-engine Lockheed Sirius floatplane christened *Tingmissartoq* by an Inuit boy. *(Canadian Aviation Museum)*

Clarence Chamberlin

A few weeks after Lindbergh's famous flight to Paris, Clarence Chamberlain (left) travelled three hundred miles further than Lindy, almost reaching Berlin. He flew a Bellanca monoplane, *Columbia*, accompanied by the owner of the aircraft, the garrulous and unpredictable ex-munitions dealer Charles Levine (right). *(Smithsonian photo 88-8613)* disagreements had been settled; then Levine stunned everyone by announcing that Bertaud had been replaced. Bertaud fought back, but he was no match for the wily Levine. His injunction was denied, and he was out. Chamberlin said nothing; Bellanca said plenty. He was furious; the bickering and backbiting were ruining the chances of glory for his plane.

||||

When Charles Lindbergh took off from Roosevelt Field on May 20, 1927, he was just another flyer, one of the crazy breed of young men who kept getting their names in the papers by risking life and limb in their frail craft. A French general named Duval called the whole business a folly: "Everyone knows that a vigorous, skillful pilot can fly for forty-five consecutive hours. The record has already been set at more than fifty-one hours. He may, if he be bold, put in these forty-five hours between Paris and New York, only all the elements of uncertainty must swing in his favour – favourable winds, clear atmosphere, no navigation mistakes, no engine trouble. Is it worth risking lives for such a demonstration? The transatlantic flight is a great sporting exploit, nothing more, and not worth the sacrifice of life, as nothing practical or scientific can be gained from even a successful attempt."[4] Many people agreed. Aviators were brave, of course, but they were madcaps. Who would want his daughter getting involved with *that* sort of individual? But after Lindbergh's flight, everything changed. Lindy underwent a magical transformation: he became, quite simply, the most admired man in the world.

He began his long journey along the same gravel and clay strip on which Fonck's transatlantic attempt had come to grief. The ground was tacky from the rain that had been falling on and off for days. The heavily loaded Ryan gathered speed with maddening deliberation. Spectators gasped, sickeningly sure that the plane could never reach flying speed while any runway remained beneath her wheels – each one of which had been rubbed with grease in a vain attempt to keep the mud from sticking. Conditions were lousy, but as far as Lindbergh was concerned, one factor outweighed all others. He had a head start. The competitors, Byrd's tri-motor Fokker and Chamberlin's Bellanca were still locked away in their hangars.

Of all the nail-biting takeoffs in that eventful era, none came closer to disaster than Lindbergh's. "The plane creeps heavily forward," Lindbergh later wrote. "Several men are pushing on wing struts to help it start – pushing so hard I'm afraid the struts will buckle. How can I possibly gain flying speed? Why did I ever think that air could carry such a weight? Why have I placed such reliance on a sheet of paper's curves? What possible connection is there between the intersection of a pencil's lines in San Diego and the ability of *this* airplane, *here*, *now*, to fly?"[5] As the Ryan slowly picked up speed, Lindbergh wondered bleakly whether the landing gear would collapse before he became airborne. Whether the enormous load of fuel would erupt and burn him to a crisp while he was struggling to get out of that tiny, cramped cabin. He had to keep his eyes glued to the edge of the strip, ignoring the splashes of water as the tires hurtled through puddles. A subtle difference in the feel of the controls. Speed was bestowing strength on the elevator and rudder. She wanted to fly! "I ease the stick forward – almost flying speed, and nearly 2,000 feet of field ahead – A shallow pool on the runway – water spews up from the tires – A wing drops – lifts as I shove aileron against it – the entire plane trembles from the shock – off again – right wing low – pull it up – Ease back onto the runway – left rudder – hold to centre – must keep straight – another pool – water drumming on the fabric – the next hop's longer – I could probably stay in the air; but I let the wheels touch once more – lightly, a last bow to earth, a gesture of humility before it."[6]

A web of telephone wires . . . he missed them by a few precious feet. A golf course slipped below. It seemed to Lindbergh that the *Spirit of St. Louis* was balanced on a pinpoint; the smallest error in his movement of the controls would cause it to topple.

Long Island slipped away behind. Ahead lay Connecticut, Rhode Island, and the broad Atlantic.

En route to Nova Scotia, he saw a few fishing boats. Soon afterward he experienced the first signs of the fatigue that would torment him throughout much of the flight. He had attempted to get a few hours' sleep before going to the field, but the hotel was crammed with people, all talking, laughing, telephoning, arguing, all eager to ask him questions or wish him luck. He had dragged himself out of bed at 2:30 a.m., having had no sleep. When he arrived at the field, he was greeted by the news that the engine was running thirty rpm low. The weather, shrugged the mechanic . . . the engine would never rev up fully in such conditions. The thought of postponing the flight was delicious, almost sensuous. A release of the tension, the simple delight of enjoying a good breakfast . . . *No! Such thoughts had to be denied!*

He ploughed on through rough weather, doggedly maintaining his course. His eyelids – which felt as if they weighed ten pounds each – had somehow become coated with glue; every time he blinked, they stuck together. He opened the side window and cupped the speeding air onto his face. It helped. Momentarily. He hadn't slept in forty-eight hours. He could think of nothing but sleep. There was no reward, no prize more desirable than oblivion. Sleep was far more important than flying to Paris. He pinched himself, he stamped his feet, he concentrated on his fuel supply

calculations and his navigation problems. The *Spirit*'s instability
was helpful, for he had to keep flying her, correcting her attitude in
the air as he switched from outer-wing tanks to central-wing tanks.

God, what he would give for a hour's slumber. Thirty minutes.
Ten. He could think of nothing else. His entire being ached for
sleep. If he didn't give in to it, something would break, some muscle,
some tendon, some nerve. Something vital. Maybe fatigue would
shut down his brain, leaving him unable to perform the multitudinous tasks that kept the plane in the air. He would dive helpless
into the sea, and the newspaper reporters would wonder why . . .

Shortly after midnight, he passed the point of no return. A
significant moment. Now he was closer to Europe than to North
America. He *had* to stay awake. *Had* to. In a semi-daze he flew on,
the shifting waters beneath him, the clearing sky above. It was daylight now. He had flown over 2,000 miles from New York; he had
only a little more than 1,300 miles to Paris. Three hundred gallons
of fuel had been consumed in the full day he had spent in the air.
Engine still performing perfectly.

At about 10 a.m., he spotted the dot in the water. A boat!
Human beings! He flew close to the surface, edged the throttle
down, and yelled, "Which way is Ireland?"

The men didn't respond. They stared at him, unable to credit the
evidence of their eyes. Just then, he saw it on the horizon dead
ahead: a thin dark line that might have been a mirage, until it slowly
evolved into a rocky shoreline and breaking waves. It was unquestionably the most beautiful sight he had ever seen. But where was
it? Scotland? Ireland? England? France? Soon, he was able to iden-
tify the glorious ground beneath him: Dingle Bay, Ireland. Now his
fatigue dissolved, forgotten. A mere six hundred miles remained!

He had been flying more than thirty hours when he crossed the
French coast at Deauville. Right on track! His navigation was

better than he thought! As if to celebrate, he fingered the neck of his paper bag and took out a sandwich. His first food since takeoff. It tasted flat and unappetizing. He drank some water to help it down. Below, lights were beginning to appear as the second night of the journey began. He scanned the scene ahead. Blackness and twinkling lights, dozens, hundreds of them. He searched in vain for Le Bourget, the Paris airport. Someone had told him it was north-east of the city. He circled, his eyes aching with the strain of staring into confusing blackness punctuated by lights that made no sense.

At last he found it – an open space punctuated by lights splash-ing on grass. Tiny figures running. But why? Had his arrival inter-rupted some sporting event? He was still wondering as he turned the Ryan into wind and descended for a landing:

Tail too high – hold off – hold off – but the lights are far behind – the surface dims – texture of sod is gone – Ahead, there's nothing but night – give her the gun and climb for another try? – The wheels touch gently – off again – No, I'll keep contact – ease the stick forward – Back on the ground – Off – Back – the tail skid too – Not a bad landing, but I'm beyond the light – can't see anything ahead – Like flying in fog – Ground loop? – No, still rolling too fast – might blow a tire – The field *must be* clear – Uncomfortable, though, jolting into blackness – Wish I had a wing light – but too heavy on the take-off – Slower now – slow enough to ground loop safely – left rudder – reverse it – stick over the other way – The *Spirit of St. Louis* swings around and stops rolling, resting on the solidness of earth, in the center of Le Bourget.[7]

He had done it! In a few hours he would be the most famous man on the planet, his youthful features splashed across newspapers from Vancouver to Vladivostok. The Flyin' Fool had become the Lone Eagle. Editors could scarcely contain themselves. His was the greatest feat of solitary man in the records of the human, according to the New York *Evening World*. The Albany *Evening News* declared that "nothing in years has brought world thought and world hope to such unity . . ." Heywood Broun in the New York *World* went further: "One had only to venture into any city street after the news of Lindbergh's landing to notice that for a little while the aspect of the world and all its people had magnificently altered. We came up out of slumps and slouches. There was more brotherhood in being than I have ever seen here since the morning of the Armistice. . . . Glory can be rationed out to every living being. Each one of us feels that in some way he shared in the mighty jump . . ." The Baltimore *Sun* declared that Lindbergh had "exalted the race of man." A Consolidated Press dispatch revelled in the diplomatic implications: "Charles Lindbergh . . . has done by a single stroke more to put Franco-American relations on a plane of human friendliness than the diplomats could have done in years." The politicians also had their say, of course. Former secretary of state Charles E. Hughes declared expansively that Lindbergh has "lifted us into the freer and upper air that is his home." He continued, "He has displaced everything that is petty; that is sordid; that is vulgar. . . . He has driven the sensation mongers out of the temples of our thoughts. He has kindled anew the fire of the eight ancient altars in the temple."

||||

When Charles Lindbergh took off for Paris, he left two competitors feeling like brides abandoned at the altar. Both had been considered far more likely to win the Orteig prize than the youngster from the Midwest. Richard Byrd, whose crew now included a second pilot, the dashing Bert Acosta, in addition to Bernt Balchen and engineer and radio operator George Noville, said he was making the flight in order to chart the best air route to Europe. Also left in the aerial lurch was the Bellanca owned by the endlessly artful Charles Levine and piloted by Chamberlin. Levine, an outspoken admirer of the Italian dictator Mussolini, whom he regarded as another Napoleon, was said to be considering a flight to Rome now instead of Paris. On the morning of June 2, the rumours buzzed when Chamberlin arrived at the field, clambered aboard *Columbia*, and took off. But he returned in the afternoon. The reason for the flight was nothing more exciting than the installation of a new carburetor heater.

The next day, June 3, came the announcement that everyone had been waiting for. Chamberlin said he would be taking off at 4 a.m. to fly the Atlantic and continue for as long as his fuel held out, to beat Lindbergh's distance record. But who would accompany him now that Bertaud was gone? No one seemed to know. The names of Charles Fields and Bernt Balchen kept coming up, despite the latter's involvement with Byrd.

It was still dark the next morning when Chamberlin arrived at the field. The *Columbia* was hauled to Roosevelt Field by truck, just as the *Spirit of St. Louis* had been. Despite the early hour, a boisterous crowd had assembled; flashbulbs kept popping as reporters fired questions at anyone who looked as if he might have something to do with the flight. John Carisi, chief engineer for Columbia Aircraft, went over the aircraft, checking and rechecking every last detail. Shortly before 6 a.m., he started the engine. Chamberlin clambered aboard and exchanged a few words with the engineer. Just then, as daylight crept over the scene, something odd happened. Charles Levine, natty in a double-breasted business suit, broke from the crowd and trotted over to the aircraft carrying an armful of charts. It looked as if the Columbia boss was going to have a last word with Chamberlin. But he astounded everyone by opening the cabin door and settling himself in the co-pilot's seat. The door slammed shut behind him.

Another figure ran to the aircraft – a woman; none other than Grace Levine. She was distraught, her voice strident with urgency. "Stop him! Please stop him!"

Carisi restrained her and tried to calm her by saying it was just a short test flight, nothing more. The Bellanca's engine roared purposefully. Chamberlin signalled to the waiting mechanics. They tugged the chocks free. The monoplane taxied to the crude strip from which Lindbergh had taken off. Chamberlin turned around when spectators overflowed onto the strip. He returned to his starting point. Grace Levine became a little calmer, apparently believing that her erratic husband was in fact merely going on a test hop.

Chamberlin, a polished and experienced pilot, handled the Bellanca with his usual skill as it trundled along the rough strip, heavily laden with some 450 gallons of fuel. Little more than halfway along, the yellow monoplane took to the air. The Bellanca demonstrated her fine qualities, soaring easily over the telephone wires that had nearly brought Lindbergh down, heading out toward Long Island Sound.

At this point, the truth appeared to hit Mrs. Levine. Charlie *was* going to fly the Atlantic – or at least, he was going to try. The idea appalled her. He had spent no more than a couple of hours at the controls of an airplane. He knew nothing about navigation. What was he trying to prove? It was too late to ask him. The Bellanca was already a mere speck in the distant sky. Mrs. Levine did not turn her tear-stained face away until the speck had vanished.

For his part, Chamberlin seemed untroubled by Levine's inexperience. He assumed responsibility for both flying and navigating. He intended to fly to Europe, keeping on going until his fuel ran out. If he couldn't beat Lindbergh across the Atlantic, at least he would better his distance.

Just before reaching Cape Cod, he made a nasty discovery. The earth inductor compass had failed. He had to rely on his magnetic compass, a quirky instrument at best. Did Levine want to abandon the flight and return to New York? Levine shook his head. No turning back, not now that they were on their way.

They flew on, hour following hour, the endless ocean sliding beneath them, unchanging, uncaring. Chamberlin had only a vague idea as to their precise position, but when they came across a large liner, he checked the name on the stern – *Mauretania* – and consulted the newspaper that Levine had brought along. It stated that the British liner was heading west and was less than a day out of Cherbourg. Figuring the ship's speed at 500 miles a day, he estimated that *Columbia* had brought them to within 350 miles of the French coast – little more than three hours' flying time! Chamberlin flew along the liner's line of direction. It brought them to Land's End, the western tip of England. Night was falling as the Bellanca crossed the English Channel, her engine humming as sweetly as ever.

For much of the trip, the weather had been superb. Now it was thickening. Chamberlin climbed to the Bellanca's ceiling, twenty-one thousand feet. To his disappointment he saw even higher clouds ahead. He decided to let Levine take the controls for a few minutes while he had a nap. It was a short one. He awoke a minute or two later to find the Bellanca in a spiral dive, speed mounting alarmingly, the ocean revolving before him like some lunatic image in a nightmare. Chamberlin got the aircraft straightened out in time, hoping the incident hadn't resulted in structural damage. He gingerly tested the controls. Things seemed to be okay. Levine grinned; he seemed to think it had all been a huge joke. He had inadvertently pulled up the nose while trying to keep the aircraft level: a common mistake among inexperienced pilots. The result was a stall, quickly developing into a spiral dive. It might have been the end. But Chamberlin merely shrugged it off. No use getting Levine in a stew. He looked out. They were over Germany, Chamberlin calculated, somewhere near the Harz mountains. The end of the journey was in sight! Chamberlin told Levine to go to the rear of the cabin to help keep the tail down in the forthcoming landing. The Bellanca was becoming nose-heavy as the fuel was consumed, the same problem that beset Byrd's tri-motor.

The engine stopped, out of gas after forty-three hours, having taken the sturdy Bellanca 3,905 miles – nearly three hundred miles further than the *Spirit of St. Louis* had journeyed. Chamberlin brought the *Columbia* in for a good landing in a field near the village of Eisleben, about one hundred miles southwest of Berlin.

In New York, Isaac Levine, father of the Columbia boss, declared proudly, "Charlie's is a greater feat than Lindbergh's!" Levine Senior had spent a sleepless night waiting for news of his son's progress. For a few delicious days, Chamberlin and Levine were the toast of the world. They were the guests of honour at ceremonies and receptions in Berlin, Vienna, Rome, Madrid, and beyond. Chamberlin soon wearied of it all, but Levine loved every moment. He had never enjoyed himself so much. As far as he was concerned, the fun could go on forever. Eager to promote his company and himself, he talked at length to anyone who cared to listen. He hinted that he intended to return to the United States in the Bellanca and, yes, his transatlantic airline would soon take to the air. He raked Pioneer Instruments over the coals for the failure of the earth inductor compass. Charles Colvin, Pioneer's president, responded bluntly that there was only one reason for Levine's bitter comments: he wanted to avoid paying for the equipment. Levine ignored him. He was still enjoying himself too much to be concerned over petty bellyaches. He continued to talk about returning to the States aboard the *Columbia*. There and back aboard the same aircraft! What an accomplishment! What lustre for the Levine name! Clarence Chamberlin didn't share his enthusiasm. He said that even if he agreed to fly the plane home, which was by no means certain, he needed at least a month to prepare. Levine balked at that. He hated waiting. The return flight had to be completed while the story was still hot. In his impulsive way he immediately hired the French pilot Maurice Drouhin to fly him home – blithely ignoring the fact that the Frenchman was under contract to the Farman company to fly a somewhat ungainly biplane named the *Oiseau Bleu* across the Atlantic. Drouhin's contract with Levine called for him to be paid three thousand francs a week while he prepared the *Columbia* for the return trip. If the venture ended disastrously, three hundred thousand francs was to be paid to Mme Drouhin. The arrangements did nothing for owner Henry Farman's blood pressure. He commented acidly, "Mr. Levine's way of doing things has certainly taken us by surprise. He did not consult us either by letter or by telephone."

Another man surprised by Mr. Levine's way of doing things was his new pilot, for the promised fee failed to materialize in Drouhin's bank account, despite numerous assurances that it was "in the mail." The fact that Drouhin spoke no English and Levine no French may have had something to do with it – although

Levine's dealings always seemed to be wondrously convoluted, no matter what language was involved.

Levine, meanwhile, had reverted to his old cantankerous self. He asked Drouhin to fly him to Deauville to see the Grand Prix. Drouhin replied haughtily that he was not an aerial taxi driver. Tempers flared; onlookers expected the pair to come to blows. They didn't, but it was a near thing. The next day Levine arrived at the field, marched into his hangar, and instructed the mechanics to wheel the *Columbia* outside. A youthful *gendarme* had been guarding the aircraft ever since Drouhin had obtained an injunction to prevent the aircraft being flown by anyone but himself. Levine, untroubled by such a minor technicality, said he intended just to test the engine and taxi the aircraft around the field. The mechanic obediently started the engine. Who could blame him? Levine was the *Columbia*'s owner – and a thoroughly persuasive character at any time. When Levine asked the young man to fetch his hat and coat from the car, there was no argument, only a quick nod. Off trotted the young man. Levine got aboard the Bellanca and ran it up. A few minutes later, he began to taxi the aircraft about the field. No one took much notice – until he suddenly opened the throttle wide and went bumping across the field at increasing speed. Onlookers gazed in fascination as the Bellanca gained speed, lurched uneasily into the air, and climbed away into the sunny sky. The authorities at Le Bourget were thunderstruck. A military aircraft took off in pursuit, but by the time it was airborne, Levine was almost out of sight, heading north.

Officials called Croydon and warned them that Levine – who had benefit of only an hour or two's instruction – had departed and seemed to be headed their way. He had never soloed. Until today, that is. Moreover, they added with some passion, he hadn't paid his bill for the *Columbia*'s hangar at Le Bourget. Reports soon began to come in from Abbeville and Boulogne . . . then from southern England. Levine had flown the Channel – in a somewhat erratic manner, it is true, but he had managed not to kill himself. At least, not yet. Now he approached Croydon, London's busy airport south of the city. Fire and ambulance staff sprang into action. Several airliners were due to arrive from various points in Europe. God knew what might happen if Levine was still buzzing about when they did. He had no radio and had never landed an airplane. Officials watched in mute horror as the Bellanca came into view. All they could do was hope. Levine reduced power, apparently intending to land. The aircraft swooped toward the field, then climbed back into the air. Four times Levine *almost* landed, coming close to the ground, then, engine roaring, climbing away, turning, preparing for yet another try. A British pilot, Fred Smith of the Surrey Flying Service, took off and led Levine down to an eventful but ultimately safe landing, a grotesque bouncing into the air, a thumping back onto the ground, followed by another bounce. And another. Eventually, thoroughly shaken, the stalwart Bellanca came to a halt.

An unperturbed Levine stepped out, rubbing his chin, saying he needed a shave. An airport official declared that he had already had a shave – a close one. Levine grinned. A good joke. He chatted with the airport people as if they were all old friends. Charlie Levine was immensely pleased with himself; he had successfully flown from Paris to London, that no one could deny. Admittedly, his handling of the long-suffering Bellanca had been something less than polished, but he could work on that. He told reporters he had forgotten about the Bellanca's adjustable tail surface; it had to be in the right position for landing. *The Times* wasn't the least bit amused, chiding the American for "the most alarming experience which has ever happened in the memory of the civil aviation traffic officers, regular pilots and aerodrome staff." Levine's life, declared the paper, had been saved by the prompt action of Fred Smith. Levine shook his balding head and professed ignorance of Mr. Smith's assistance – claiming, in fact, that he had never seen him. He shrugged off complaints that he had endangered the lives of airport personnel and had flouted Croydon's regulations. Wide-eyed, Levine said no one had told him about any regulations, adding that he had become disenchanted with French control and intended to fly back to the U.S. from British soil. It was a master stroke. Britons suddenly became oddly fond of the troublesome Levine. When he turned up for a performance of the musical comedy *Blue Skies*, the West End audience stood up and applauded – although no one was sure whether the cheers were for Levine's hair-raising flying or for his apparent victory over the French. Few things delighted the British more than seeing their Gallic neigh-bours at a disadvantage.

Two days later, Levine announced he had engaged Captain Walter Hinchliffe to fly him and *Columbia* home to America. Hinchliffe was a highly skilled pilot who had worked for years for Imperial Airways. The *Columbia* had been installed with extra fuel tanks and, Levine claimed, could stay aloft for sixty-five hours. But Levine was destined never to make another record-breaking flight. In September, he and Hinchliffe set off on a non-stop flight to India, but landed with engine trouble at Vienna. From Vienna the two of them set off for Venice to see the Schneider Cup races, after which Levine went to Rome to fulfill a long ambition to meet the Pope and Mussolini. In the presence of Pius XI, Levine became almost incoherent, although he was able to utter a few phrases to his dictator hero. He promised to drop a silver watch by parachute to *Il Duce*'s newborn baby girl. After *Columbia* suffered some damage in a forced landing, Levine abandoned his plans to fly over

Mussolini's villa and went by commercial liner, from which he duly dropped his gift. He abandoned his plans to fly home and went by ship. His reception on arrival in New York was tepid; the controversial Mr. Levine had ruffled too many feathers on his travels.

IIII

Richard Byrd's tri-motor Fokker still occupied the hangar bearing the name "America Transoceanic Company." Preparations for the big flight had been going on for weeks – too long for the impetuous Anthony Fokker. He had been counting on a triumphal flight to bolster sales of his aircraft. Precious time was slipping away. He threatened to buy back his plane and make the flight himself if Byrd didn't act soon. Byrd, scion of a distinguished family, began to receive mail accusing him of cowardice: "I am sick of seeing your name," one correspondent huffed. "You are a disgrace to America. You have never had any idea of flying across the Atlantic."[8] Byrd ignored them.

Late in June, the weather forecasts, while far from perfect, could be considered acceptable. Byrd delayed no longer. In the grey early hours, the ground crew manhandled the hefty Fokker tail-first up the incline at one end of the Roosevelt landing strip. Bert Acosta, burly and good-humoured, was in the left-hand seat; Bernt Balchen took the right-hand seat, George Noville was at the radio, Byrd himself was to navigate.

The idea was to run up the engines while the Fokker was still secured. In the event, the line snapped before the engines had been fully warmed up. Acosta had only a split second to make up his mind. Keep going, or start again? He decided to keep going. The Fokker rumbled along the taxi-way and rose easily, to the intense relief of everyone concerned.

Soon after takeoff, the Fokker ran into misty weather, which soon became thick fog. Balchen, in the co-pilot's seat, was unwrapping a sandwich when, horrified, he realized that the Fokker was in a spin, heading straight for the sea. He got the aircraft back on an even keel, then glanced across at Acosta, who grinned sheepishly and admitted that he knew nothing about instrument flying. It is an interesting comment on the state of aviation at that time that a pilot could be selected for a project of this significance without possessing an instrument rating – and that other aviators would have no qualms about trusting their lives to him. Acosta was a highly respected flyer, but strictly a seat-of-the-pants man.

The visibility didn't improve much – indeed, as they neared the French coast, it deteriorated dramatically until even the Fokker's wing tips were invisible. Le Bourget was socked in completely. Balchen glimpsed what he believed were the spires of Rouen Cathedral thrusting up through the mist. Byrd, concerned about the possibility of hitting something in the poor visibility, instructed the pilots to land on the shore as best they could. Three carbide drift flares provided a little light, but the crew still did not know just where they were – and after forty hours aloft, the airmen were weary and disinclined to spend any more time circling blindly, searching for a landing field. They splashed down, their long journey finally over. The landing gear sheared off, but the plane did not flip onto her back as they had feared. Cold water flooded into the cabin as the aircraft settled by the nose, dragged down by the weight of the engines. The four airmen clambered into their rubber raft and paddled to shore only a few yards away. They had arrived at the village of Ver-sur-Mer, part of what soon would be better known as the invasion beaches on D-Day.

||||

Publisher William Randolph Hearst's name kept cropping up in aviation stories. In 1927, he formed a new newspaper, the New York *Daily Mirror*. To promote it, he sponsored a flight from Old Orchard, Maine, to Rome in a single-engine Fokker named *Old Glory*. One experienced airmail pilot, Lloyd Bertaud, was hired to fly the plane; a second, James D. Hill, was enlisted as navigator. The editor of the *Mirror*, Philip Payne, wanted to go along. The pilots said no, the plane was loaded to its limit. Payne said one more wouldn't make any difference. Bertaud was in a difficult position. The plane belonged to Hearst; indeed, the newspaper mogul was paying for everything. Reluctantly, he agreed to take Payne along, although he had to reduce his fuel supply by one hundred gallons to compensate for the additional passenger.

When at last *Old Glory* began her takeoff run along the Old Orchard beach, it was one of the classic nail-biters of the era. Police on motorcycles roared along beside the aircraft as she picked up speed, exhorting the hundreds of onlookers – including comedian Fred Allen – to get back out of the way. For some two miles, the heavily laden monoplane thundered along the sand, her broad wings rocking from side to side as if testing the air. Then at last she left the sand, engine howling. Onlookers held their breath as the big plane roared over the pier, clearing it by one or two feet. It was 1:25 p.m. Soon she was reported over Monhegan Island; at 3:55 p.m. the freighter *Empress* spotted her near Digby, Nova Scotia. Three hours later, she flew low over North Sydney. At 9:25 p.m. the *Berlin*, then some 1,200 miles east of New York, reported hearing the plane. Little more than an hour later, the station at Cape Race, Newfoundland, picked up a message from *Old Glory* indicating that all was well.

But at 4:03 a.m., alarmed ships' radio operators picked up a message from the monoplane telling of trouble. The aircraft was about six hundred miles east of Cape Race. Several ships altered course to look for her. They searched for more than twelve hours. They found nothing. Tony Fokker declared that the problem must have been with the engine, for the aircraft was in perfect condition.

IIII

In Canada, the Carling Brewery decided to get in on the long-distance action, although the idea is believed to have originated with a newspaper reporter, Arthur Carty, of the London, Ontario, *Advertiser*. Carling announced a twenty-five thousand dollar prize for a flight from London, Ontario, to London, England, by any Canadian or British airman. Scores of applications came in, but only one applicant could provide his own aircraft – and since he was an American, he wasn't eligible. The company then purchased a Stinson Detroiter, named it *Sir John Carling* after the firm's founder, and started interviewing airmen to fly it. Two experienced pilots, Terence Tully and James Medcalf, both of whom worked for the Ontario Provincial Air Service, were selected. At the same time, a group of Canadian businessmen sponsored another Stinson to fly from Windsor, Ontario, to Windsor, England. Duke Schiller, a well-known Canadian bush pilot, and Phil Wood, brother of the American motorboat racer, would crew the aircraft, named the *Royal Windsor*. Competition was keen between the two teams. In the event, however, the *Sir John Carling* got away first, on August 28, 1927 – only to run into thick fog near Kingston, Ontario. Sensibly, Tully and Medcalf turned around and flew back. Originally, the intention had been to fly direct to England. Now, in view of weather problems, it was decided to head first for Harbour Grace, Newfoundland, before setting out over the

Atlantic. The fog persisted for several days, causing the two flyers to remain at Harbour Grace until September 7. They took on a large load of fuel and set off, using the entire strip before rising. The trim Stinson climbed steadily and headed out to sea. No doubt Tully and Medcalf congratulated themselves on getting away ahead of the competition. They might have been less sanguine had they known that as they took off, word was received that *Old Glory*, the Fokker that had taken off from Old Orchard beach a few hours earlier, had broadcast an SOS.

No one knows whether Tully and Medcalf ever heard about *Old Glory*; they vanished over the broad Atlantic, just as surely and finally as had so many flyers. Carling announced that the twenty-five thousand dollars would be divided up among the flyers' widows.

The backers of the *Royal Windsor* decided to call the whole thing off, and no one argued with the decision. A few days later, a section of wing was found floating in the sea, distinctive because an American flag had been painted on it. It belonged to *Old Glory*. The fuel tanks in the wing section were partially filled. Pieces of the landing gear were also found. It appeared that the Fokker had flown into the sea, ripping the wing free, leaving the fuselage, weighed down by the engine, to sink into the depths. Despite the chilling evidence, Mrs. Bertaud bravely insisted that it all added up to good news: "I am terribly happy. Everything tells me that the condition of the parts found indicate that they were able to keep afloat until they were picked up by some vessel. I am absolutely certain they are safe. Lloyd has been in many tight squeezes before and he has always come through safely. An awful load has been lifted from my mind since I heard about the finding of the wreckage."[9]

The brave Mrs. Bertaud wished as hard as a certain Mrs. Hawker had wished eight years earlier. But the fates weren't as kind. Nothing more was ever heard of Bertaud and his fellow flyers. Or of *Old Glory*. Or of *Sir John Carling*.

The disasters led inevitably to harsh criticism in the press. These suicidal flights had to stop. There should be a law. Something had to be done. But nothing ever was.

CHAPTER SIX | *Promoting*
Pineapples

J ames D. Dole, president of the famous canned fruit company,
had a brainwave. With all the world still talking about Charles
Lindbergh and his New York-to-Paris flight, Dole thought, why
not promote air travel between the U.S. mainland and Hawaii by
setting up a race and offering substantial cash prizes? It seemed a
great idea.

Dole dearly wanted Lindbergh to participate, to bring the sort
of glory to Hawaii that he had brought to St. Louis. In that city,
the businessmen who had backed Lindy's Atlantic flight were more
than prepared to do the same for the Pacific flight, if he decided to
participate. He turned the offer down, his reasoning characteristically sound. Although the 2,407-mile long flight to Hawaii was
considerably shorter than the trip to Paris, in some ways it was
much tougher. For one thing, it was entirely over water – more
than six hundred miles farther than the longest over-water stretch
of the earlier flight. But perhaps the most daunting aspect of all was

the need for superlative navigation. An error of more than a degree or two would mean missing the Hawaiian Islands altogether, and Lindbergh had no illusions about his skill as a navigator.

James Dole was bitterly disappointed, and more disappointments were on the way. Dole didn't know it, but the U.S. Army Air Corps was about to steal his thunder. For several months two lieutenants, Lester Maitland and Albert Hegenberger, had been preparing to fly a Fokker tri-motor from the mainland to Hawaii. The Army was anxious to demonstrate that Hawaii could be quickly reached in the event of war. Late in June, the Fokker, bearing the curiously inappropriate name *Bird of Paradise*, was flown to the West Coast equipped with the latest navigational equipment. The flight, scheduled weeks ahead of the Dole Derby, would also test the concept of radio directional beams: riding one beam out of San Francisco, then picking up another emitting from Hawaii.

A civilian pilot, Ernie Smith, was bent on beating the big Fokker to Hawaii. He had a Travel Air monoplane named *City of Oakland*, and a navigator, Charles Carter, and was all set to take off from the Army's Crissey Field, San Francisco. To the flyers' surprise – and anger – the Army abruptly decreed that no civilian airplanes could use the field – even to take off to go to another field. Although the Army declared that the ruling had nothing whatever to do with the Maitland–Hegenberger flight, no one believed them. The Travel Air had to be dismantled and trucked to Oakland Municipal Airport at considerable expense to Smith and Carter.

Now a third contender put in an appearance. His name was Dick Grace and he was better known for wrecking airplanes than flying them great distances. Grace had survived no less than sixteen staged crashes for the movies, including one for *Wings* which broke his neck. Grace planned to fly from Hawaii to the mainland, taking off from the island of Kauai.

The Army Fokker got away first, in the early morning of June 28, and went roaring away to the west. The *City of Oakland* followed a couple of hours later, Smith confident that he could overtake the Fokker. But bad luck dogged him. The windshield of the navigator's cockpit suddenly collapsed. Carter found it impossible to take navigational observations in the ferocious gale. The Travel Air returned to Oakland – where no one could find a replacement windshield for Carter's cockpit. Smith dissolved in tears, his disappointment too much to bear.

Maitland and Hegenberger droned on, making good progress, although their much-vaunted navigational equipment proved to be of dubious value. The radio beam signals were intermittent. The earth inductor compass failed. High winds and turbulent seas rendered their smoke bombs useless for navigational purposes. But Hegenberger was up to the challenge, bringing the Fokker to Hawaii "on the nose." The Army flyers landed at Wheeler Field, having flown for twenty-five hours, forty-nine minutes, a new record for the longest over-water flight.

Dick Grace got away from Kauai a few days later. He had control problems with his Ryan and turned back. He landed safely but ran into a tree. Disappointed, he went back to flying for the movies.

Ernie Smith obtained a new windshield for his Travel Air, but dismissed Carter. He needed a navigator made of sterner stuff. He recruited a master mariner, Emory Bronte, and the choice proved excellent. The flyers set off for Hawaii. The journey was not easy, for solid cloud obscured the ocean from start to finish. To compound their problems, they ran low on fuel before reaching Hawaii. Bronte transmitted an SOS, telling the world their position and the news that they would soon be landing in the sea. Several ships immediately changed course to hurry to their aid. Among the aircraft being readied for the search was the Army's *Bird of Paradise*. But it wasn't needed. A message arrived stating that the flyers had landed safely on the nearby island of Molokai, famous for the leper colony and the Belgian priest, Father Damien, who had worked there. It was a rough landing, for Smith had to stall into the upper branches of a tree. But both airmen crawled out of the wreck uninjured.

Now the Dole Derby – as it had become known – gathered momentum. The newly formed Aeronautics Branch of the U.S. Department of Commerce sent a team of inspectors to supervise the event. They decreed that every plane had to have "sufficient fuel range" and a qualified navigator aboard. At that time, pilots' licences were not essential for all private flying, although provisional licences were issued for this event. Entries streamed in, including one from Mildred Doran, from Caro, Michigan. The attractive schoolteacher had some experience as a pilot but was considered insufficiently qualified for this trip. She was, however, given permission to travel as a passenger in the Buhl CA-5, the *Miss Doran*, the only biplane among the entries. Augie Pedlar was the pilot and Cy Knope the navigator. Two other women had wanted to participate in the race: Pauline Rich of Los Angeles had intended to accompany Garland Lincoln but he pulled out of the competition. Constance Erwin, the twenty-year-old wife of pilot Bill Erwin, had intended to accompany her husband as navigator in *Dallas Spirit*, a Swallow monoplane, but was disqualified due to a rule forbidding anyone under the age of twenty-one to participate in a National Aeronautics Association (NAA) event. Other early entries included John W. Frost in a new Lockheed Vega, *Golden Eagle*, owned by the Hearst organization, and former movie stunt flyer Art Goebel and Bill Davis in a Travel Air called *Woolaroc*. The unusual name derived from "woods, lakes, and rocks" and was also the name of oilman Frank Phillips's ranch; Phillips helped to finance the entry, as well as that of the *Oklahoma*, another Travel Air, this crewed by Benny Griffin and Al Haney. Two U.S. Navy flyers entered a "home-built," designed by Naval pilot Norman Goddard, named *El Encanto* ("*The Charm*"). Goddard's navigator was Lieutenant K.C. Hawkins, USN. Also entered was *Pabco Pacific Flyer*, a Breese, to be flown solo by Livingston Irving.

Some odd birds put in an appearance: an ungainly International triplane bearing the name *Pride of Los Angeles*, didn't even make it to the starting line, stalling into San Francisco Bay, fortunately without killing anyone. Other hopeful entrants were not so lucky. Lieutenants Covell and Waggener of the U.S. Navy died when their Tremaine monoplane *Humming Bird* crashed into Point Loma, San Diego, during a test flight. Captain Arthur Rodgers took off in an aircraft designed by Leland Bryant, dubbed *The Angel of Los Angeles*. A veteran pilot who had flown in the Lafayette Escadrille during the war, Rodgers couldn't handle the viciously unstable Bryant plane. He bailed out – but he was too low. His wife saw his body hit the ground. "Thank God he left me a daughter," she managed to gasp. An Air King, *City of Peoria*, flown by Charles W. Parkhurst, was forcibly withdrawn when government inspectors decreed that the aircraft had insufficient fuel capacity to make the trip.

The great race, originally scheduled to take place on August 12, was now set for Tuesday, August 16, to give the competitors as much preparation time as possible. Fifty thousand people swarmed onto the field at Oakland to see the fun. It was a sunny day with slight haze. Eight aircraft remained in the contest, with fifteen men and one woman aboard. Promptly at noon, the official starter, Edward Howard, brought down his checkered black-and-white flag. First off the mark was the Travel Air *Oklahoma* with Griffin and Haney aboard. A huge cloud of dust billowed up, obscuring the aircraft. The Travel Air used up more than 4,500 feet of the cinder runway before lifting off. Officials waved the next aircraft, *El Encanto*, into the starting circle. At 12:04 p.m., the monoplane began its takeoff roll. The speed increased – but the aircraft didn't leave the ground. After roaring more than halfway along the strip, Goddard lost control of his heavily loaded aircraft. It slewed off to the right of the runway, sending spectators fleeing for their lives. The landing gear then collapsed; a wing crumpled. The bent and broken remains slithered to an untidy halt, but few of the onlookers could see anything because of the dust. The flyers, Goddard and Hawkins, emerged, a little wobbly but unhurt. In minutes, the *Pabco Pacific Flyer* was on its way, engine howling, gathering speed along the strip. But the aircraft stayed resolutely on the ground; the pilot, Livingston Irving, had to cut the throttle to prevent a crash off the end of the runway. The *Pabco Pacific Flyer* didn't. Ground staff towed her away to make room for competitors to come.

The Vega *Golden Eagle* started to roll at 12:29. The sleek monoplane was in the air halfway along the strip and had climbed to two hundred feet at runway's end. The pilot was John Frost, the navigator Gordon Scott. The Vega turned to pass over San Francisco before heading out into the haze. Next to go was the only biplane, the red and white Buhl Air Sedan *Miss Doran* with the attractive Michigan schoolteacher aboard, sporting a military-style uniform of her own design. But no sooner had the Buhl taken to the air than the engine started backfiring. The pilot, Augie Pedlar, promptly turned, dumped most of his fuel in the bay, and landed, taxiing to the end of the takeoff line for a set of new plugs. The *Oklahoma*, with Benny Griffin at the controls, reappeared close behind, also experiencing engine woes. It landed and taxied to the flight line for servicing. Now Irving in the *Pabco Pacific Flyer* tried again. Shortly after 1:00 p.m., the aircraft started its takeoff roll. It seemed to be going well – until it ground looped, smashing a wing. The *Flyer* was out, although Irving was not hurt. Two aircraft then made successful takeoffs: *Aloha*, with Martin Jensen at the controls and Paul Schluter, navigator, followed by *Woolaroc*, the porky Travel Air monoplane flown by Art Goebel with a naval officer, Lieutenant W. V. Davis, as navigator. It took to the air after a run of only three thousand feet.

The Swallow monoplane *Dallas Spirit*, with Bill Erwin at the controls and Alvin Eichwaldt sitting in as navigator for Constance, climbed away in good order after running almost the entire length of the strip, but not long after it came into view again through the dust, heading back to the field. The navigator's drift sight hatch in the bottom of the fuselage had come unfastened and was furiously beating against the body of the plane, ripping fabric. It looked as if the rear fuselage was disintegrating, but Erwin pulled off a successful landing at 1:15 p.m. Little more than half an hour later, Augie Pedlar took off again in *Miss Doran*, his engine serviced and his tanks topped up.

Of the eight aircraft that had tried to get away, four were now headed for Hawaii. Soon the last murmurs of their engines were silenced. The crowds began to disperse, leaving the field quieter than it had been for days. There was nothing to do but await news of the triumphant winner.

At Wheeler Field, outside Honolulu, an estimated twenty thousand people gathered, chattering excitedly. A band played popular songs. Colourful Hawaiian shirts mingled with a kaleidoscopic collection of kimonos, flowered jackets, and pajama pants. It was the most exciting day in Hawaii that anyone could remember. Unfortunately, the three thousand employees of the Dole company could not be present. The pineapple crop had ripened more rapidly than expected, and the workers had to remain in the canneries to ensure that the precious fruit was packed before it spoiled.

Shortly after noon, several aircraft took off and headed out to sea. They were the aerial welcoming committee. They returned a few minutes later escorting Art Goebel's Travel Air *Woolaroc*. He and navigator Bill Davis were soon on the ground, grinning, shaking hands, saying how glad they were to be there. They meant it, for it had been a long and dangerous trip: many lonely hours with nothing to look at but sea. Goebel said he and Davis weren't tired or sleepy; they wanted only to cable home, have a shave, and take a dip at Waikiki.

In between the handshakes, Marguerita Jensen, whose husband was piloting *Aloha*, grabbed Goebel's arm. Where was he, she asked? Why hadn't he arrived? Goebel didn't know. He had seen nothing since takeoff, not even a steamer.

Mrs. Jensen dissolved in tears. They soon dried, however, for the Breese monoplane appeared. The *Aloha* came in for a good landing. Martin Jensen emerged, weary but overjoyed, followed by Paul Schluter of San Francisco, his navigator. More handshakes, more official words of congratulation. Eyes turned seaward. The others should appear at any moment. The crowds waited. Hours ticked away. The excited chatter had become an intermittent drone of uneasy conversation. How long could they keep flying?

A big celebration had been scheduled for that evening, but it was a cheerless affair. The morning brought no news. *Miss Doran* and *Golden Eagle* were down. Somewhere. The U.S. Navy sent out an armada of thirty-nine ships and dozens of aircraft to search more than a half-million square miles of ocean. They found nothing. Predictably, Jim Dole believed that the problem could be solved by the application of sufficient cash. He promptly offered ten thousand dollars for the rescue of either crew, twenty thousand dollars for both. Bill Malloska, who had sponsored the *Miss Doran*, offered ten thousand for the trio aboard his Buhl. Another pledge of ten thousand dollars came from George Hearst for the men on the *Golden Eagle*. It was all in vain. Nothing was ever heard of them – although the ghouls came out to play as they invariably did at such times. One report told of the *Miss Doran* making a safe landing on the island of Maui. In Michigan, movie audiences cheered when the news was flashed on the screen.

Two of the Dole flyers, Erwin and Eichwaldt, were determined to find the downed aircraft. They took off from the mainland in *Dallas Spirit* carrying an enormous load of fuel: 460 gallons, enough to keep their aircraft flying for forty hours or more. They kept in touch by radio, but at about 9:00 p.m., they tapped out a final, urgent message. They were in a spin, they said. Then silence.

Constance Erwin said her husband had a life raft and emergency rations with him; she was sure he would come out of this alive. But a radio engineer who had followed the flight from the takeoff at Oakland studied the varying pitch of the radio signals transmitted by the aircraft and concluded that the *Dallas Spirit* had spun into the ocean from an altitude of two thousand feet. Nothing more was heard of the aircraft or its occupants.

Prayer meetings were held for the Dole racers in Flint, Michigan, and San Francisco. In Detroit, Chevrolet and Buick workers turned out to bow their heads in remembrance. There was intense criticism of the event. And with good reason. The race had cost ten lives. The Navy used more than $100,000 worth of fuel in their unsuccessful search for survivors. Four winners divided a total of $35,000. (According to Martin Jensen, every penny of his second-place winnings of $10,000 went to pay creditors; he and his wife divorced a few years later.)

The press didn't hold back. The Syracuse *Post-Standard* declared, "This is no sport at all, it is a gamble at long odds against suicide." The Norfolk *Virginian-Pilot* totted up the cost: four airman alive and victorious; three racers killed in the preliminaries; five racers dead; two would-be rescuers dead; value of prizes won, $35,000; cost of aircraft lost, more than $300,000; useful contribution to aeronautics, none. "Now there are plenty of voices to point out that the Dole race was a big mistake," the *Virginian-Pilot* continued, "that the prize money and the glory dazzled many of the contestants into a disregard for their own safety, that the planes were 'pick-up' affairs designed for land cruising and not for cross-ocean racing, that they were hastily and imperfectly remodeled, that they were, for the most part, not subjected to full-load tests; in short, that the most exacting of flying enterprises was organized and managed in the spirit of the country-fair ballyhoo and in the presence of a national audience resembling, in its naive hunger for thrills and in its criminal indifference to consequences, the crowds that assemble to witness the performance of prehensile acrobats who climb the perpendicular walls of tall buildings."

The Brooklyn *Eagle* had the last word: "A foolhardy and useless enterprise."

CHAPTER SEVEN | *Enter*
the
Ladies

By now, the Atlantic had been flown again and again. But only by men. Now it was the women's turn. An astonishingly large number of them decided that they *had* to be the first of their sex to fly across the ocean. One was the sixty-two-year-old Princess Alice of Lowenstein-Wertheim, better known to British society as Lady Anne Savile. She was the widow of a German prince who had been killed fighting for Spain in the Spanish-American War in 1899. Fond of flying (she flew across the Channel shortly after Harriet Quimby), this doughty lady was brave but not foolish. She recognized that the trip might be beyond her flying skills, so she hired two experienced airmen – the quiet, good-natured Fred Minchin and his younger co-pilot Leslie Hamilton, a dashing man about town with a twinkling smile and, it was said, a veritable treasure trove of names, addresses and telephone numbers of attractive and available females.

The princess planned to make the trip in the passenger seat, flying direct from England to Ottawa, Canada, in a single-engine Fokker F.VII monoplane. There was strong opposition from her brother, the Earl of Mexborough, but the imperturbable princess went ahead with her plans anyway. The late summer of 1927 found her at the RAF station at Upavon on Salisbury Plain, where the aircraft – named *San Raphael* – was made ready for the big trip. Onlookers said that Minchin and Hamilton seemed noticeably edgy, saying little, whereas the princess was all smiles, chatting freely and apparently looking forward to her adventure. She wore a blue flying suit of her own design and carried two attaché cases, a small wicker basket, and two red hat boxes. Upavon was one of the largest airfields in the country – an air force "aerodrome" and therefore unavailable to civilian flyers, unless they happened to have the right connections, which Lady Savile undoubtedly did. The Roman Catholic Bishop of Cardiff, the Most Reverend Frances Mostyn, blessed the aircraft, sprinkling holy water on the wings. Moments later, the two pilots and their passenger clambered aboard, the princess settling herself into a wicker easy chair in the cabin behind the pilots' seats and waving gaily to onlookers, looking as unconcerned as if she were taking a taxi to Leicester Square. The 450-horsepower Jupiter air-cooled engine bellowed as Minchin began his takeoff run. Every foot of the grass strip was needed to get the hefty aircraft off the ground with its load of eight hundred gallons of fuel and three occupants. *San Raphael* lifted off at 7:32 p.m. and climbed away slowly, almost painfully. If the engine missed a beat, the spectators mused, the plane would surely tumble. She would become better behaved, the knowledgeable said, when she had used up some of her fuel.

In mid-Atlantic, the Fokker was spotted by an oil tanker. In Ottawa, the Mounties prepared for bedlam at the airport: the flight would undoubtedly attract the sort of crazy hordes who swarmed Lindbergh at Le Bourget. The authorities were determined to keep control. They had plans. As it turned out, however, they had no need of them. The *San Raphael* never reached Ottawa. It vanished somewhere over the ocean. No trace of the aircraft or its occupants was ever found.

IIII

There was another titled lady of mature years active in aviation. She was in her sixties when she first flew in an airplane, and the experience changed her life. Flying, she discovered, was not only enjoyable, it was beneficial. For many years she had suffered from ear trouble, the result of a bout with typhoid fever as a teenager. Flying gave her some relief from the maddening ringing sounds that plagued her. She soon bought her own aircraft, a Gipsy Moth, and set out to earn her pilot's licence. She could afford such indulgences for she was the Duchess of Bedford, one of Britain's wealthiest women. Born Mary du Caurroy in 1865, the daughter of a clergyman, she married a lieutenant in the Grenadier Guards, Lord Herbrand Russell. It was an advantageous match. In 1891, Lord Herbrand's father died, followed two years later by his elder brother. Herbrand became the eleventh Duke of Bedford, inheriting enormous wealth and a vast estate of some three thousand acres.

The Duchess worked hard on her flying and soon became an able pilot, although she always liked to have experienced aviators close at hand in case of trouble. She employed several highly skilled pilots and became fond of all of them, although at times she could be heard addressing them in the same stridently peremptory tones that she used on coachmen. On one occasion, when her pilot flew her into the country, she chastised him loudly for making too much noise and frightening the animals. The Duchess was an aristocrat of the old school and had not the slightest hesitation in making her views known, to anyone, at any time.

In 1929, she decided to fly to India – as a passenger. She travelled in her own airplane, a hefty Fokker F.VIIA, flown by her pilot, the "ribald and golden-haired"[1] Charles Barnard, with his co-pilot Alliott. The flight went smoothly until the Middle East. Soon after takeoff from Bushire, on the Persian Gulf, they had trouble. The cabin began to fill with smoke, and oil spattered the windshield. Barnard turned and managed to get the big aircraft – with its load of 350 gallons of fuel – down without damage. The Duchess called his performance "truly miraculous." She was obliged to return to England by ship.

The experience did nothing to diminish her enthusiasm for long-distance flying. Determined to complete an eight-day there-and-back flight to India, the Duchess renamed the Fokker *The Spider*, after Robert Bruce's indefatigable spider that kept on trying in spite of innumerable setbacks. She set off again. Once more, Barnard was in the pilot's seat, with Robert Little as navigator on this occasion. They left Lympne on August 2 and returned on August 9, the job done with remarkably few problems. The Duchess professed to be astonished by the size of the crowd that greeted her at Croydon: "A perfect hornet's nest of reporters and press photographers swarmed upon us. . . . Telegrams and letters poured in upon me for days afterwards, and the greatest surprise and pleasure of all was to receive a very kind telegram from the King. It really was all very funny and bewildering. Flying over England a few minutes before landing, I was feeling a little depressed that our flight had come to an end. The early starts, the long hours in the air, the pleasant but irregular and rather sparse meals had all become such a matter of routine that I felt I could have gone on with it for weeks. . . . I doubt whether anyone who was about to be lionized could have been so utterly unconscious as I was, five minutes before we landed, that I should be held to have done anything wonderful. It had all seemed so easy."[2]

The following month, she experienced the sensation of looping; later she went for her first solo from a field near Dunstable – an event which seems to have been harder on her instructor than it was on the duchess; he was overheard telling a fellow pilot he would shoot himself if anything untoward happened to his titled pupil.

In April 1930, the Duchess set off for South Africa in *The Spider*, with Barnard in command and Little again in charge of navigation. On this trip, she handled the controls regularly, and took her turns at pumping fuel from the cabin tanks to the wing tanks, a vital function because of the extra tanks that had been installed. The Duchess kept a meticulous record of every leg of the journey, sparing no one's feelings when it came to her accommodation. She noted in her journal that Dodoma, Tanzania, "has a nice aerodrome and a nice climate and a perfectly detestable hotel. Uncomfortable, horribly dirty, a very unattractive bathroom with all sorts of evil-looking livestock creeping and flying about it, bad food and exceedingly ill-lit rooms, and they added insult to injury by turning off the only electric light before I got into bed."[3] At Bulawayo, she experienced the Carlton Hotel, recording that "some of its arrangements were quite indescribably horrible."[4]

There were some worrying moments when a forced landing seemed likely due to what appeared to be an oil leak. Characteristically, the Duchess analyzed her emotions instead of giving in to them: "It is rather interesting to experience just how one feels when one knows that the end may come at any moment. My own experience is that with a little determination panic can be lived down."[5] (The problem turned out to be with the gauge.) *The Spider* performed admirably and landed at Croydon before another large and effusive crowd. The welcomers included Sir Sefton Brancker, who made "a pretty little speech in our honour."[6]

In 1931, the Duchess sold *The Spider* and bought a Puss Moth, a high-wing cabin monoplane, much smaller than the Fokker. She parted company with Barnard at the same time and engaged Flight Lieutenant J.B. Allen, formerly of the Royal Air Force, as her personal pilot. They became close friends – or as close as society's strictures permitted. She flew to Spain and North Africa with Allen, later touring the Middle East. It was probably the happiest period of the Duchess's aeronautical career, but it ended tragically when Allen crashed in a Monospar ST-4 twin-engined monoplane. Her journal notes were typically philosophical: "And so ends a chapter of my flying times, which I think we both enjoyed equally. For him it has been the best of deaths for an airman to die, and the suffering for the tragedy was only for those who knew him."

She replaced Allen with Flight Lieutenant Preston, a former test pilot for General Aircraft, makers of the Monospar. He became the Duchess's pilot for one thousand pounds a year and a house on the estate, generous terms at the time. Preston held the Duchess in high regard: "She was a terrific character, and so innately kind and generous under a formidable exterior brought about probably by her 'noises in the head' – which was worse than just deafness. She used to describe this as being 'like railway trains rushing through stations.' She could hear better against a background of noise, and frequently would have the engine of the car running if she wanted to speak to me at my house. In an aeroplane she heard almost better through the speaking tube than some of normal hearing would. But at the same time she could be a little 'deaf-minded' and fail to hear things which she didn't want to hear."[7]

In March 1937, the Duchess took off on a round trip of about ninety miles. She should have returned home to Woburn Abbey by late afternoon. It began to snow. The police were informed and a full-scale search began. The searchers found nothing. Not until April 2 was there a clue as to the Duchess's fate. On that day, aircraft wreckage washed ashore at Yarmouth. Preston identified it as belonging to the Duchess's aircraft. In the next few weeks, more wreckage washed ashore, unquestionably parts of the Duchess's Gipsy Moth. Nothing more of her fate was ever learned. Why did she alter course and fly out over the sea? An error in navigation? Or was it suicide? At the time of her flight she appeared to be in good health, although her hearing had worsened. There was always the possibility that she suffered from some other ailment, but her body was never found, so that could not be determined. Thus passed a truly unique figure in aviation history, an aristocrat from another era who found her spiritual home in the air.

||||

Undoubtedly the prettiest of the ambitious early aviatrixes was Ruth Elder of Florida. She saw long-distance flying as a means to an end, a chance to create a better, more exciting life for herself. Look what it had done for Charles Lindbergh. Why shouldn't she achieve just as much? An epic long-distance flight was a gamble, admittedly – but didn't the potential rewards make it worthwhile? Wasn't it better to risk everything on a chance at better things – and a *good* chance at that – than to curl up and accept second-rate status for the rest of her days? Ruth knew that her looks were exceptional; heaven knows how many men had told her so. Again and again. She should be in the movies, they said. Ruth agreed. And with the cachet of being the first woman to fly the Atlantic behind her, the future would be glittering indeed. This, Ruth decided, was her moment of destiny. She broached the subject to her flying instructor, a genial fellow and an excellent pilot named George Haldeman. To her delight, the idea appealed to George. The fact that the pair had no suitable aircraft and no money to buy one was incidental.

Born in Anniston, Alabama, now living in Lakeland, Florida, and employed as a dental assistant, Miss Elder was married to an advertising salesman named Lyle Womack. Lyle did not possess the sort of funds needed to mount a transatlantic flight; in fact, he seemed not to take the enterprise very seriously. No doubt he regarded it as nothing more than his wife's latest craze, something that would soon be forgotten. To her surprise, Ruth found that raising money was the easiest part of the entire venture; in those ebullient days of stratospheric stocks and apparently limitless profits on Wall Street, there were always funds available for sufficiently intriguing projects, particularly if they involved long-distance flying. Ruth and Haldeman contacted businessmen in Florida and West Virginia, all of whom salivated at the thought of generating the same sort of publicity for their towns as Lindy had won for St. Louis. A consortium was formed; an aircraft, a Stinson Detroiter, was purchased; the flyers' lives were insured for $250,000 each. Ruth and Haldeman named their striking orange Stinson *American Girl*, and they planned to make the ocean hop as soon as possible. They had to. The summer was drawing to a close. Although still pleasantly warm, the weather was acquiring a hint of fall. It was now or never.

American Girl's arrival at Roosevelt Field caused a mild sensation. Mr. J.J. Lannin, owner of the field from which so many Atlantic flights had been made, had decreed that any aircraft taking off from Roosevelt and heading out across the Atlantic must have two or more engines. It must also be capable of landing on the water and be equipped with radios. *American Girl* met none of these criteria, but Mr. Lannin seemed not to care. Possibly the striking Miss Elder had something to do with that. It certainly wasn't a question of insufficient time, for Ruth and Haldeman had to camp out at Roosevelt for no less than three weeks waiting for favourable weather. While she was there, Ruth became almost as famous as Lindy himself. The papers were full of pictures of her smiling face, invariably adorned with multicoloured bandeaux matching her outfit of the day. Ruth was always ready to talk to reporters or pose for photographs. Or both. When a report from Florida revealed the startling – and for many young men, positively tragic – news that she was married, she dismissed it all with a toss of her pretty head. But one reporter persisted. Wasn't it true that she was the wife of Lyle Womack? She smiled. She *knew* a Lyle Womack, she allowed, but he was just a dear, dear friend. Later, admitting to her married state, she said she had misunderstood the reporter's question. The reporters were far less interested in Haldeman, satisfied to learn that he was twenty-nine, with a wife, Virginia, and son. He remained in the background, concentrating on preparing *American Girl* for the big test. The Stinson would carry more than five hundred gallons of fuel, resulting in a takeoff weight of some 5,600 pounds, greater than either Lindbergh's or Chamberlin's. Two of the Stinson's seats had been removed to make room for extra fuel tanks. The redoubtable J-5 Whirlwind provided the power.

Haldeman put *American Girl* through a series of tests, checking on her instruments and fuel consumption. The Stinson passed them all with flying colours. He announced that, because it was so late in the season, they would fly due east instead of taking the Great Circle route; it would mean a longer flight, but it would speed them to warmer climes, reducing the risk of icing. Everything appeared to be taking shape satisfactorily – then another female contender for Atlantic glory arrived at Roosevelt. Her name was Frances Grayson. She too yearned to be the first woman to cross the ocean by air. Frances Grayson didn't possess Ruth's good looks, but she was far better equipped financially. Formerly a successful realtor, she had joined forces with a wealthy woman named Mrs. Aage Ancker, the daughter of a Pittsburgh steelman. These two unlikely ladies caught a bad case of the Atlantic fever and purchased a twin-engined Sikorsky s-38 amphibian, calling it *Dawn*. They hired a good crew, consisting of Wilmer Stultz, pilot, and Bryce Goldsborough, navigator. Though smaller, *Dawn* bore an odd resemblance to the Curtiss NC flying boats of 1919 with its boat-like hull to which were attached wings and tail by means of multitudinous struts and booms. The two Atlantic hopefuls, Frances Grayson and Ruth Elder, were often together, posing for photographs in which they were seen shaking hands or pretending to study charts. The fiction was created that they were firm friends and that they regarded the race for the Atlantic as friendly fun. It was nothing of the sort. Both women craved success as alcoholics crave booze. They could think of little else. They were more than willing to risk their lives in winning it. In spite of what the newspapers said, the two women had no contact socially. Neither would have shed too many tears if the other had met with an unfortunate accident – hardly an improbable eventuality under the circumstances. It was perhaps just as well that Frances Grayson decided that her takeoff would be from the long, hard-packed beach at Old Orchard, Maine, rather than the cinder runway at Roosevelt.

Early in October, the Grayson entourage set off for Maine. Mrs. Grayson (she had long since divorced Mr. Grayson) seemed to regard herself as a sort of field marshal of feminism – and possibly it pleased her to be commanding an all-male crew. On the way to Maine, she instructed Goldsborough to tap out a message to the *New York Times* with a request that it be forwarded to all news agencies – although what interest they would have in its contents is hard to gauge: "The plane took off beautifully. Pilot Stultz began to lift our graceful Sikorsky ship when 2,000 feet from the starting line. We were off the ground in twenty-five seconds flat and headed out over the Sound. Weather fine for the first leg of our transatlantic flight. After further tests with ship, weather permitting, will carry the progressive American woman's greeting to my splendid associate, Mrs. Ancker, in Denmark. Goldsborough navigating and radioing. 'Doc' Kimball timed the take-off and is listening to motors. Chief Engineer Libinsky getting much-needed sleep. I am enjoying the trip. FRANCES GRAYSON."

Libinsky was a mechanic employed by Sikorsky; he must have been flattered to be described as Chief Engineer. Frances relaxed in a wicker seat in the cabin watching the view and hoping against hope that she had stolen a march on her rival, Ruth Elder.

In fact, the *Dawn's* departure galvanized the *American Girl* team into action. Topped up with 520 gallons of fuel (200 in the wing tanks, 180 in the fuselage tank, plus five 28-gallon cans in the rear cabin), with various items of emergency equipment stashed in any available spot, the Stinson started down the "Byrd ramp" at the east end of the field at 5:40 p.m. the next day. It was another touch-and-go takeoff, but the skillful Haldeman got the plane into the air after a run of only about three thousand feet and the Stinson climbed away, heading for the ocean. The weather, which had been pleasant for the departure, rapidly deteriorated. Violent up and down drafts sent *American Girl* lurching about the sky – to the extreme discomfort of the occupants. Both wondered bleakly how long the Stinson could take such punishment. They had no cause for concern; the plane came through magnificently. So did Ruth, according to Haldeman, saying that she was "extremely courageous and very helpful with the controls." As they flew on, into slightly better conditions, Ruth and George Haldeman had every reason to feel optimistic about their chances – despite the adverse publicity the flight had engendered. Eleanor Roosevelt was widely quoted when she declared, "My personal feeling is that it is very foolish to risk one's life, as well as that of a pilot in the face of contrary advice from almost everyone who knows anything about aviation. All the experts told Miss Elder that she should not try it, but she was determined to go ahead." But then all was forgiven. "Of course, there is no denying that she exhibited marvellous courage and for that we must pay her tribute."

During the evening, a message was received from the freighter *American Banker*, reporting that the Stinson had been spotted some four hundred miles off the coast. It was the last news of the aircraft for more than a day. At dusk on October 12, crowds began to gather at Le Bourget; there were murmurs of concern, because nothing had been heard of Ruth and Haldeman. The usual calculations were discussed endlessly: so much fuel, so many hours, so much hope.

Aboard the *American Girl*, things were going well. Ruth took her turn at the controls from time to time, to relieve Haldeman. Both flyers began to feel that success was within their grasp.

But fate had other ideas. The oil pressure – lifeblood of the engine – began to drop. Quickly. Was it a faulty gauge or a break in a pipe? Haldeman throttled back; the airspeed dropped to seventy miles per hour. The engine continued to function but its exertions were taking their toll. How long would it keep working? It was already emitting nerve-racking clatterings: mechanical death rattles. How long before it stopped and dumped them in the cold sea?

No ships appeared. The world seemed to consist entirely of grey, restless water, and impenetrable overcast. Then – a wonderful sight! A tanker dead ahead! They flew low overhead and dropped a weighted message asking the distance from land and the direction. It splashed into the sea. Ruth penned another note. This time her aim was better. It landed on the tanker's deck.

A few minutes later, a message was whitewashed on the deck: *True 40 360 miles Terceira Azores.*

That made up their minds. The oil pressure had dropped to five pounds. They couldn't possibly make it to land. They had to ditch, after a remarkable thirty-six hours in the air. It was a tragedy, but they were still alive. After circling the tanker – the Dutch ship *Barendrecht* – to use up as much fuel as possible, Haldeman stalled the Stinson on the crest of a swell. It was done so expertly that the aircraft floated like a bright orange leaf. Its occupants clambered out of the tiny cabin. Ruth put on her inflatable safety suit. Haldeman didn't have one, so Ruth told the boat crew from the *Barendrecht* to rescue him first, which they did. Then it was Ruth's turn to be plucked from the ocean. They were safe.

American Girl wasn't so lucky. While she was being hauled onto the tanker's deck, an explosion ripped through her, possibly caused by gasoline spilling on the still-hot engine, or by water splashing on the carbide drift flares. Whatever the cause, it was the end of the aircraft. Cut loose, she flopped back in the water and, as the flames were snuffed out, she disappeared for all time.

The two flyers were the luckiest since Hawker and Grieve beat the odds back in 1919. And the attractive Ruth Elder's presence sparked even more excitement among the media back home. They asked Lyle Womack for his reactions. Gamely, he said he was sorry she didn't succeed, but he was glad she was safe. In a New York hotel, Virginia Haldeman broke down, weeping for joy. The *New*

York Times reported receiving some two thousand telephone calls a day while *American Girl* was aloft.

As for Ruth Elder, she was having a bully time in the Azores, adored and admired by the crowds – who studied her as if she belonged to some rare species. Haldeman again kept in the background, happy to let her have her day.

While in the Azores, Ruth met another aviatrix, a comely Austrian actress named Lilli Dillenz, who had journeyed from Germany aboard a Junkers float plane. Her mission was similar to Ruth's; she wanted publicity as the first woman to fly the Atlantic. The businessmen who sponsored her demanded 50 per cent of whatever she made as a consequence. Offers for personal appearances and even acting jobs were indeed flooding in. Unfortunately for Lilli, they were all for Miss Elder. Lilli and Ruth parted company when the Junkers team set off for America. They didn't make it; the Junkers crashed and was wrecked, but the occupants, though shaken, survived.

Ruth and George Haldeman set sail for Lisbon aboard the Portuguese steamer *Lima*. In the Portuguese capital, officials twittered about what sort of reception should be accorded the two Americans. After all, they had *failed*, hadn't they? How should they be received? What was their *situation*? Didn't they have husbands and wives in the background? Officials shuddered at the thought that they might actually be encouraging an illicit relationship. But they had nothing to worry about; although the two flyers were on the best of terms, there was no romantic involvement. Airplanes circled the *Lima* as she made her way up the Tagus; flowers were dropped on the deck. Ruth was in her element. The crowds adored her – and they probably adored George too, although no one bothered to find out. Ruth felt as if she had miraculously acquired demigod status. The crowds were positively worshipful. After

Lisbon it was Madrid, then Paris, where Ruth and George were driven through crowded streets to the Hotel Lotti for a reception to which leading French aviators were invited.

While in Paris, Ruth indulged in a little shopping, picking up a mink coat, an assortment of sports outfits, two evening gowns, and a few hats, shoes, and bags. An Italian sculptor immortalized her in bronze. She spoke to the French public on the radio. They loved her in Paris as much as they had done in Lisbon. She had come a long way from the dentist's office in Lakeland. On November 11, she arrived back in the United States, to participate in a tickertape parade, to have a bite of lunch with President Coolidge, and to meet that well-known ladies' man, New York mayor Jimmy Walker. Never at a loss for words in the presence of a pretty face, he declared: "Pulchritude is no bar to courage."

Lyle Womack met her in New York. Sad to say, their reunion was less than effusive. Ruth seemed curiously reluctant to embrace him in public. Lyle hung about New York for a week or two while Ruth busied herself buying more clothes, meeting more people, and picking up contracts worth some two hundred thousand dollars for personal appearances. She had already earned seventeen thousand dollars from newspaper stories and photographs. Offers from Ziegfeld and the movies were said to be imminent.

Less than a year later, Lyle Womack filed suit for divorce on the grounds of cruelty. He declared that his wife's aerial adventures had caused him endless worry; her lack of enthusiasm on their meeting in New York had been a source of much humiliation. She had, he said, shown him no affection since returning to the United States. The suit was uncontested.

||||

When tall, athletic South African Lady Heath (formerly Mrs. Elliott-Lynn) took off from Pretoria in February 1928, she had stowed away in her light Avian more than a hundred pounds of engine spares, medicines, various items of wardrobe (including an evening dress), tennis racquets, a Bible, and a shotgun complete with a supply of cartridges. As she flew over East Africa, most of these items went over the side when she had trouble getting the Avian to climb over high land. In Sudan, local authorities refused her permission to fly on alone because of trouble among the natives, whose restlessness manifested itself in the killing of a district commissioner. Fortunately she met Dick Bentley, a young officer in the South African Air Force. He volunteered to accompany her over the dangerous areas, whereupon the authorities relented.

The pair flew to Nimule, Sudan, after which Lady Heath flew on alone to Khartoum. There she met another titled woman, Lady Bailey, heading in the opposite direction. The wife of South African millionaire Sir Abe Bailey, she had taken off from Stag Lane, London, on March 9, 1928, with the intention of flying her Moth to Cape Town, "sublimely unaware of the function of the verge ring on her compass."[8] After brief stops at Paris, Marseille, Naples, Catania, Malta, Tripoli, Serti, Benghazi, Sollum, Alexandria, and Cairo, Lady Bailey ran into the same restrictions that had delayed Lady Heath. But the *Johannesburg Star* made arrangements for Dick Bentley to accompany her as he had done for Lady Heath. Bentley later wrote, "On Sunday April 1st Lady Bailey arrived in Khartoum after a very gallant and plucky flight with a badly behaving engine and a forced landing in the desert. It hurt me to see her looking tired and weary after it. I cannot speak too highly of Lady Bailey's gallant and plucky attitude in making this flight when she had never flown outside England before."[9] Hard luck continued to plague the Bailey venture. She crashed her Moth at Malakal,

Sudan, after landing to ask for directions. Undaunted, she promptly telephoned her husband, and twelve days later a replacement aircraft arrived, flown by the South African Air Force. Lady Bailey flew this aircraft on to Cape Town, greeting her husband with: "Hullo, Abe, how are you? I'm a bit late, but I got muddled up in the mountains." On September 21, the redoubtable Lady Bailey took off from Cape Town for the return journey, reaching London on January 16, 1929, and thus completing the first solo return flight.

Lady Heath arrived at Croydon on May 17 after suffering sunstroke in Rhodesia (now Zimbabwe) and damaging her fuselage landing on a stony airfield in Italy. Characteristically, she was elegantly attired in a fur coat and high heels; not for her the slacks and bush shirts favoured by most aviatrixes of the era. Lady Bailey's flight was widely praised, being described as "Not only by far the most remarkable feat ever achieved by a woman, but the greatest solo flight ever made by a pilot of either sex." But Lady Bailey, "so modest, so vague, so charming, was surprised that anyone should make a fuss about her journey."[10] She was the very picture of embarrassment when a luncheon was given in her honour at the Savoy the next day.

IIII

A new contender came on the scene, as eager as all the others to make her mark in aviation. She too yearned to be the first woman to fly the Atlantic. Her name was Elsie Mackay. Strictly speaking, she was the *Honourable* Elsie. Her father was Lord Inchcape, chairman of the great Peninsular and Orient shipping line. The thirty-three-year-old Elsie was a delightful individual, attractive, vivacious – and wondrously wealthy. She had made a name for herself on the stage and screen, and she could fly an airplane. While that may have been enough for some, Elsie wanted more. She had talked to a former Imperial Airways pilot, an outstanding airman named Ray Hinchliffe, about the possibility of joining forces to conquer the Atlantic. Her timing was perfect.

Ray Hinchliffe had been looking for just such an opportunity as this. Earlier in the year he had been approached by Mabel Boll, an heiress from Rochester, New York, and yet another unlikely candidate in the First Woman Across the Atlantic stakes. Miss Boll had far too much money and time on her well-manicured hands. Known to the press as "The Queen of Diamonds," she was inordinately fond of jewellery and particularly prized one snappy little number, a sweater made of solid gold links. Mabel realized the crossing was something she couldn't do by herself. No matter, she would hire a pilot. And a plane. But Hinchliffe, like Charles Levine before him, declined her offer of twenty-five thousand dollars to fly her across the Atlantic. He could afford to; at the time, he had a well-paid job as a pilot. But then the outlook darkened. He had lost an eye during the war, and although he was still regarded as one of the best pilots on the Imperial line, the bureaucrats were busy formulating rules and regulations that would transform the airline business from its somewhat free and easy beginnings to a strictly regulated monolith. There would be no room for a one-eyed airline captain in the brave new world of aerial transport. Hinchliffe had enjoyed a fine career: his logbook recorded some nine thousand hours in the air. But now what? How would he support his wife? Another child was on the way.

There was one way to solve all his problems: make a great, record-breaking flight with Miss Mackay. Quite apart from the rewards that would inevitably come his way, Miss Mackay said she would insure his life for ten thousand pounds – a fortune. Hinchliffe didn't take long to say yes. Elsie was pleased, but she cautioned the pilot about discussing the matter too freely. It was vital that her father, Lord Inchcape, didn't find out about their plans, otherwise he would put a stop to them. He had the power and the connections.

Hinchliffe let it be known that he planned to tackle the Atlantic alone – or possibly with a fellow flyer, Gordon Sinclair. Or someone else. If he sounded vague it was because he wanted to. That winter, he resigned from Imperial to take the position of "personal pilot" to Elsie Mackay. Now on salary (at eighty pounds per month, an excellent income), Hinchliffe took a trip to the United States to purchase a Stinson Detroiter, the same aircraft that had been used successfully in several record-breaking flights. He ruffled more than a few feathers at home by declaring that he couldn't find a suitable British plane. He returned to England aboard the *Aquitania*, with the Stinson carefully stowed on deck. Hinchliffe estimated that the aircraft, to be named *Endeavour*, would be able to fly for forty hours with a load of 480 gallons of fuel. The two rear seats were replaced by a large tank with a capacity of 225 gallons which fed fuel to the Whirlwind engine via an intricate system of metal arteries threading their way through the cabin.

The *Endeavour* would need a long take-off run. Hinchliffe favoured Cranwell, the site of the air force college. But how could he, a civilian, obtain permission to use the facility? Elsie solved that problem. She had friends in high places – specifically, Sir Samuel Hoare, the air minister. Permission was granted to use Cranwell provided the *Endeavour* stayed there no longer than a week.

Toward the end of February, the aircraft was ready. Painted jet black, with wires and struts attractively picked out in gold, it looked capable of anything. Hinchliffe told reporters that he was preparing for a non-stop flight to India on which he would be accompanied by his good friend, Sinclair. Where was Sinclair? Temporarily indisposed, responded Hinchliffe, and until he was better Miss Mackay would be occupying the co-pilot's seat during tests.

It was a tense time. Hinchliffe lived in a state of nervous tension, concerned about the forthcoming flight yet even more concerned that it might be called off at a moment's notice. His family's future hung in the balance. Complicating matters, Hinchliffe's New York agent suddenly – and inexplicably – released the news that the former Imperial Airways pilot would indeed attempt to fly the Atlantic. The reports reached Lord Inchcape, who was in Egypt. He suspected that Elsie might be involved, so he immediately wired his son in England. If there was any truth in the story, Elsie was to be dissuaded from going along. At all costs. It didn't help that the *Endeavour* had outstayed its welcome at Cranwell by several days because of bad weather. Hinchliffe could do nothing but fret, which he undoubtedly did, for everything depended upon the forthcoming flight.

The weather turned worse, with unusually heavy falls of snow. The conditions were, however, less threatening to Hinchliffe than they would have been to almost any other pilot in Europe. During his days at the controls of Argosies and Hercules, he had main-tained an astonishing record, flying through some of the worst weather that nature could throw at him. The *Endeavour* would take off next morning.

Elsie was in a quandary. She *had* to fly with Hinchliffe, yet she hated the thought of opposing her father. In the end, though, the thought of staying safe at home and letting him go ahead was insupportable. At 5 a.m., a maid woke her. She had slept fitfully, her mind abuzz with thoughts of the adventure to come. She pulled on her leather flying suit and covered it with a fur coat. She hid her flying helmet with a silk scarf. Peeking through the window, she saw her car pull up, the driver swathed in scarves. It looked chilly down there. No time for second thoughts. She ran downstairs and through the darkened lobby. Only the night porter saw her. In a moment she was in the car, to be joined by Hinchliffe, the recently recovered Gordon Sinclair, and a mechanic.

Daylight was breaking when they arrived at the airfield. The *Endeavour* waited, her black flanks dramatic against the pristine snow. The forecast was optimistic, promising an east wind in the Atlantic. Hinchliffe and Sinclair walked to the Stinson, pausing to exchange a few words with well-wishers. Hinchliffe then informed Sinclair that Miss Mackay would be going on the flight. Sinclair nodded, as if he had been expecting the news all along. Hinchliffe clambered aboard and, as was his custom, settled himself in the right-hand seat, the seat normally occupied by the co-pilot. The reporters were bewildered; no one seemed to know who was aboard the black Stinson as it began to roll across Cranwell's grassy acres. Progress was painfully slow at first, but then the aircraft gathered speed, as if relishing the prospect of flight. The Whirlwind engine bellowed. The onlookers held their breaths. It took more than a mile, but eventually the Stinson rose, heaving her burden into the frosty air. The onlookers breathed again.

Three hours later, the *Endeavour* was sighted over southwest Ireland. The weather forecasters continued to promise improving conditions over the Atlantic. The liner *Majestic* reported gales in mid-ocean, but on the U.S.–Canadian coast, conditions were good for the time of year.

Fishing boats from Newfoundland were keeping a sharp lookout for the *Endeavour*. They saw nothing. The hours accumulated; the odds lengthened. The usual hopes were expressed. The flyers were down somewhere and would be picked up – like Hawker and Grieve. And consider the man in control – a master of his craft, possibly the best pilot in Britain, if not the world. But eventually the truth could no longer be denied. The *Endeavour* and her crew were lost to the unforgiving ocean.

The story has an eerie postscript. In mid-April, Hinchliffe's wife, Emilie, received a telephone call. To her surprise the noted author and spiritualist Sir Arthur Conan Doyle was on the line. He told her that word had been received from her husband. Dubious but willing to pursue any lead, Emilie attended a seance in London. A message was delivered to her, supposedly from Ray. It stated that the *Endeavour* had flown some nine hundred miles past Mizen Head, Ireland, before running into violent weather. The left wing strut broke under the stress, and fabric was ripped from the wing. Hinchliffe, according to the report from the beyond, then turned to the south, heading for the Azores. The engine started to give trouble and the compass became erratic. At 3 a.m., he ditched in the ocean within sight of land.

"I took a last drink from my flask and set out to swim for the shore," Hinchliffe communicated to Emilie. "I swam for twenty minutes, but the currents were too strong, and I became unconscious and finally drowned. Miss Mackay's end was peaceful. She was drowned in the machine while unconscious."[11]

While it is easy to scoff at the story, several aspects of it are interesting. The times, speeds, and weather conditions seem to be consistent with the information available. Was there something in the spiritualist's report after all? It's questionable, because for months later, wreckage washed up on the coast of County Donegal. An examination by experts revealed that it undoubtedly belonged to *Endeavour* and its position indicated that Hinchliffe had probably turned around and had almost made it back to Ireland when he crashed.

Elsie Mackay left an estate of about half a million pounds. It went to the government, for the family did not wish to benefit by her will. Unhappily, Emilie Hinchliffe was denied the insurance her husband had arranged with Miss Mackay; the insurance company demanded another two thousand pounds premium. The letter requesting the additional premium arrived shortly after *Endeavour* took to the air on its last flight.

||||

Most pilots approached long-distance attempts with the care and caution such potentially hazardous enterprises deserved. In contrast, the Honourable Mrs. Victor Bruce always claimed that the idea of flying a light airplane around the world occurred to her on the spur of the moment. In London, indulging in an hour's window-shopping, she spotted an unusual sight in a shop in Mayfair: a Blackburn Bluebird, a light biplane about the same size as the ubiquitous de Havilland Moth. Mrs. Bruce, who had already established a name for herself in motor and speedboat racing, went into the shop and examined the plane. What was the aircraft's range? Some seven hundred miles, the salesman told her, but that could be increased by placing a fifty-gallon fuel tank in the passenger cockpit. The Blackburn Company would be only too happy to handle this modification. She enquired as to the price of the airplane. Five hundred and fifty pounds, she was told, plus another fiver if she wanted more chromium plating. Could the Bluebird fly around the world? Undoubtedly, replied the salesman, managing to sound as if he was asked such a question every day. Mrs. Bruce promptly wrote a cheque.

Fortunately, perhaps, she did not know of the Bluebird's habit of spinning off imperfectly executed turns, a peculiarity apparently stemming from the type's very wide fuselage, housing side-by-side seating. But Mrs. Bruce had more immediate concerns on her mind:

"Coming out of the shop, I suddenly remembered something rather serious. It *was* rather serious. I had never been up in the air."[12] At Blackburn's airfield in Brough, Yorkshire, she was told that she would have to wait two weeks before learning to fly. She shook her head. That was far too long. She intended to be flying around the world by then. She made her point successfully, and "that day I had my first lesson in flying, and at the end of the week I went solo."[13] Rank was not without its advantages.

On September 25, 1930, with her logbook recording a mere forty hours of solo flying, Mildred Bruce prepared to take off from Heston (now Heathrow) airport. The little Bluebird IV biplane was heavily loaded with fuel and carried such diverse items of equipment as a spare propeller and a Dictaphone. "You couldn't fly light aeroplanes with your hands off the controls in those days," she wrote, "and I wanted to keep a record of the flight. When Norman Blackburn noticed the Dictaphone being fitted, he said to the mechanics, 'She can't take that extra weight.' My husband immediately spoke up and said, 'Oh yes, she can. Don't you stop her taking the Dictaphone, she'll never be happy unless she's talking.' So in order to lighten the load I threw out the parachute."[14]

The Bluebird took to the air with astonishing ease. In her eternally optimistic way, Mildred told herself that the worst part of the journey was now over. In spite of morning mist, she had little difficulty finding her way to Munich, her first stop. Delighted with her progress, she telephoned her husband – but the line wasn't clear. He kept asking her where in Kent she had landed.

So far the trip had been the smoothest of sailing. Such good fortune couldn't last. Four days later, she was over the Persian Gulf, hoping to reach Jask, on the Gulf of Oman, before nightfall. She had barely got out of sight of land when she saw the needle on the oil pressure gauge drop to zero. Probably a burst oil pipe. No time to waste. At once she turned back toward the coast.

She was lucky – and unlucky. She was able to glide down for a landing on what looked like golden sand. It turned out, too late, to be a muddy salt flat. The Bluebird buried its nose in the stuff. She banged her head, blood streamed down her face, but otherwise she seemed to be unhurt. The aircraft wasn't badly damaged either; the propeller had shattered, but thankfully there was that spare, fastened under the fuselage. She was examining the mess when she became aware of company: Baluchis, local African-Persian natives. They seemed friendly enough, though unsure of the strange white woman with the clock that sang – an alarm clock that they persuaded her to sound every few minutes. In between performances, they helped her drag the Bluebird out of the mud.

A chilly night was followed by another searing day. The Baluchis brought her a sheepskin full of water – foul-tasting stuff, but more than welcome. Later, the Baluchis pointed toward the mountains; a cluster of horsemen was approaching. Typically, Mildred went out to meet them, shaking hands with the man who appeared to be the leader and who kept muttering "Rupee" in a threatening manner. She handed over five pounds and attempted to win the group over with a performance by the alarm clock. It failed to amuse. The horsemen prepared to depart – and the leader, presumably having seen Valentino in *The Sheik*, had his heart set on lifting Mildred up to join him on the saddle. She politely declined, saying that she had to stay with the Bluebird. Somewhat to her surprise, he accepted this and rode off, leaving Mildred with only an elderly Baluchi for company.

Three days after her crash, Mildred heard an English voice offering her sausages for tea. It was Mr. Murray, an officer of the Jask cable station. He had brought a mechanic and a doctor.

Although the Bluebird's engine was in dubious condition, having taken in sand and dirt from the violent desert landing, Mildred was able to take off from a nearby beach. She pushed on to Calcutta, then crossed the Bay of Bengal to Rangoon. From there she struck out for Bangkok, despite the entreaties of officials, who pointed out that the flight would involve traversing some fourteen hundred miles of virtually uninhabited jungle without weather information or fuel supplies – except for a tiny military establishment five hundred miles away in a village called Korat. It had a small parade ground where a Bluebird *might* land. Also, fuel *might* be obtained there. At dawn, Mildred was on her way, flying above a seemingly endless expanse of trees and other vegetation, the monotonous green broken only by the occasional river.

Again luck was with her. Mildred found Korat – and fuel *was* available. But the delay at Jask had cost her dearly; now she was caught in the northeast monsoon. The rain thundered down in torrents, drenching her in the open cockpit. She had to wait several days until the weather improved enough for her to tackle the mountains before the valley of Hanoi. She had to climb to thirteen thousand feet, the Bluebird's ceiling, to clear the towering peaks – and then, because of poor visibility, it was largely a matter of hoping for the best. Again, her luck held. She negotiated the crags successfully and landed at Hanoi to a great reception – and the award of the Order of the Million Elephants and White Umbrella.

At Hong Kong, as there was no landing ground on the island, she landed on the mainland at Kowloon. She was soon busy making arrangements for the next leg of the trip, to China. She wanted to land at Foochow, about four hundred miles east of Hong Kong, but local wars made it a dangerous place to touch down. Eventually, through a sort of Oriental old-boy network, she was granted permission to land on a private golf course a few miles to the north of the town. From there she went on to Shanghai. She had intended to fly across the Yellow Sea to Japan. It turned out, however, that the Japanese were conducting naval manoeuvres, attended by the Emperor. Since it was forbidden for anyone to look *down* on the Emperor, Mildred had to fly to Seoul, Korea, to await further instructions. After two days, she was given permission to make the trip to Japan. At Tachikawa airfield, enthusiastic Japanese clustered around her Bluebird, thrusting flowers into her cockpit. Later, grappling inexpertly with chopsticks, she endured countless banquets in her honour.

She sailed to Vancouver, with the Bluebird, wings folded, safely stowed away, ready for action when the ship reached shore. In Seattle, she was given a huge key, a symbol of the freedom of the city. She had time for only a brief glimpse of San Francisco, her mother's birthplace, before she hurried on to Los Angeles. In Texas, she encountered vigorous headwinds that cut her ground speed to little more than 40 mph – and a train cheekily overtook her, the passengers waving at her from their windows. At Baltimore, Maryland, she stalled the Bluebird and seriously damaged the small aircraft. But her remarkable luck didn't desert her. She could hardly have chosen a better spot to descend; she was almost beside the Glenn Martin aircraft plant. Mildred appealed to Martin himself for help – and he promptly assigned ten of his workers to repair her plane. He also extended the airstrip to facilitate her departure. She returned to Europe aboard the *Île de France*, with the Bluebird secured on the boat deck.

Mrs. Bruce flew the Bluebird from France to Croydon, arriving on February 20, 1931, and so completing the first solo "flight" around the world. The long-suffering Bluebird went on display at Charing Cross station in London.

CHAPTER EIGHT | *"Impenetrable Mediocrity"*

Mrs. Frederick Guest was another of that determined band of women who yearned to be the first of their sex to conquer the Atlantic by air. American by birth, she was stout and middle-aged, wife of the wartime British air minister and a wealthy woman. She had never learnt to fly; she intended to hire a pilot and travel as a passenger. She happened to know that Commander Byrd, the well-known explorer, had a Fokker tri-motor for sale. He thought highly of the type, and if it was good enough for the hand-some, well-connected commander, it was good enough for her. Mrs. Guest bought the aircraft and named it *Friendship*, as an expression of Anglo-American amity. She hired Wilmer Stultz as her pilot on the strict understanding that the arrangement be kept secret. As far as the world – and in particular, the media – were concerned, Commander Byrd still owned the big Fokker and the work being done on her was in preparation for another of his expeditions. With only the vaguest knowledge of aircraft and their idiosyncrasies, she demanded that the Fokker be equipped with pontoons – in case of a forced landing on the ocean. Although Byrd had installed skis on his Fokker, no one had ever mounted pontoons on the type before, and there were many dark comments about how the modification would affect the big aircraft's performance and handling.

Eventually – probably inevitably – Mrs. Guest's family heard of her intentions. They were horrified. Four women had already met their deaths in ocean flights. Did she want to be the fifth? After some heated discussions, Mrs. Guest agreed not to participate – but she insisted on continuing to finance the flight – provided the "right sort of girl" could be found to take her place. She turned for help to a member of the advisory committee they had created for the venture: Hilton H. Railey, grandnephew of Mrs. Jefferson Davis and head of a public relations firm. Railey was more than willing to find a suitable aviatrix. It was essentially a matter of asking questions of enough people. In Boston, he met retired Rear Admiral Reginald K. Belnap. The admiral said he knew of just the girl: a young social worker who flew her own plane. "Call Denison House," he told Railey, "and ask for Amelia Earhart."

She looked enough like Lindbergh to be his sister. Tall, close-cropped fair hair, a touch of shyness combined with a hint of determination. She had owned two airplanes and had acquired some five hundred hours in the air.

"How would you like to be the first woman to fly the Atlantic?"

Only a flicker of her steady grey eyes revealed the excitement the question created. Amelia nodded, carefully. She made it clear that she had no experience of flying by instruments or of handling a multi-engine aircraft. It didn't matter. The committee wanted her as a passenger, a presence. She spoke well, lucidly, and grammatically – an important quality, all part of being the "right sort of girl."

The committee would never consider a girl whose grammar and manner reflected negatively on the project.

Amelia Earhart pondered later that the interview "found me in a curious situation. If they did not like me at all, or found me wanting in too many respects, I would be deprived of the trip. If they liked me too well, they might be loath to drown me. It was, therefore, necessary for me to maintain an attitude of impenetrable mediocrity."[1]

It's an interesting reflection on the times that the pilot (as yet unnamed as far as Amelia was concerned) would be paid a fee of twenty thousand dollars, and the mechanic five thousand dollars, sizable sums in 1928. Amelia herself would receive nothing but fame, yet she would be described as "captain." Two days later she received a letter from the committee announcing that she had been selected for the flight and enclosing a contract absolving the committee of any blame if she lost her life. Amelia rented a safety deposit box and placed her will in it, together with letters to her father and mother, to be delivered "in case." The missives told a lot about her. To her father, she wrote, "Hooray for the last grand adventure! I wish I had won, but it was worthwhile anyway. You know that. I have no faith that we'll meet anywhere again, but I wish we might."[2]

In East Boston, near the harbour, she saw the Fokker for the first time. With a span of more than sixty feet and powered by three engines, the high-wing monoplane was a giant by the standards of her day. Strikingly finished in red and gold (to aid in any search-and-rescue attempts that might be required), the Fokker was a well-tried airplane, probably as good a machine as could be procured at that time.

Amelia met her pilot, Wilmer Stultz, a blond young man, short but sturdy and possessing a wealth of aeronautical experience.

Only one thing dismayed her: according to fellow airmen, Stultz was more than a little fond of a drink. Amelia thought long and hard about this. She had some knowledge of drinkers; her own father had his problems with alcohol. She was assured, however, that Stultz would be fine once he was in the cockpit. Amelia decided to take a chance on him; heaven knew what problems would be generated by changing the pilot at this late stage. The third member of the crew was a mechanic, a laconic individual named Louis "Slim" Gordon.

The weather kept delaying the *Friendship*'s departure from Boston. It was either fog or wind – or a lack of wind – that kept holding the flight up. May gave way to June. On the third of the month, conditions seemed to be propitious for the first leg of the trip, to Newfoundland. After two failed take-off attempts, the *Friendship* took reluctant leave of the waters of Boston Bay. Amelia, crouched on the floor behind the pilots' seats, was kept busy with the logbook. The trip to Newfoundland had to be curtailed because of thick fog, a common enough condition in that part of the world. They landed at Halifax, Nova Scotia, where reporters and photographers swarmed about, eager for a glimpse of the woman who was taking on the broad and thoroughly beastly Atlantic. She cringed at what the newspapers wrote about her; most of the stories seemed to be about a total stranger. One paper declared that she hoped to make enough money from the flight to pay off the family mortgage.

The flight to Trepassey Bay, Newfoundland, was uneventful, but after they had landed amid a flotilla of small boats, a storm blew in – and continued to blow for an incredible thirteen days. While Amelia and Lou Gordon waited as calmly as they could, Bill Stultz found comfort in the brandy bottle. Amelia came close to giving up on Stultz – a replacement pilot, Lou Gower, was on standby in

Boston. But the others persuaded her to give Stultz another chance.

During the evening of June 16, Amelia and Lou Gordon were playing rummy in the front parlour of their rooming house while Bill Stultz, his brandy bottle close at hand, was thumping around in his room upstairs, thoroughly frustrated and ill-tempered. A wire arrived from New York: the weather forecast was at last favourable for the transatlantic trip. Amelia abandoned thoughts of replacing her pilot. The trip was on!

In the chill light of early morning, they roused the badly hungover pilot and stuffed him into the cockpit. He pulled himself together sufficiently to attempt the takeoff – which was tricky in that overloaded aircraft. Three tries failed. On the fourth, Stultz succeeded, after a lengthy run. The grey water fell away. The Fokker rose, straining, complaining. Amelia had nothing to do but note the essentials of the flight in her logbook: speed, altitude, weather conditions. They flew steadily, through rain, through fog, through sunshine. Night fell. They flew on instruments, guided through the darkness by flickering needles. The aviators munched malted-milk tablets and sandwiches. Eventually, after what seemed a lifetime of droning through darkness, dawn glimmered on the horizon. They descended gently, cautiously. They spotted a large ship. It was the *America*. Soon afterward they saw land. Was it Ireland? England? Like many Atlantic flyers, they didn't know. Neither did they care. The fact that it was land was enough.

Friendship landed at Burry Port, Wales, a few miles from Swansea, with a mere twenty-five gallons of fuel left in the tanks. To Amelia's considerable embarrassment, she found herself the focus of all the media attention. In vain she told reporters that she had done nothing but sit – she was just "baggage," she said, claiming that she suffered housemaid's knee from kneeling so long in the Fokker's confined cabin. U.S. President Calvin Coolidge wired his congratulations, and she responded saying that the success of the flight was entirely due to Bill Stultz. She kept talking about the contribution of Stultz and Gordon, but it was no use; male flyers were tired news; she was the latest thing. Railey had chosen well; she handled the fervent admiration of the public with an attractive combination of shyness and modesty. She was not without vanity, however; she tried to avoid smiling broadly in photographs because of the gap between her two front teeth.

Within days, Amelia had hundreds of offers to speak of her adventures. Magazines wanted her to write articles. Advertisers wanted her endorsement of everything from cigarettes to spark plugs. She was famous – yet she felt she didn't deserve her fame. She resolved to fly the Atlantic again – solo, as soon as she could. In the meantime she had agreed to write a book about her first Atlantic flight. It was to be published by Putnam, George Palmer Putnam being a member of the committee that had organized the flight for Mrs. Guest. GP had little trouble persuading Amelia to use his house in New York for her writing. The completed work – *20 Hrs. 40 Min.* – was a success and earned her a considerable income. She came to rely on Putnam for advice in many aspects of her new life. He had no objection; he admired her. He had divorced his wife in 1929 and it was no great surprise when he proposed to Amelia. She turned him down, having no desire to get involved in marriage. He persisted, proposing five more times until he was accepted. At the time of their marriage, he was forty-two, she thirty-two. Characteristically, she insisted on a prenuptial agreement stipulating that they would separate if they found no happiness together. "I shall not hold you to any medieval code of faithfulness to me, nor shall I consider myself bound to you similarly."

It was an unusual arrangement for the time, but it seemed to work, despite the predictions of many. Putnam's enthusiasm for deals of every complexion did, however, precipitate a few marital crises. An example was the affair of the "AE hats." Putnam entered into an agreement with a manufacturer of children's hats to produce replicas of the tan cloche Amelia had worn on her return to the United States following the *Friendship* flight. Putnam handled all the negotiations. The hats were to be sold for three dollars each, with Amelia realizing a profit of fifty cents per hat. She was in California at the time of the negotiations, so knew nothing of the deal. To Putnam's astonishment, when she learned the details, she rejected it outright. The hats weren't worth three dollars, she said, and she refused to have her name associated with the enterprise. Putnam bowed to the inevitable and cancelled the whole thing. Considerably more successful were her ventures into sports clothes and other items. She had genuine talent as a designer. But aviation remained her first love – and she was determined to fly the Atlantic solo.

||||

Frank Courtney, a noted British test pilot, had bad luck over the Atlantic. In 1926, Courtney had talked to a number of shipping lines in an attempt to get them to add flying boats to their fleets to act as high-speed auxiliary transports. Several expressed interest, and Courtney embarked on a zigzagging demonstration flight between England and Canada, via the Azores, Newfoundland, and New York. The flight had one overriding purpose: to impress the shipping people, which, it was hoped, would lead to further developments. Courtney chose the German Dornier Wal (Whale), which he regarded as "by a long way the fastest and most seaworthy seaplane of its class,"[3] and the Dornier company was pleased to make one available for the venture. Its twin engines were mounted in tandem above the wing. Courtney also got good support from such companies as Napier, which supplied two 450-horsepower Lion engines, Marconi, which installed a complete long-range radio system, Shell Oil, which supplied fuel, and Lloyd's, which insured all the borrowed equipment. Courtney had, however, been far too optimistic in his estimate of "incidental expenses." Fortunately, a London newspaper, acting in collaboration with a U.S. news syndicate, offered an attractive fee for the exclusive story of the flight. But the timing was a problem. Courtney's flight coincided with the Orteig "stampede," and his newspaper friends wanted him to start while transatlantic flying news was still "hot."

Courtney took off from Plymouth on England's south coast with his radio working badly and his direction finder completely out of action. After journeying a thousand miles, he was forced to turn back, bitterly disappointed. A well-to-do Canadian named Elwood Hosmer came to Courtney's aid, offering to buy a new Dornier seaplane and to take care of other financial problems. His only condition was that he be taken along for the ride. Whatever misgivings he may have had, Courtney agreed. He had little choice. He hired a flight engineer named Fred Pierce and a radio operator, sight unseen, who was to join the crew at Lisbon. When word came from the Dornier factory in Pisa, Italy, that the aircraft was ready, Courtney got a shock. He found that the all-important radio direction finder was useless, completely drowned out by engine ignition interference. Courtney developed an ingenious solution to the problem. He would climb, throttle the engines down until they were only just turning over, then hurriedly take the necessary bearing. It was by no means an ideal arrangement, but it was the best that could be done under the circumstances. In mid-June, Courtney left Pisa, reaching Lisbon after a thirteen-hour flight. There, Hugh Gilmour, the sight-unseen radio man, introduced himself to Courtney, saying that he had never before been up in an airplane, but as far as he was concerned, it mattered not a jot whether he was on a ship or in a plane.

After a delay for repairs to the direction-finding equipment, Courtney took off, headed for the Azores. He soon ran into rough weather with high winds and heavy rain. Gilmour raised a Cunarder some four hundred miles ahead. He was told that the weather was little better there. Courtney turned back to Horta, in the Azores.

On August 1, he took off again – and once more ran into stormy skies: "Suddenly everything hit us; torrential rain with snatches of hail, lightning flashes that lit up the enveloping cloud to almost continuous incandescence, and a wild turbulence that tossed the plane around in all directions."[4] Courtney flew from one storm into another and still another, tossed about by violent up- and down-drafts. That was bad enough but worse luck was lying in wait:

> With no warning, disaster struck. And then things happened with frantic rapidity. Suddenly came the bangs of a backfiring engine. A strange orange glow flickered on my windshield and, almost at the same moment, Pierce shouted in my ear, "The rear engine's on fire." I looked back just as the lower cowling released a flood of flaming fuel, which – as we knew later – had been fed into it by a broken fuel line. An in-flight fuel fire is blood-curdling enough in the daytime, when all you can see is the torching flame with its trailing plume of black smoke. But at night it is a far more fearsome sight, for the flames appear longer and brighter and, instead of the smoke, there is a train of brilliant sparks that pour out far behind, swathing the tail and turning the plane into a winged comet. Any number of things must have

come to my mind during those few hectic seconds; but the only thing that seemed to matter was to get down on the water, somewhere in the blackness fifteen hundred feet below, before something blew up, or the tail burned off, or some equally final disaster took place. I cut the engine switches and shoved the nose down as steeply as I dared – if I dived too steeply I could plunge into the waves before I could see them soon enough to level off. At the same moment Fred Pierce performed a feat of quick thinking and courage that probably gave us the margin that saved us. He remembered that for reasons connected with the fuel-system design, the only fuel cutoff from the gravity tanks to the engines was up in the nacelle, and with the propellers still spinning, the pumps were continuing to feed fuel into the flames. With the agility of desperation he clambered out onto the hull and up through the small access hole into the nacelle. Fumbling in the small space between the two engines, he started to turn off the cock under the rear gravity tank. He was still up there when we hit the water. Gilmour behaved as though this sort of thing happened to him every day. He shouted something about "Looks nasty," rapidly wound in the trailing antenna as I had instructed him always to do when we were approaching the water, and then sat back to await developments. Hosmer's little cockpit was right under the blazing engine; for a while he stayed there to avoid getting in the way of any crew activities, but the heat soon forced him to squeeze his way forward through the little bulkhead door.[5]

Courtney was down to two hundred feet when he glimpsed the white of the wave crests. The water had a kind of yellow glow in the light of the Wal's flames. The actual contact with the far-from-calm sea was surprisingly gentle. A sizable wave brought the aircraft to a halt. The engine fire still blazed and appeared to be destroying the connections to the tank. It looked as if it might collapse, with a very real danger of setting off the main fuel tanks in the hull. Pierce and Gilmour dragged out the aircraft's sea anchor and lowered it over the bow. The fire spluttered into silence as the fuel was exhausted. Acutely conscious of the danger of having the rear engine crashing down onto the hull, Courtney wondered if he could get the Wal into the air with only one engine. Dawn brought calmer seas. Up came the sea anchor followed by a quick check of the controls. Everything appeared to be functioning properly. The forward engine started well. Courtney taxied along the swell, gaining speed – until Pierce bellowed an alarm. The useless rear engine was rocking violently in its blackened and buckled mount. It would surely break away at the first real jolt.

The airmen gave up. Disappointed and drenched, they sent out an SOS, which the Cunarder *Cedric* picked up. The twenty-two-thousand-ton liner *Minnewaska* came to the airmen's aid. The unfortunate Dornier had to be left in the sea, as the ship had no means of hoisting it aboard.

To the astonishment of the airmen, they were treated as heroes when they landed at New York. A motorcycle escort rushed them noisily to City Hall, after which they settled in at the swanky Ritz-Carlton hotel and picked up clothes and other supplies "on the house." Courtney even got the Wal back. The Italian freighter *Valprato* came across it floating in mid-ocean, picked it up and brought it to Montreal – although the aircraft suffered grievous damage in the process. Napier got their engines back – an examination revealed that the cause of the fire was the crystallization of a copper fuel line through vibration.

Elwood Hosmer said he didn't regard the flight as a financial disaster; he had never had so much fun for his money.

|||||

Ireland's small air force was based at Baldonnel, near Dublin, an advantageous spot from which to launch a flight over the Atlantic. An Irish air force pilot with more than his fair share of blarney, Major James Fitzmaurice, tried to interest his government in such a venture. He received a frosty refusal. The young country was hard up; money couldn't be wasted on such frivolities, he was told. All was not lost, however, for out of the blue came a request from Germany: a Baron von Huenefeld and a Hermann Koehl, who was a Lufthansa captain, wanted to try an east-west crossing of the Atlantic, and Baldonnel seemed an ideal spot to start from. Could they have permission to use the airfield?

They had an aircraft, a Junkers W33, a sturdy, all-metal monoplane that was achieving a reputation for reliability and strength. The previous years two W33s, named *Bremen* and *Europa*, had set off to fly the Atlantic in formation. They had to abandon the attempt. Now, on March 26, 1928, the *Bremen* turned up at Baldonnel. Aboard was an unusual trio, looking like characters out of an espionage movie. Baron von Huenefeld, wearing a monocle and a supercilious smile, was a Prussian aristocrat, currently working in public relations. If he seemed testy, he could hardly be blamed; he was dying of cancer and would in fact be gone within the year. His pilot was a burly, aggressive man named Hermann Koehl, who had quit his job with Lufthansa because of disagreements over this flight. The third member of the crew, Arthur Spindler, resigned after an argument with the baron and caught the next ship back to Germany. Major Fitzmaurice offered to take his

place. His offer was accepted. Thus, the flight took on an unusually international flavour with Irishmen and Germans working in
close co-operation – and having little familiarity with each other's
languages. The flight was big news in Ireland, and the Free State's
president, William Cosgrave, journeyed to Baldonnel to see the
Bremen off in the early hours of April 12.

As soon as the Junkers was airborne – her flanks coated with
paraffin to reduce the risk of icing – she faced vigorous headwinds.
To minimize their effect, Koehl and Fitzmaurice (they alternated
at the controls) kept low, only about fifty feet above the water.
Because of the limitations on engine size imposed on Germany
after the Great War, they had to cope with an engine delivering a
mere 310 horsepower. Patchy fog added to the airmen's difficulties.
The weather was consistently awful, creating serious navigational
difficulties. For hour after endless hour, they droned over dense
banks of fog, battling through rain and snow. Visibility varied from
poor to impossible. They flew right over Newfoundland without
seeing it. The miserable visibility continued until they were well
inland. By this time the fuel was running low. The ground was
rocky, an unappealing place to attempt a forced landing. They flew
on, coming to what seemed to be an enormous frozen lake (it was
in fact the Gulf of St. Lawrence). With the fuel almost gone, they
had little choice but to land. Koehl did a superb job, and although
the landing gear was torn off and the aircraft pitched onto its nose,
the occupants were unharmed. They had landed on Greenly
Island, Labrador, more than a thousand miles from their intended
destination of New York, but the first east-to-west transatlantic
flight had been completed. In Ireland and Germany, celebrations
were unrestrained, although the *Bremen* crew still languished in
Labrador – well-fed and warm, but bored and anxious to get home.

Herbert Bayard Swope, executive editor of the New York *World* newspaper, smelled a good story in the making. He knew that Commander Byrd was preparing an expedition to the South Pole. He lost no time contacting Byrd and offering to rent his Ford tri-motor for the rescue mission, carefully pointing out that the publicity would undoubtedly result in more funds becoming available for the polar expedition. Byrd, never averse to promoting his projects, agreed at once and ordered that the aircraft be made available. It had just travelled to Manitoba with Byrd's usual crew to test its ski gear and, unfortunately, chief pilot Floyd Bennett had caught influenza on the trip. Nevertheless, he insisted on going on the rescue mission. He was in poor condition with a high fever and a violent cough. Soon his co-pilot, Bernt Balchen, was similarly afflicted but kept going. They reached Lake Ste. Agnes in Quebec, where Bennett was put to bed in a farmhouse and later moved to hospital in Quebec City, semi-delirious, the flu having become pneumonia.

Balchen, with the affable Fitzmaurice at his side, flew the Ford to Labrador and landed on the ice near the downed Junkers. They attempted to get the Junkers' engine started without success, so towed the aircraft to the mainland and left it to be brought out by ship after the breakup of the ice. Meanwhile, Floyd Bennett's condition deteriorated. Byrd went to his bedside; so did Charles Lindbergh, who flew a supply of pneumonia serum from New York. Although gallant, the gesture served no purpose, because it was the wrong sort of serum.

Bennett died – and Byrd promptly named the Ford tri-motor the *Floyd Bennett*. The first municipal airport in New York would also bear his name.

‖‖

Among the array of airmen and airwomen attracted to the lure of long-distance flying was Bert Hinkler, who hailed from the village of Bundaberg, Australia. In 1928, he amazed the world by flying there from London in a small Avro Avian biplane powered by an eighty-horsepower engine. It took him a little over fifteen days. No suitable maps were available for much of the route, so Hinkler used pages cut from an atlas and had little difficulty finding his way, although exhaustion became a serious problem during the last lap, crossing the dangerous Timor Sea. He landed at Darwin, having completed the 11,250-mile odyssey in 128 hours, cutting the 1919 time of the Smith brothers in half. "Hustling Hinkler" was the new Aussie hero, the unassuming working-class bloke who had captured the hearts of an entire nation. Soon, men all over Australia were sporting "Hinkler Homburgs." Dancers practised the "Hinkler Quickstep." King George V awarded him the Air Force Cross; the Australian government made him an honorary Squadron Leader – but he wasn't knighted, as the Smith brothers had been. Some said it was because of his humble family background. Hinkler seemed not to care.

Three years later, he appeared in New York with another air-craft of modest proportions, a de Havilland Puss Moth cabin monoplane. It was a little higher-powered than his Avian, sporting a ninety-horsepower Gipsy engine. He had told no one that he was coming, nor had he made public his intentions. Typical Hinkler. He flew down the Atlantic seaboard through the West Indies to South America. The Brazilians arrested him; some problem with his documents, soon sorted out. On November 26, 1931, Hinkler took off and headed out across the vast expanse of the South Atlantic. The weather turned violent. He ran into terrifying elec-trical storms, and the Puss Moth was flung about the sky like a leaf. He couldn't climb above the storm, so he went down low – so low that his wheels touched the churning waves. The Gipsy engine didn't let him down. After twenty-five hours and five minutes, he landed safely at Senegal, West Africa. He cabled his wife: "Landed at Gambia OK. Bert."

In January 1933, he set off from London in an attempt to set a new record to Australia. His first scheduled stop was Brindisi, Italy. He failed to arrive there. Three months later his body was found in northern Italy. His luck had run out at last.

| *Distant Destinations*

*I*f the Atlantic was formidable, the Pacific was absolutely terrifying. Its size was awesome, a barely comprehensible seventy *million* square miles, the deepest of all the oceans, the graveyard of countless ships and many aircraft – the unfortunates of the Dole Derby among them. Yet in 1928 two Australians set out to conquer the Pacific by air, from San Francisco to Brisbane. It was an undertaking of truly heroic proportions: nearly eight thousand miles of ocean, with the only stops being Honolulu, after 2,400 miles, and Fiji, another 3,200 miles, before the final hop to Australia. The man in charge was a laconic ex-air force pilot, Charles Kingsford Smith – Smithy to his mates. During the war he had risen from dispatch rider to commissioned pilot; many people considered him the finest long-distance airman of his time, superior even to Lindy himself. His co-pilot was another Australian air force veteran, Charles T.P. Ulm. They were enthusiastic about the idea but lacked two important things: money and an airplane. Part of the problem appeared solved when the Australian government came up with a grant of 3,500 pounds. Smith and Ulm immediately sailed for San Francisco. At the time, the Dole Derby was the biggest news in aviation – and the two Aussies were offered the use of an aircraft with which to enter the ill-starred event. They turned it down; the thought of a lot of single-engine airplanes heading out across the wide Pacific, most of them flown by crews sadly lacking in navigational skills, failed to arouse the Aussies' enthusiasm.

Kingsford Smith and Ulm spent a lot of time planning their flight, analyzing the factors that had led to the success or failure of recent attempts at long-distance flights. Right from the start, they decided that single-engine aircraft were out. Too little margin of safety. And a radio was a must. Wright Whirlwind engines had proved themselves on many demanding flights, so had Fokker aircraft. So the flyers had their specifications. But the means were again a problem. The government grant suddenly vanished, a casualty of shifting political winds. A general election had ousted the former government, and the new political bosses didn't warm to the idea of public funds being used for such frivolous pursuits as long-distance flying. Smithy was ordered to dispose of the second-hand Fokker he had just acquired from the noted explorer George H. Wilkins (soon to be *Sir* George). A California financier, G. Allan Hancock, saved the day by purchasing the airplane and placing it at Smithy's disposal, an extraordinarily generous gesture from a total stranger. Two Americans joined Smithy's crew: Harry W. Lyon, navigator, and James Warner, radio operator. The Fokker was now named *Southern Cross*, as a tip of the hat to the constellation that would, the flyers hoped, steer them to their destination, or as a salute to a small town near Perth; it all depended on who you asked.

The flight began in California, at Oakland, on May 31, 1928. The meticulous preparations paid off; despite some stormy weather en route, the big Fokker arrived in Hawaii in good order, touching down at Wheeler Field after a twenty-seven-hour flight.

The aircraft was too heavy to take off from Wheeler for the flight to Fiji, so the departure took place on June 3 from the big beach of hard-packed sand on the Hawaiian island of Kauai. On this leg of the trip, the crew encountered more stormy weather, necessitating several major detours – and the radio failed. After a gruelling thirty-four hours they landed in Fiji at Suva.

The final leg was twenty-one hours, through some of the most violent weather of the entire trip, the journey being made even more difficult by compass problems. They made it, though, and a massive crowd greeted the flyers at Brisbane's Eagle Farm Airport.

Smithy was the hero of the hour. The politicians decided that perhaps they liked long-distance flights after all, awarding the airmen twenty-five thousand dollars. A public subscription harvested a similar sum. Things looked healthier for Smithy. In December 1928, he and Ulm formed Australian National Airways. They ordered four Avro Ten airliners (Fokker F.VII/3Ms built under licence in England) and opened a daily service between Sydney and Brisbane, charging nine pounds, thirteen shillings one-way for the five-hundred-mile journey. In June, a daily service was inaugurated between Sydney and Melbourne. Smithy's airline did well – until March 21, 1931, when the Avro Ten *Southern Cloud* crashed in the Snowy Mountains between Sydney and Melbourne, killing everyone aboard. (The wreckage – and the bodies – would remain undiscovered for almost thirty years.) The loss was the beginning of the end of ATA. Within a few months the airline had been liquidated.

Despite this setback, the irrepressible Smithy developed plans for two more long-distance flights: an east-to-west Atlantic crossing and a solo flight from England to Australia. He and co-pilot

Evert Van Dyke, on leave from KLM, took off in the *Southern Cross* from Portmarnock Beach in southern Ireland, intending to fly direct to New York. The weather was against him; after thirty-one and a half hours he had to land in Harbour Grace, Newfoundland, but New Yorkers, when he finally arrived, still gave him a great welcome complete with tickertape parade.

Smith next set off from England in a diminutive Avro Avian biplane, *Southern Cross Junior*, and flew to Australia in less than ten days. Landing at Darwin, he commented, "This shows there is nothing in these long air trips beyond the reach of the ordinary pilot."

IIII

Not only airplanes were breaking records in those exciting years. In Germany, a magnificent new airship emerged from the Zeppelin works in the fall of 1928, the name *Graf Zeppelin* resplendent on her flanks. The Count would have been proud. The *Graf* was the biggest, most luxurious airship ever built. Known officially as the LZ127, she was christened by Count Zeppelin's daughter on what would have been her father's ninetieth birthday. The LZ127 had been designed by Ludwig Durr, who had worked for Zeppelin since 1899. More than seven hundred feet long, she had a gas capacity of 3.7 million cubic feet and could maintain a cruising speed of seventy miles per hour. Power was provided by five 530-horsepower Maybach engines, each mounted in a separate gondola large enough for a mechanic to enter to see to minor repairs and service work. Ten sleeping cabins were provided for passengers, with a lounge sixteen feet square. Countless German citizens had contributed to the cost of the airship, coming up with about half the necessary funds; the government provided the rest.

In October 1928, the *Graf* made history by embarking on the first transoceanic flight ever made by an airship carrying fare-paying passengers. There were twenty passengers on board for the journey to New York – or, more precisely, Lakehurst, New Jersey – plus 66,000 pieces of mail. It was not a totally tranquil voyage. South of the Azores, the *Graf* ran into turbulence at breakfast time. The result was chaotic, with furniture and condiments, dishes and decorations flying about the dining room. A correspondent for Hearst, Lady Grace Drummond-Hay, wrote feelingly of the incident: "Coffee, tea, butter, sausages, marmalade formed a glutinous mess and overspread the unlucky ones with their backs to the stern. I in my chair slid the length of the saloon, crashing into the unfortunate artist, Professor Dettmann, who in turn fell over Robert Hartman's heavy movie camera, which fell full weight on Frederick Gilfillan. Breathless moments passed, leaving not a few blanched faces, and the thought – we were facing death."[1]

Their concerns were understandable. The storm had ripped off part of the fabric skin of the airship; fragments fluttered in the slipstream like disconsolate flags, threatening to jam the rudder and elevators. Courageous crew members – including the twenty-six-year-old son of Hugo Eckener, the airship commander, volunteered to go out onto the hull and repair the damage. It was no minor feat, working in driving rain and fierce winds. As the crippled ship sank helplessly toward the ocean, Eckener faced the unsavoury prospect of endangering the lives of the volunteers, for at some point he would have to pour on the power to climb away from the water. Fortunately, it didn't come to that. The repair team had returned inside by the time the power was increased. Later, when the ship had regained a safe altitude, the engines were slowed once again to permit the crew to attend to the fluttering fabric. It took hours to complete the repairs – hours in which the world's media hinted at the probable loss of the ship. They had received no word from the airship; the worst had probably happened.

But then – good news! The *Graf* was safe! To prove it, Eckener steered inland along Chesapeake Bay, circling Washington, D.C., and Baltimore, then New York itself. The sight of the huge ship – still bearing the "wound" in her tail fabric – practically brought the city to a standstill. A tickertape parade attracted many thousands to gape at this incredible ship, this triumph of modern engineering, this glimpse into the future of international travel.

It should have been the crowning moment in the history of the Zeppelin organization. It wasn't. In spite of the publicity, in spite of the intense, fervid enthusiasm of millions, the plain, unvarnished truth was that the Zeppelin organization wasn't making money. Although the fares were astronomical – some three thousand dollars per person – they weren't high enough to make the enterprise profitable, not with an aircrew of forty-three to maintain, plus another hundred brawny souls required for every takeoff and landing, as well as countless administrative and production people. Eckener had counted on this trip to America to establish meaningful contacts with businessmen and politicians as a first step to the creation of an airship airline and the construction of four Zeppelins even larger than the *Graf*, true giants of the air that would cruise across the Atlantic carrying hundreds of passengers. There was plenty of keen interest; the International Zeppelin Transport Company was formed, but that was as far as it went. Eckener pondered the problem long and hard. Eventually, he came to a decision: what was needed was a spectacular flight to reignite public interest in lighter-than-air travel. He would fly the *Graf* around the world. He would dazzle everyone with the *Graf*'s capabilities. It would be an expensive proposition – he estimated the cost at about $250,000 – but an excellent investment in the future

of the Zeppelin company. The Hearst organization – always on
the lookout for good stories – found out about Eckener's plans and
offered $150,000 for the exclusive rights. Eckener was tempted,
but he couldn't exclude the German press – to do so would alien-
ate half the country. Reluctantly, the Zeppelin CEO agreed to a
two-tier deal: Hearst would pay $100,000 for the English-
language rights to the story; the German papers would contribute
$12,500. Eckener had nearly half the money he needed. A major
contribution came from the world of philately; collectors were
ecstatic at the prospect of securing correspondence franked in
Friedrichshafen, Tokyo, Los Angeles, and Lakehurst. By August
1929, when plans for the round-the-world flight were nearing
completion, the profit and loss statements were in the black – quite
an achievement, considering that only two of the twenty passengers actually paid for their tickets.

Eckener chose to fly a northerly route, across central Russia,
south to Tokyo, although this necessitated travelling over immense
stretches of Siberian wilderness very far from help, should it be
needed. The fact seemed not to concern any of the passengers. The
epochal voyage began before dawn on August 15, 1929, from
Friedrichshafen (although most Americans considered that it had
begun a week earlier, when the *Graf* had left from Lakehurst,
New Jersey, since Hearst, the principal backer, had insisted on an
American starting point). Aboard was a cosmopolitan group,
including correspondents from papers in America, Germany,
Japan, and France, plus representatives from the Soviet Union and
Japan, as well as Sir George Wilkins, the noted Arctic explorer. This
heterogeneous assembly had its tense moments. Eckener and the
Soviet representative, Karklin, exchanged undiplomatic words on
the very first day. Karklin said the airship *must* pass over Moscow;
any other course of action was unthinkable. Eckener snapped back

that favourable winds were blowing farther north, and he intended to take advantage of them, no matter what anyone said. Karklin simmered, but the moment passed. For three days the huge airship purred across the endless plains and forests of Eastern Europe before crossing into Asia. The very harshness of the land over which they were passing seemed to break down everyone's reserve; soon the sounds of accordion music and a portable phonograph filled the airship's cabins. The terrain below was as bleak as the surface of the moon – and apparently just as empty of life. On the fourth day, the airship approached the Stanovoi mountains, the last natural obstacle before reaching Tokyo. With questionable navigational data at hand, Eckener had to make a perilous passage between walls of rock – although Charles Rosendahl, captain of the U.S. dirigible *Los Angeles*, wondered if Eckener hadn't arranged the whole thing to demonstrate to the passengers that the flight hadn't been *too* easy.

The *Graf* arrived at Tokyo on the evening of August 19, four and a half days after leaving Friedrichshafen. A huge crowd, perhaps as many as a quarter of a million, watched as Eckener brought the airship in for a smooth landing. After leaving Tokyo (with some relief because of the oppressive heat) the *Graf* sailed five thousand miles across the Pacific, aided by vigorous winds, and arrived at San Francisco in sixty-eight hours, just in time for a superb sunset to provide a breathtaking backdrop as the dirigible purred over the Golden Gate Bridge – a deliberate bit of stage-managing by Eckener, who knew the value of an eye-catching picture in the papers. It continued without stopping, and at 5:00 a.m. on August 26, after a flight of seventy-nine hours, three minutes from Tokyo, the *Graf* touched down at Mines Field, Los Angeles (later Los Angeles International Airport). On the twenty-ninth came the arrival at Lakehurst, followed by the mandatory tickertape parade up Broadway and a reception at the White House. On September 4, the *Graf* arrived at Friedrichshafen, having dazzled the world – and having convinced most people that the future of air travel lay in airships. After all, weren't the British building *two* grand new airships at that very moment? And the Americans two more? No wonder Hugo Eckener felt confident about the future. The economy in the U.S. was breaking record after record; soon the big Zeppelin airline would be a glorious reality. Nothing could stop it. Except a stock market crash of catastrophic proportions.

The market crashed just weeks after the round-the-world flight, and the event changed all Eckener's plans. Many men in similar positions might have given up. Not Eckener. He had no intention of letting this economic hiccup wreck the plans that he had formulated with such care. He concentrated on ways of keeping the *Graf* – and indeed the whole concept of airship travel – alive in the public consciousness. He set his sights on South America, where there were sizable German communities. He saw Rio de Janeiro as the future terminus for the South American service, and set off on a proving flight. The intense heat created a special set of problems for the hydrogen-filled dirigible – and a shortage of water forced passengers to wash in cologne in the last stages of the trip.

In 1931, the *Graf* explored the Arctic, stopping briefly at the scientific station on Hooker Island, Franz Joseph Land, to exchange mail. The airship was becoming one of the best known aircraft in the world, guaranteed to thrill crowds wherever she appeared. Within a few years, however, the fiery destruction of the *Graf*'s successor, the *Hindenburg*, would end the dream of airship travel forever.

||||

In Tacoma, Washington, Canadian-born Harold Bromley, test pilot and operator of a flying school, was determined to conquer the Pacific. He intended to fly to Tokyo, alone, and in a single-engine airplane. He enlisted the aid of several local businessmen, most notably a lumberman, John Buffelen, and raised enough money to acquire a Lockheed Explorer, a handsome monoplane of modern lines. Internally braced, the Lockheed had none of the struts and wires of most aircraft of the day. The lacquered plywood fuselage was of semi-monocoque construction, with the external skin carrying much of the stress in flight. Lockheed had developed the system in 1918 for an unsuccessful sport aircraft: The technique made use of "a concrete mold that looked like a 27-foot bathtub."[2] The wooden components were placed in the mould: first the spruce strips coated with glue, followed by a second set bent into a semi-circular shape placed crosswise over the first, then treated with a coat of glue. A third set of strips completed the structure. A lid containing an inflatable rubber bag was then tightened in place. When pumped to the highest pressure, it exerted enough force to press the wooden strips against the sides of the mould. Left to cure for twenty-four hours, the result was a completely formed half fuselage, only a quarter-inch thick yet possessing remarkable strength. The finished shells for both halves of the aircraft were fastened together using barbed nails and copious quantities of glue. The result: an immensely strong and clean fuselage, a "plywood bullet" in contemporary jargon. The technique was used on a whole series of successful Lockheed aircraft, from the Vega to the Orion.

At the time, Tacoma had no airport, but citizens approved a three-hundred-thousand-dollar bond issue to finance an airstrip, the first stage of what would become a municipal facility. The takeoff strip was 5,400 feet long, with a nine-foot high ramp at one end to give Bromley's Lockheed a boost on its takeoff run, like the

"Byrd ramp" at Roosevelt Field. The city also bought a gold watch for Bromley to present to the Emperor of Japan. Bromley himself would earn no money from the flight; glory and prestige would be the only rewards. No doubt he also hoped to pick up a bountiful array of contracts and offers.

Bromley's bright orange aircraft was christened *City of Tacoma* before an enthusiastic crowd estimated at seventy thousand on July 28, 1929. The Japanese consul, Mr. S. Okamoto, declared that the flight would result in a new depth of friendly feeling between the United States and Japan. Everyone thought that an admirable sentiment. Mechanics had filled the *City of Tacoma*'s tanks to the brim. It was time to go. With a confident wave to the crowd, Bromley opened the throttle. Revs up to 2,000. The restraining rope was cut. The Explorer heaved herself into motion, engine roaring, as she sped down the ramp and along the takeoff strip. Everything seemed to be going splendidly – until gasoline suddenly spurted from the overflow vents, spraying back over Bromley in his open cockpit at the rear of the fuselage. Half blinded, he pushed his goggles up. Gas streamed into his eyes. Before Bromley could throttle back, the *City of Tacoma* swerved violently, ground-looping, and ending up in a pile of broken parts, all of them gasoline-soaked and in imminent danger of bursting into flames. Incredibly, there was no fire. Bromley scrambled uninjured from the cockpit, wiping his eyes and cursing his luck. The accident had been caused by overfilling the fuel tanks; as the heat rose, the fuel had expanded and it had nowhere to go but out through the vents.

Bromley's backers were remarkably understanding, promptly ordering another Lockheed Explorer, also dubbed *City of Tacoma*. During a test flight, the rudder broke away and the aircraft crashed, fortunately without killing anyone. Lockheed executives must have begun to entertain some doubts about this customer, but they agreed to supply yet another monoplane, a Sirius this time. On a test flight over the Mojave Desert, it crashed, killing a Lockheed test pilot named Hugh Catlin. It was an extraordinary run of bad luck for the people at Lockheed, who had a well-deserved reputation as a most successful and innovative corporation. Perhaps no one should have been surprised when Bromley chose an Emsco monoplane as the fourth *City of Tacoma*. Bromley took a navigator along this time, a well-regarded Australian named Harold Gatty, who ran a navigation school in San Francisco and who would later achieve fame as Wiley Post's crewmate in the Lockheed Vega *Winnie Mae*. Gatty undoubtedly had a hand in the decision to fly east instead of west. It made good sense. Why battle the prevailing westerlies? Why not make use of the winds to help the flight along? Bromley and Gatty sailed to Japan, intending to fly back to the U.S. But the fates continued to conspire against Bromley. He had to abandon his first takeoff attempt; the strip proved to be too short. His next attempt was from a naval airfield near Tokyo. It failed when Bromley nearly flew into trees. He dumped fuel to reduce the Emsco's weight, turned, and managed to land safely back on the field. The two flyers then travelled to Sabishiro Beach, 350 miles north of Tokyo. This time they were successful, lifting off from a makeshift runway of hard-packed sand nearly seven thousand feet long. The airmen heaved huge sighs of relief. They were on their way at last.

Twelve hours out over the Pacific, they heard a bang. The cabin began to fill with smoke, vile, noxious stuff. It didn't take long to sort out what had happened. There had been a break in the exhaust system – something that couldn't be fixed in flight. The foul air had to be endured. Opening the cabin windows helped a little, but both men felt their consciousness fading. They managed to turn the faltering airplane around. Somehow, they made it back to the

Japanese mainland, coming down on the cape of Shiriya Saki, passing out as they touched down. Fishermen found the two airmen lying on the beach, semi-comatose. They soon recovered, and the following year began planning for the trip again. But it was 1931; the Depression was deepening; Tacoma businessmen had enough problems making a living without worrying about Bromley and his dreams of flying halfway across the world. They refused to fund him. Disappointed, Bromley withdrew from the long-distance flight scene, no doubt to the intense relief of his family. Thus it was that his navigator, Harold Getty, became available to Wiley Post.

Now the Tokyo newspaper *Asahi*, picking up where Hearst, Northcliffe, and numerous other circulation-hungry newspaper publishers had left off, announced a prize of 50,000 yen (then about $25,000) for the first non-stop flight between Japan and the United States. The first to respond was an American, a carefree character by the name of Thomas Ash. He cabled Tacoma businessman John Buffelen, who owned the Emsco that Harold Bromley had used, requesting permission to use it for a shot at the big prize. Buffelen agreed, and Ash became an instant celebrity when he announced his intention of making the trip solo. He had the Emsco thoroughly overhauled and renamed her *Pacific*. Next, he transported the aircraft to Sabishiro Beach, the site of Bromley's takeoff on his last attempt to fly the big ocean. The ramp was still there. So was a sizable crowd of Japanese, chattering among themselves and gazing at Ash and his aircraft as if afraid that they would suddenly vanish, as apparitions were known to do. They shied away when Ash ran up the engine; then they edged forward, a tide of humanity, as he came speeding down the ramp and hurtled off along the beach. In vain. After a run of a mile and a half, he stopped, lightened his fuel load and tried again. But he couldn't get the

Emsco aloft with enough fuel on board to make the trip. Since Bromley and Gatty had succeeded in taking to the air carrying two men and a full fuel load, Ash began to doubt his abilities in the long-distance stakes. Sensibly, he decided to forget the whole thing.

Another Tokyo paper, the *Hochi Shimbun*, jumped on the bandwagon, sponsoring a Tokyo-to-San Francisco flight by a pilot named Seiji Yoshihara. The paper wrote reams about the superlative skills of the young man, calling him a second Lindbergh. Unhappily, his performance didn't live up to the advance billing. After less than a thousand miles, he damaged his Junkers float plane. The paper provided another, which crashed during a test flight. The managers of the paper still had confidence in their man, for they supplied him with a third aircraft. It was shipped to the United States in 1932 – and became yet another pile of shattered dreams when, still equipped with pontoons, it came down on dry land. It was at this point that Yoshihara lost his enthusiasm.

Hoping to stimulate the ultra-conservative Japanese aircraft industry into producing some outstanding airplanes, the Imperial Aviation Society announced a prize of 100,000 yen (then worth about $50,000) for the first Japanese airman to fly non-stop between Japan and the United States. The prize was never claimed. In the U.S., however, a $28,000 prize was offered for a flight from Seattle to within fifty miles of Tokyo. Simultaneously, William Easterwood put up $25,000 for the first flight between Dallas and Tokyo in either direction. Two young Americans, Reginald Robbins of Fort Worth, and a wealthy New Yorker named Harold S. Jones, decided to try for both the Seattle prize and that offered by Easterwood. They had a white Lockheed Vega named *Fort Worth*, the range of which they planned to extend by employing an innovative new technique: in-flight refuelling. They arranged for a Ford tri-motor, crewed by Jimmy Mattern and Nick Greener, to fly ahead to Fairbanks, Alaska. The plan was for the Ford to take on a load of fuel and have it ready for transfer, mid-air, to the *Fort Worth* at the appropriate time. It should have worked. The Vega took off on July 8, 1931, journeying from Seattle to Fairbanks, where two hundred gallons of fuel gurgled from one aircraft to another. The flyers intended to rendezvous again near Nome for a second fill-up, but Nature put a stop to it. Violent winds sprang up, making any attempt at refuelling suicidal. Robbins and Jones headed back to Seattle. In August they tried again, and again ran afoul of uncooperative weather, this time a front of thick clouds over the Yukon Valley, which caused the two aircraft to lose contact. Robbins and Jones abandoned the mission.

Clyde Pangborn was a veteran barnstormer who had been a performer with the Gates Flying Circus in the early twenties. In 1931, he became friendly with a wealthy New Yorker, Hugh Herndon, Jr., who offered to finance a shot at the round-the-world speed record, held at that time by the airship *Graf Zeppelin*. Herndon bought a Bellanca, named *Miss Veedol* as a nod to the oil company that provided financial assistance for the flight. Herndon delayed the takeoff when he met a girl from Albany, New York, and they decided to marry. Eventually the *Miss Veedol* got away from Floyd Bennett Field on July 29, 1931. Coincidentally, another Bellanca, the *Cape Cod*, flown by Russell Boardman and John Polando, was also at the field, preparing to fly to Istanbul. The two aircraft took off little more than fifteen minutes apart. The *Cape Cod* eventually reached Istanbul with a few drops of fuel remaining in the tank, having broken the distance record with a flight of just over five thousand miles in forty-nine hours. *Miss Veedol* wasn't so fortunate. Encountering horrible weather, the two flyers abandoned the flight in Siberia. They expected to go home, but out of the blue came a wire from Tokyo, from the paper *Asahi*, urging them to try for its Pacific prize. The two Americans thought this a good idea, and immediately set off for Tokyo, not bothering to obtain up-to-date maps. On the way, they unwittingly traversed restricted areas, plunging themselves into hot water with the Japanese authorities, who were totally unimpressed when told that the Americans were there because of the newspaper *Asahi*. Newspapers had little influence in the Japan of the thirties; the two airmen were placed under arrest and questioned repeatedly. The authorities apparently saw them as thoroughly undesirable characters, possibly spies. Their aircraft, the *Miss Veedol*, was locked up, in spite of entreaties from the U.S. Embassy. After weeks of delay, they were eventually released – although the suspicious authorities sent an army aircraft to make sure they kept to a prescribed route which took them some four hundred miles out of their way. But at least they were clear of Japan. They ran into icing over the Aleutians, but made it safely to Wenatchee, Washington, where they made a spectacular landing on the aircraft's belly (Pangborn had rigged the gear to fall off once it was in the air, thus reducing drag and extending the plane's range), skidding some fifty feet before coming to a safe halt.

The first non-stop Pacific flight in history was over.

IIII

One of the most important aviation events of the thirties was the MacRobertson England-to-Australia contest of 1934, officially the Victorian Centenary Race. Sponsored by a seventy-three-year-old philanthropist, Sir Macpherson Robertson, known as the "Australian Carnegie," the race was open to pilots and aircraft of all nations. It had two divisions: a speed race and a handicap event. All aircraft had to conform to the regulations of the International

Commission on Aerial Navigation, and all crews were checked for professional competence – a repeat of the Dole debacle was to be avoided at all costs.

The timing was perfect for Boeing and Douglas in America, which had both just unveiled revolutionary new airliners. Here, with all the world watching, was an opportunity to show off the capabilities of the 247D from Boeing and the DC-2 from Douglas.

The Boeing entry was owned by Warner Brothers, the motion picture company. Their pilot was the colourful Roscoe Turner, probably the best-known racing pilot in the United States. Turner had a positive genius for self-promotion. Not for him the leather jackets and scarves common to most pilots. Roscoe was usually to be seen garbed in uniforms that might have been left over from the movies *Hell's Angels* and *Wings* – except that Roscoe liked them in attractive pinks and bright blues. These togs, combined with his six-inch-wide waxed moustaches, his diamond-studded pilot's badge – made, he claimed, of gold and platinum – plus his uniform buttons sporting the initials RT, ensured he would never go unnoticed. When Gilmore Oil hired him, he had a bright idea. The company's trademark was a lion, so Turner talked the World Jungle Compound of Ventura, California, into lending him a lion cub, which he took for walks along city streets. In case anyone missed the connection, he named the cub Gilmore. The cub flew too, equipped with his own parachute, logging some thirty thousand air miles at Roscoe's side. Fellow pilots made fun of Turner's flamboyant habits. Turner didn't care. He let other pilots razz him as much as they pleased; it all added up to good advertising. And highly effective advertising it was. The names Turner and Gilmore became famous even among people who had no interest in aviation. Hotels provided both flyer and feline with luxury accommodation free of charge. Newspapers couldn't resist printing their pictures.

The DC-2 in the race belonged to KLM and was to be flown by two Dutch pilots, Parmentier and Moll, carrying three passengers and a load of mail – although the company declared that it was not interested in winning prizes, only in demonstrating the future of air travel via KLM.

The British had no airliner to compare with the Boeing and Douglas aircraft. Imperial Airways still favoured the "slow but sure" approach typified by the stately Handley Page biplanes and the plodding Armstrong Whitworth monoplanes. In January 1934, however, the de Havilland company decided to build an aircraft capable of winning the race. Thus was born the Comet, a beautifully streamlined twin-engine racing monoplane with retractable landing gear. The Comet's Ratier propellers featured a primitive means of changing pitch during flight. At 150 mph, the disc on the spinner on each propeller was pushed in by air pressure, releasing internal air pressure that automatically changed the pitch to coarse. The pitch could only be changed back to fine on the ground, using a bicycle pump. A curse of the system for multi-engine aircraft was that, in flight, the two propellers seldom changed pitch simultaneously, resulting in some odd, if temporary, handling problems. The aircraft had two 230-horsepower de Havilland Gipsy Six R engines. Orders for the new racer had to be placed by February 1934 so that construction could be completed in time for the race. The first Comet took to the air on September 8, 1934, a mere six weeks before the big event.

At dawn on October 24, 1934, a crowd estimated at sixty thousand watched the start of the race at Mildenhall, Suffolk, England. The racers were flagged off at forty-five-second intervals. The first leg, to Baghdad, was 2,350 miles. The husband and wife team of Jim Mollison and Amy Johnson was in the lead in a Comet named *Black Magic*, averaging about two hundred miles per hour. Another

Comet, *Grosvenor House*, was in second place; the crew of this aircraft consisted of Charles Scott and Tom Campbell Black. The next
leg, Baghdad to Allahabad, India, proved unlucky for the
Mollisons. After their excellent start, they had to retire with engine
trouble. So did the notoriously tricky Gee Bee racer crewed by
Americans Jacqueline Cochran and Wesley Smith. Roscoe Turner's
Boeing was several hours behind the leader, as was the KLM DC-2.
At Singapore, *Grosvenor House* had an impressive eight-hour lead
over the DC-2, with Turner a further eight hours behind.

It was apparent to Scott and Campbell Black that their big lead
was far from secure. The DC-2's Wright Cyclone engines were
operating at normal cruising power, whereas their Comet's Gipsy
engines were being pushed to the limit. Soon they would pay the
price. Crossing the Timor Sea to Darwin, *Grosvenor House*'s port
engine began to lose oil pressure. Shortly afterwards, it failed
entirely. When Scott and Campbell Black arrived at Darwin on
only one engine, mechanics worked frantically to make the necessary repairs. And luck played a big part. Frank Halford, the designer
of the engine, heard about the problem and happened to know
that a London newspaper had a telephone line open to Australia
– a rarity at that time. Geoffrey de Havilland later related what
happened: "He was soon talking to Scott and heard what the
symptoms of the trouble were. It was obviously connected with oil
pressure, and Halford realized that it might possibly be only a
defective oil pressure gauge that was the cause. He told Scott to go
ahead, forget the gauge, and give the engine a rather easier time
when in the air."[3] The crew of Scott and Campbell Black took
turns catnapping as they nursed the Comet toward Melbourne.
They arrived first, to an enthusiastic reception from the huge
crowd. Sir Macpherson Robertson handed them the winning
cheque for ten thousand pounds as well as a gold cup.

Mechanical problems had plagued many of the flyers. A British Airspeed Viceroy had to withdraw at Athens with electrical problems. The Dutch Pander S-4 Postjager experienced difficulties with its retractable landing gear. Two British airmen were killed when their Fairey Fox crashed in Italy.

The KLM DC-2 ran into bad weather and was forced to land at the small town of Albury some 150 miles northeast of Melbourne. Hearing the airliner circling, the residents made use of the town's lights, spelling its name in Morse code. As torrential rain battered the area, Parmentier made a perfect landing on the local racecourse. The DC-2 became bogged down overnight, so in the morning dozens of residents helped to haul the hefty machine out of the soggy area. In Parmentier's capable hands, the airliner took off, flew to Melbourne, and landed, coming in second in the speed category. Parmentier and Moll, neat in their KLM uniforms, accepted the runner-up cheque from Sir Macpherson Robertson.

Roscoe Turner, who was fond of saying, "There's no excuse for an airplane unless it goes fast," couldn't get Warner's Boeing 247 to go fast enough. He flew the aircraft flat out trying to catch up to the KLM DC-2. He was unsuccessful, arriving at Melbourne two and a half hours behind the Dutchmen with worn-out engines.

||||

Earlier that year, a former oil field worker, an intense young Texan named Wiley Post began to think about flying around the world. He was an excellent and experienced pilot, despite the fact that he had only one eye, a souvenir of an oil field accident in which a roughneck chipped an iron bolt while pounding it with a sledgehammer. A sliver of steel shot into Post's left eye. The injury cost him peripheral vision and impaired his depth perception – but Post had no intention of giving up his ambition to fly. This was just the latest in a lifetime of hard knocks; virtually uneducated, he had grown up in a poverty-stricken home. Unemployed and desperate, he tried his hand at crime, and failed, spending a year in the Oklahoma State Reformatory.[4] Oddly enough, the jail term seemed to mark the beginning of better times for Post. He received a payment of $1,800 from the Oklahoma State Industrial Commission as compensation for the loss of his eye. The award wasn't princely but it enabled him to do something he had long wanted to do: buy an airplane. He settled on an elderly Canuck, the Canadian-built version of the famous Curtiss Jenny. While he learned to fly, he trained himself to improve his vision: "I practised gauging depth on hills and trees. Then I would step off the distance. At first, my mental calculations were far off, but by the end of two months I was a better judge of distance than I had ever been."[5] He found work with Burrell Tibbs' Flying Circus as a "featured parachute jumper" – although he had never used a parachute in his life. No problem, Tibbs said, when Post raised this technicality, all he had to do was climb out of the cockpit and jump; he'd be okay, Tibbs assured him, as long as he remembered to pull the rip cord. He earned fifty dollars per jump. He soon developed his own routines, delaying the chute's opening to the last split second, and using two parachutes, dropping one to make the crowd (a bloodthirsty species in the main) think he was doomed. Post made more than a hundred jumps. It was a lucrative business; some days he cleared as much as two hundred dollars, at a time when an average American man with a family was doing well to earn fifty dollars a week. He became a good pilot and earned a reasonable income flying oilmen to their rigs and teaching students to fly. In 1927, Wiley married Mae Laine, a rancher's daughter from Sweetwater, Texas. At her request, he gave up the weekend parachute jumping. Soon afterward, he became the personal pilot for a wealthy oilman, F.C. Hall, who needed fast transportation to bid on oil contracts. Late in 1928, Post went to Burbank, California, to pick up a brand new Lockheed Vega for Hall – who named the plane *Winnie Mae* after his daughter. Post could hardly have found a better or more generous employer. When Hall didn't need the Vega for business, Post could use it. It was a perfect arrangement – and, of course, it was too good to last. Hard times hit Hall's business, and reluctantly he decided he could no longer afford the *Winnie Mae* or its pilot. A downcast Wiley Post flew the Vega to Lockheed's used-plane park at Burbank. He cheered up when Lockheed hired him as a test pilot and salesman. Post did well, and stayed a little over a year. Then Post's ex-employer called. Business had picked up; he wanted Wiley back. He wanted the *Winnie Mae* too, but Wiley had to tell him that the aircraft was now flying with Nevada Airlines. Hall instructed him to order another Vega, also to be named *Winnie Mae*. Post won the 1930 Men's Air Derby in the new Vega, speeding non-stop from Los Angeles to Chicago. His prize: $7,500. The magnanimous Hall told him to keep the money.

Early in 1931, Wiley Post began to plan his round-the-world flight in earnest. He selected Harold Gatty as his navigator. Gatty, an Australian, had been a master navigator in the British Merchant Marine and had flown with Harold Bromley. Post had the Lockheed people modify the Vega for the big flight, installing the latest equipment to facilitate blind flying as well as huge fuel tanks, behind which was Gatty's cramped office. The aircraft also had a drift-speed indicator, a device invented by Gatty. The two aviators went into intense training for the flight, sitting in the same position for hours on end and accustoming themselves to sleeping at irregular intervals. Post and Gatty flew to Roosevelt Field in May. There they had to endure an excruciating thirty days' delay because of bad weather. Not until June 22 did they leave for Newfoundland, their first stop, where, seven hours later, they touched down at Harbour Grace.

They paused only long enough to refuel, then they were off again, heading out over the Atlantic. The visibility was dreadful; after flying blind across the ocean, Post was unsure whether he had arrived over England, Scotland, or Ireland. It turned out to be England. The flyers had lunch at the RAF mess at Sealand, near Liverpool, before leaving for Germany. Utterly weary by now, Post forgot to refuel at Hanover; he had to return to that city. Thousands of people greeted the flyers at Berlin; but at Moscow, only airport workers were to be seen. The *Winnie Mae* touched down at October Field at 5:40 p.m. after flying through violent, blinding rain. The Soviets did not officially recognize the flight, so no reception had been organized. The airmen didn't care; what they did care about was the fact that Russian mechanics measured out the *Winnie Mae*'s fuel in imperial gallons, which were twenty per cent larger than U.S. gallons. The flyers had to wait while the surplus gasoline was siphoned off, then, after a bumpy takeoff, the Vega sped away, pushed by vigorous tailwinds. In Siberia, they found Blagoveshchensk airport under water. The landing was an event. "We thought we were in a seaplane," Post said. "Spray flew all over the place. As long as the ship kept moving, we were all right, but I couldn't keep her going. I felt her left wheel sink. There I sat – in a mud hole in the last 300 miles of Siberia."[6]

Eventually, the Vega was dragged out of the muck by a team of horses. The incident cost the flyers more than fourteen hours. Now behind schedule, Post decided to fly direct to Alaska instead of making a last refuelling stop in Russia. He landed on the beach near the village of Solomon, exhausted after flying seventeen hours through wet weather with poor visibility. He took on just enough

The Stinson Detroiter *Royal Windsor* at Harbour Grace, Newfoundland, September 1927. The aircraft, crewed by Canadians Duke Schiller and Phil Wood, had been prepared for a flight from Windsor, Ontario, to Windsor, England, but the flight was cancelled following the disappearance of the *Sir John Carling*. *(Canadian Aviation Museum)*

Terence Tully and James Medcalf with their Stinson Detroiter *Sir John Carling* in which they hoped to fly from London, Ontario, to London, England, in August 1927. The flight ended in disaster, with both men lost somewhere in the ocean. *(Canadian Aviation Museum)*

Amelia Earhart was a skilled pilot, yet when she became the first woman to cross the Atlantic by air, she flew as a passenger – though she was listed as captain of the Fokker tri-motor, *Friendship*. Wilmer Stultz was the pilot, Louis "Slim" Gordon the engineer. *(Smithsonian photo SI 81-1431)*

The Junkers W33 *Bremen* high and dry on Greenly Island in the Strait of Belle Isle after completing the first east-west crossing of the Atlantic in April 1928. The crew consisted of two Germans, Baron von Huenefeld and Hermann Koehl, and an Irishman, James Fitzmaurice. *(Canadian Aviation Museum)*

Two famous Aussies prepare for the first trans-Pacific flight on May 31, 1928: Charles Kingsford Smith (right) and Charles Ulm. They were accompanied by Harry Lyon, navigator, and James Warner, radio operator, in the Fokker *Southern Cross*. *(Smithsonian photo 78-16944)*

The Bellanca *Miss Veedol* at Wenatchee, Washington, after the first nonstop crossing of the Pacific. Hugh Herndon and Clyde Pangborn flew the aircraft. It landed on its belly, having dropped its landing gear after takeoff to reduce drag and extend the range. Despite the damage, the crew was unhurt. *(Smithsonian photo 89-4506)*

Wiley Post's Lockheed Vega *Winnie Mae* is refuelled at Harbour Grace, Newfoundland, on June 23, 1931, during a record-breaking round-the-world flight. Harold Gatty was the navigator. The flight took eight days, fifteen hours, including about 106 flying hours. Two years later, Post did the trip alone. *(Canadian Aviation Museum)*

Beryl Markham flew the first direct, solo, east-to-west crossing of the Atlantic by a woman in September 1936. *(Canadian Aviation Museum)*

Beryl Markham's borrowed Percival Vega Gull, *The Messenger*, in an undignified position in a bog in Cape Breton after her successful crossing. Beryl was enthusiastically greeted in Canada and later in New York and London. *(Canadian Aviation Museum)*

Amy Johnson became an instant heroine in England and the Commonwealth when she flew her diminutive Moth from London to Australia in May 1930. She was a shy individual who exhibited remarkable resolve and courage in all her flights.
(Smithsonian photo SI 72-19187)

Comfort was a minor consideration for long-distance flyers. Here, Jim Mollison shares the limited space in his Puss Moth's cabin with outsize fuel tanks. Mollison had just landed at Pennfield Ridge, New Brunswick, after completing the first solo crossing of the Atlantic from east to west. *(Canadian Aviation Museum)*

Jim Mollison enjoys a cup of tea after his successful crossing, although he usually partook of stronger stimulants. Mollison married Amy Johnson in 1932, but the union was short-lived. *(Canadian Aviation Museum)*

Soviet general Kokkinaki in earnest conversation with a Canadian doctor on tiny Miscou Island, New Brunswick, 1939. The Russians had attempted to fly nonstop from Moscow to New York, but strong headwinds caused a fuel shortage, leading to a wheels-up landing – without serious injury. *(Canadian Aviation Museum)*

fuel to reach Fairbanks, a trip of some five hundred miles. As he taxied to the takeoff point, Post felt the *Winnie Mae* sinking in soft sand. He reacted quickly, switching off the engine – but not quickly enough. With a bang and a flurry of sand, the propeller hit the beach. No replacement was available in this remote spot, but Post managed to straighten the propeller with the aid of a wrench, a hammer, and a small boulder. The propeller hadn't finished with the flyers, though. When Gatty tugged on a propeller blade to start the engine, a backfire sent it into the navigator's shoulder, a sharp, painful blow that could have killed him. He was lucky, although in considerable discomfort. Since nothing appeared to be broken, he clambered back aboard the *Winnie Mae*, and a few minutes later, the aircraft soared into the Alaskan sky. At Fairbanks, Post and Gatty had a couple of hours' sleep while mechanics refuelled their aircraft and installed a new propeller.

The cumulative effects of too many hours in noisy cockpits and too little sleep were slowing their reactions, but they pushed on, zombie-like, painstakingly performing the duties which normally were almost automatic. Pushing their way through thick cloud over the Rockies, they found themselves at Edmonton – with the airfield covered by water, just like the one in Siberia. Post managed to prevent the Vega from sinking into the mud by landing at high speed and keeping the aircraft's full weight off the wheels until the last moment. But how to depart? Was the flight going to end there? Would it be a matter of waiting until the field dried out? A Canadian airmail pilot saved the day. He pointed out that Portage Avenue was a paved thoroughfare linking the airport and town – and it was almost straight. Why not use it as a runway? Obliging local officials removed electric cables overnight. In the morning, Post "taxied out to the unused streetcar tracks and faced the nose toward the hotel, two miles away, at which we had stayed. People crowded uncomfortably close to the ship, and I'm afraid we seemed impolite to them. Dirt, mud and spray flew all around while I revved the motor up one last time before letting go the brakes. We were to bobble off headed straight for the centre of town and I didn't want to take any chances of being let down among the corners of the buildings . . . I let the Wasp have her head. . . . Curbstones and electric-light poles clipped by the wing tips so fast that I was just a little scared myself. The wind was slightly across our path and if one wing had ever dropped, it would have been just too bad. I'm not sure Harold nor I ever went or ever will go down a street so fast again. I got a new idea of the ground speed of the *Winnie Mae*. Loafing along an airport runway, with nothing upright nearer the plane than 100 yards or so, reduces the sensation of high speed, but I know now what 75 miles an hour feels like!"[7]

Wiley Post didn't breathe again until he was well clear of the ground, then, with a waggle of his wings to say thank you, he set off for Cleveland and New York. The *Winnie Mae* arrived back at Roosevelt Field after girdling the globe in eight days, fifteen hours, fifty-one minutes – a new world record.

F.C. Hall was so impressed that he gave the now-famous Vega to Wiley Post, who then began planning a *solo* flight around the world. He relinquished a second crew member in favour of a new Sperry automatic pilot and a controllable pitch propeller. On July 15, Post took off, flying direct from New York to Berlin. He planned to reach Novosibirsk, Russia, the same day, but violent thunderstorms necessitated a stop near the Russian–Polish border. He tried to beat his own time crossing Siberia – but damaged his propeller and landing gear coming down at Flat, Yukon Territories. He landed back at Floyd Bennett Field just before midnight on July 22, having beaten his old record by a whopping ten hours.

Wiley Post was now a world-famous hero. Despite the economic chill that gripped the country, he picked up thousands of dollars for personal appearances and became famous for his high-altitude research work in which he was garbed in a strange rubber suit that looked like something worn by deep-sea divers. He replaced the *Winnie Mae* with a hybrid, a Lockheed Explorer wing mated to the fuselage of a Lockheed Orion and equipped with pontoons. He and his good friend, homespun humorist Will Rogers set off on a trip to Alaska. On August 15 they were killed when the aircraft crashed, apparently the result of engine failure moments after takeoff. The notoriously nose-heavy float plane turned on its back and plunged into the water. The world lost two of its favourite people.

||||

In distant East Africa (now Kenya), Beryl Markham learned to fly in the late twenties largely because a flame at the time was a pilot. An energetic individual, always eager to try something new, she had been born Beryl Clutterbuck in England in 1903, moving with her family to Africa four years later. She soon acquired a fine reputation as a horse trainer. She married three times, but kept the name of her second husband, Mansfield Markham. She demonstrated exceptional aptitude as an aviator, becoming the first woman in East Africa to possess a pilot's licence.

When she first gained her licence, she made a reasonable living as a bush pilot, flying all over Africa, carrying mail and passengers, delivering supplies to safaris, and acting as an aerial game-spotter. Long-distance flying held no fears for her; she flew from East Africa to London four times. In 1934, she decided to attempt the east-west crossing of the Atlantic, which had been done only by the German-Irish team of Von Huenefeld, Koehl, and Fitzmaurice back in 1928. If successful – and she was sure she would be – she would be the first person to do it solo.

The Moths and Avians she had been flying in Africa weren't up to the task at hand. Although Beryl didn't have the money to purchase a suitable aircraft, she had no hesitation in seeking the aid of a titled acquaintance, Baron Carberry, an Irish peer, who was having a Vega Gull built for himself at the Percival factory at Gravesend, near London. Carberry agreed to let Beryl use the Gull as long as she returned it in time for him to use it in a forthcoming race to Cape Town. Beryl agreed with alacrity. She hoped to have the new machine in late July or early August, but delivery was repeatedly postponed. Not until August 15 did she fly the Vega Gull, which had already been named *The Messenger*. Her flying instructor was Tom Campbell Black, and Jim Mollison helped her with charts and routes. Beryl had hoped for a quiet departure on her big adventure, but as the days slipped by, newspaper interest increased. They referred to her as a "society woman," which irritated her. In the end, she was persuaded to write a short piece for the *Daily Express*: "Two weeks from now I am going to set out to fly the Atlantic to New York. Not as a society girl. Not as a woman even. And certainly not as a stunt aviator. But as a pilot-graduate of one of the hardest schools of flying known, with 2,000 flying hours to my credit. And I have a definite object. It is true that I am known as a society woman. But what of it? The only thing that really counts . . . is whether one can fly. I have both tickets ["A" and "B" licences]. I can take an engine apart and put it back. I can navigate. I am fit, and given ordinary luck I am sure I can fly to New York. This is to be no stunt flight. No woman's-superiority-over-man affair. I don't want to be superior to men. I have a son. If I can be a good mother to him, and a good pilot, I'll be the happiest creature alive."[8]

Her departure was scheduled for September 4, 1936, from the air force field at Abingdon near Oxford. (She had originally intended to depart from Gravesend, but the experts advised her to use the longest strip available because of the monstrous fuel load weighing close to two thousand pounds.) She took a package of chicken sandwiches, plus nuts, raisins, and dried bananas, topped off by five flasks of tea and coffee, brandy, and water. Jim Mollison and Edgar Percival, the plane's designer and builder, saw her off. Mollison gave her his watch and made a play of being concerned that it didn't get wet. Then she was off, using only six hundred yards to become airborne. The rumble of her engine quickly faded. Jim Mollison turned to Percival and said in a resigned tone, "Well, that's the last we'll see of Beryl."[9]

At ten o'clock that night *The Messenger* was spotted off Castletown Berehaven, County Cork. The winds strengthened and the rain fell in torrents as the little monoplane battled her way across the ocean, making a mere 90 miles per hour because of the conditions. Beryl had anticipated speeding along at about 150. The journey was "terrible," she later said, with the small aircraft constantly battered, bouncing about the sky. When she opened her flask for a much-needed cup of coffee at dawn, a violent lurch knocked it out of her hand, spilling the contents. It brought her to the brink of tears. Crushing loneliness beset her, as it beset all long-distance flyers. There seemed to be no world outside this thrumming cockpit, this insecure, swaying perch in the sky. The dials, the airspeed indicator, the compass, the altimeter, were her only companions. A moment of near disaster . . . one tank ran dry. The engine, the wonderfully reliable Gipsy, hiccuped into silence, leaving only the dirge-like moaning of the wind. Beryl hastily switched to the next tank. The Gull glided down, down toward the churning sea. Then, with a growl, the engine caught as the new fuel supply – her last – wended its way along the pipes in the passenger cabin. Now she had plenty to complete the journey. Or had she? As she monitored the gauges it became apparent that her fuel was being consumed more rapidly than she had anticipated.

The journey seemed endless. It felt as if she had spent half her life up here in the lonely sky with nothing but sea to look at.

More calculations. They confirmed her suspicions about the fuel. She decided to land at Sydney airfield in Nova Scotia and refuel before going on to New York. But then she heard a heart-stopping sound: a splutter from her engine. An airlock? It seemed the most likely explanation. She hastily adjusted the valves on the fuel tanks, one after the other. It didn't help. But at least the Gull was now over solid ground. The airfield at Sydney couldn't be far away. Could she reach it? No, the engine cut out entirely. Beryl eased the nose down to maintain flying speed. She would have to land without her engine, like a glider. No missed approaches and going around again for another try.

She described what happened in her autobiography: "The earth hurries up to meet me, I bank, turn and sideslip to dodge the boulders, my wheels touch, and I feel them submerge. The nose of the plane is engulfed in mud, and I go forward striking my head on the glass of the cabin front, hearing it shatter, feeling blood pour over my face.

"I stumble out of the plane and sink to my knees in muck and stand there foolishly staring, not at the lifeless land but, but at my watch."[10]

Local fishermen helped Beryl to a nearby farm, where she asked for a cup of tea and the use of the telephone. In nearby Louisbourg, a Dr. O'Neil attended to the cut on her forehead.

Soon the news of her arrival was speeding around the world. The Carberrys called from New York, and Beryl had to tell them that *The Messenger* had suffered considerable damage in the landing on the bog. Carberry told her not to worry about it – though he would be less sanguine about the incident later.

After a fitful sleep and a light breakfast, she began to realize that what had seemed to be an abysmal failure to her, most people viewed as a triumph. Telegrams poured in. One was from Mayor Fiorello La Guardia of New York, who talked about her "epochal achievement" and invited her to the city. She was informed that an airplane was waiting at a nearby airfield, ready to whisk her off to Halifax on the first leg of the trip to New York. At Halifax, after more speeches, she stepped aboard a Beechcraft 17 Staggerwing and settled down to enjoy the journey to the Big Apple. They gave her a tumultuous welcome there, the crowds cheering her as she got out of the Beech and into a limousine. Her blond good looks were no handicap. The city rated her a Class "A" celebrity and pulled out all the stops, providing a suite at the Ritz-Carlton. Radio interviews with Milton Berle and other personalities soon followed. It was an unreal few days, a kaleidoscope of swarms of people, reporters with acres of open notebooks, flashlamps exploding in her face, souvenir hunters trying to get into her hotel room, a telegram from Jim Mollison thanking her for taking care of his watch, offers from theatrical producers, offers for lecture tours, offers of marriage, offers of jobs. She revelled in the attention – and in the clothes that kept being delivered following her announcement that she had arrived without a stitch of clothing, "nor a toothbrush, comb, nor pair of stockings." She found herself in a motorcade, escorted by dozens of police motorcycles, with grinning New Yorkers waving at her as if she were an old friend. She met the diminutive La Guardia, who kept mopping his forehead.

It was all breathtaking and great fun. But while it was happening, Jim Mollison telephoned her to tell her of Tom Campbell Black's death at Liverpool in a "million-to-one accident." It was a terrible shock for Beryl. She and Black had been lovers for years.

She returned to England on the *Queen Mary*, still grieving for Tom, the man who had taught her to fly, the only man she had really loved. In Southampton, and later in London, she had to go through what she called "the trial by press" all over again. The same questions. The same poses. It was all rather silly and time-wasting, and vaguely unreal in light of Tom's death. She went to Portsmouth to watch the start of the race to Cape Town, sponsored by I.W. Schlesinger, in which Baron Carberry was to have participated. For the next few weeks, she dined out at the best restaurants and hotels. She appeared to be on top of the world, but Tom's death had been a dreadful blow – and financial troubles were beginning to nag. She had made very little money out of her flight. It was galling, after all the publicity. No doubt most people thought the flight had made her wealthy. The theatrical offers were of no interest; she had no intention of becoming a musical hall act. In the meantime she was living off friends and relatives. It didn't trouble her greatly. In East Africa such behaviour was common – and Beryl's attitude to money was never conventional. Money was useful stuff to have around, but why worry if you happened to be short? Debts? They were tiresome but unimportant. Something would come up. It always did. In the spring of 1937, after accumulating a mountain of bills from various shops and dressmakers, she declared herself bankrupt. She agreed to pay her creditors five shillings in the pound (that is, one-quarter of the amount owed). Typically, she regarded the matter as nothing more than an irksome formality. At the time she was far too busy preparing for an important transatlantic race to worry about such mundane matters. The event was sponsored by the French government to commemorate the tenth anniversary of Lindbergh's famous flight. Initially, the ex-boxer Jack Doyle said he would sponsor her, but he quickly dropped out. Beryl herself soon withdrew; the race was being modified almost out of recognition, becoming semi-military in character. Beryl then travelled to the United States, sponsored by several wealthy South Africans, including I.W. Schlesinger, to find an aircraft capable of high speed and long range. Her intention was no doubt to attempt an around-the-world flight. When Amelia Earhart embarked on a similar mission, these plans also fell apart.

When the news of Amelia's disappearance broke, Beryl was staying at the splendid California home of the well-known aviatrix Jacqueline Cochran and her husband, Floyd. Beryl had received an offer from Columbia Pictures concerning a film about her transatlantic flight. It was an exciting prospect – but the film was never made. In December, Beryl sailed for Africa, then she returned to London, after which she sailed to New York aboard the *Manhattan*. Another offer came her way, this time from Paramount to be technical adviser on a film named *Safari* starring Douglas Fairbanks, Jr. and Madeleine Carroll. For a time, that pesky problem, money, slipped into the background. In California she met the French writer and aviator Antoine de Saint-Exupéry, and, probably with his encouragement, she began to make notes that later became the basis of her autobiography, *West with the Night*. It would become a classic of aviation literature.

| *Amy,
Wonderful
Amy*

A my Johnson grew up in the north of England, in Hull,
Yorkshire, on England's east coast. She was a paradox: shy yet
possessed of a steely determination, intensely emotional yet utterly
single-minded. She agonized over the provincial "twang" in her
voice. She longed to possess an "Oxford" accent like one of the
sophisticated actresses who trod the boards in the local "rep" theatres
– yet she became far more famous than any of them. She was the
eldest of four daughters born to a moderately prosperous fish merchant, growing up in comfortable if not luxurious circumstances.
She entered Sheffield University in 1922 at the age of nineteen –
in itself unusual for a young woman at that time and place. She
earned her B.A. and took various jobs, all of which she found
excruciatingly boring. An antidote to the tedium came in the form
of a young man, a Swiss named Hans Arregger, with whom Amy
fell deeply in love. It was to prove an unhappy affair, for her feelings were diametrically opposed to his. To Amy, it was a grand

passion, a once-in-a-lifetime romance; to him it was something far less significant, something to fill the moment, to be enjoyed then forgotten. She managed to convince herself that she would soon be his wife – even if it meant converting to Catholicism, which would have been a jolt for her strictly Methodist family. For several years, Amy alternated between bliss and total dejection as the relationship waxed and waned.

In 1926, she moved to London, principally to be closer to Hans, who was now working in the capital. But the relationship was almost over; Hans had met another girl. Heartbroken, Amy went through the range of emotions so common in such situations, ending up by writing to him that she no longer cared one way or the other. Nothing could have been further from the truth, but it was a way of salving a modicum of pride. At the time, she was living in rented quarters near a small airfield (or "aerodrome" as it was known at the time) called Stag Lane, home of the London Aeroplane Club. Small Moths were constantly overhead, landing or taking off, filling the air with intoxicating dronings. Still smarting from the breakup, Amy looked for a way to demonstrate her independence. What better way than by learning to fly? At once the notion captivated her. She immediately set off for the club. She was informed that dual instruction cost two pounds an hour; solo flying in a club Moth cost thirty shillings an hour. In addition, there was an entrance fee of three guineas (three pounds, three shillings) and another three guineas subscription. It all added up to a major expenditure. But Amy was determined to go ahead. She wrote to her father for financial assistance, and got it.

She started her flying lessons in September 1928. Amy's first lesson was hardly a triumph. Given a flying helmet several sizes too large, she put it on and took her seat in the open-cockpit Moth. It was a thrilling moment. But the wind played tricks on her, whistling under her helmet and making her instructor's directions unintelligible, a jumble of utterly confusing sounds coming through the communications tube. On landing, the instructor told her not to waste her money on any more flying lessons; in his opinion, she showed not the slightest aptitude. It may have been enough to deter some aspiring pilots, but not Amy Johnson. She was determined to learn to fly, and no misogynist-instructor was going to stop her. She knew she could do it, and she was right. Amy became a good pilot, although she never quite came to terms with landing, a problem she shared with a number of prominent flyers. When she got her "A" licence in mid-1929, she immediately set out to get her "B" licence, which would permit her to fly passengers "for hire."

Whenever she wasn't flying, Amy haunted the club's hangars, working on engines and learning about rigging. She became the first woman in England to become a licensed ground engineer. She met a club member, James Martin, who later founded Martin-Baker and developed the ejector seat. Martin was clearly impressed by Amy; at the time he was busy designing a monoplane with its engine placed in the middle of the fuselage rather than at the front. He told her of his project and suggested that she might like to demonstrate the plane, no doubt thinking of the publicity value of having a girl doing the test flying. The idea captivated her; for weeks she could think of little else. But it all fell through, largely because of lack of funds. At the same time, she began to think of an ambitious plan: a solo flight to Australia. It was madness, of course. She had a mere couple of hundred hours of flight time in her log. No experience of long-distance flying. No aircraft. No navigational skills. No money. And, in the opinion of most people, no hope of attaining her goal.

But Amy Johnson could never be accused of not trying. She wrote letters to everyone who might be able to help, every day carrying a bundle to the mailbox. Her father said he would support her to the tune of five hundred pounds, but it began to look as if that might be the end of her fundraising. Then one evening she attended a meeting at the Royal Aeronautical Society at which the Director of Civil Aviation, the personable, monocle-wearing Sir Sefton Brancker, was speaking. After the meeting, Amy sat down and wrote a letter to Sir Sefton. In the sort of incident that would never make it into a work of fiction, she forgot to sign her name. By outrageous coincidence, Brancker had just read an article in *Flight* magazine in which Amy was mentioned; he guessed it was she who had written to him and took the trouble to trace her address through the magazine. So Amy received a reply to her letter, telling her that the oil magnate, Lord Wakefield, would be contacted on her behalf. It was the turning point. Wakefield must have been impressed by the young woman with the Yorkshire accent. He agreed to provide 50 per cent of the cost of a suitable aircraft and to supply oil and gasoline along her route. Jubilant, half wondering if she was dreaming, Amy went out and bought a second-hand Gipsy Moth. The red and silver biplane had been owned by Walter Hope of Air Taxis, a small charter company operating out of Stag Lane. The Moth had been specially built for the company and was equipped with a long-range fuel tank occupying the front cockpit. It was the ideal machine for Amy. She had the Moth repainted with a bottle-green fuselage and silver wings. She called it *Jason*, the trademark of her father's wholesale fish business.

The days leading up to the big flight were hectic; Amy was busy studying navigation and discussing her intended route with the Wakefield organization so that they could arrange for fuel and oil along the way. Her plan was to reach each stopping point before dark. She organized the visas and other documents she would require en route. To assist her navigational efforts, Walter Hope suggested roller maps; they would be easier to manage in her windy open cockpit. He also instructed her to wear a sun helmet in the tropics and advised her on such matters as her first-aid kit, emergency rations, and a stove. He suggested that she take a revolver; after all, there was no telling who or what she might encounter in those foreign parts.

At four in the morning of May 5, 1930, Amy's father woke her in the Aerodrome Hotel, Croydon. She had slept poorly, disturbed by the din of traffic from nearby Purley Way and by her own twitching nerves. Never the most quiescent of individuals, she must have endured moments of sheer hell as she waited for the minutes to pass. It was chilly that morning as Amy, bundled up in a flying suit complete with a parachute — a gift from her parents — settled herself in the Moth's narrow cockpit. No doubt a sense of unreality overcame her. Was this really happening? Was she really about to take off to fly to *Australia?* A spare propeller had been lashed to the centre-section struts. She was all set. Or was she? The cockpit reeked of gasoline. Fuel dripped from one of the tubular connections. She was advised to go back to the hotel to rest until the fault was corrected. More frustration, more waiting. It was nearly 8 a.m. before she was finally ready to depart. Then, more problems. Heavily overloaded, the Moth was reluctant to leave the ground. She didn't make it the first time and had to taxi back to her starting position and try again. She took off on the second try, the gallant little biplane shouldering its sizable load and climbing into the morning air. She waved farewell to the handful of people who had seen her off, then set a course for Vienna.

She got there ten hours later. At four the following morning, she prepared to depart on the next leg and was surprised to find the maintenance staff on hand to assist her. They, like all the mechanics she encountered in her odyssey, were impressed by her mechanical abilities and her willingness to get her hands dirty servicing her plane. They had never met a lady pilot like her.

She had to fly eight hundred miles to Constantinople, through punishing rainstorms. In addition, the fuel pump leaked again, sending gas squirting into her face. The Turkish airport people were pleasant but dilatory. Her morning departure was delayed by bureaucratic problems, followed by more work on the engine. It was 10 a.m. before she got away, heading for the Taurus Mountains. She had to climb to eleven thousand feet in her search for a way through the rocks. Her engine coughed in the thin air, and Amy was chilled to the bone despite her Sidcot flying suit. It was an intense relief to get into the safer country beyond. The French air force personnel greeted her warmly when she landed at Aleppo, Syria, then a French mandate. Although the bed they provided was painfully hard, she felt secure because the windows were barred and an armed sentry paced back and forth all night.

The next day, the fourth, she flew almost five hundred miles across the desert to Baghdad. Nearing the city, she encountered a sandstorm which tossed the Moth about like a scrap of paper, almost slamming it into the ground. Amy decided to land until the storm had gone on its way. It wasn't easy. Visibility was terrible and sand and dust kept coating her goggles, but she got down safely. Then for the next several hours she had to sit on the Moth's tail to prevent it from being whipped into the air. When she heard the unearthly howling of desert dogs, she tugged the revolver from her baggage. She didn't need it; the dogs kept their distance. The storm eventually abated, and Amy, much relieved, put her gun away, started the engine, and completed her journey to Baghdad.

But on landing . . . disaster! A strut in her undercarriage sheared, probably weakened by the desert landing. Disappointment enveloped her like a hair shirt. Was this the end? She started to walk to the hangars when a truck pulled up alongside her; she climbed aboard and was driven to a lounge used by Imperial Airways passengers. The local Imperial representative took it upon himself to send the damaged strut to a nearby RAF field, where a new one was rapidly fabricated by competent mechanics. Amy's lucky star was working overtime.

By now the British newspapers were starting to take an interest in the "flying secretary." Her story had everything: LONE GIRL FLYER BATTLES TROPICAL STORMS, LANDS ON DESERT, FIGHTS OFF WILD DOGS . . . Reporters swarmed around the Johnson home in Hull; neighbours stared, amazed, barely able to believe the evidence of their eyes. Was this their *Amy* all these blokes were talking about? The one who had the unhappy love affair and went to live in London? *Her?* Offers for stories kept coming in; Amy's father handled them in his no-nonsense way, acting on her behalf as makeshift agent. There was money to be made, and Will Johnson, even though his business experience was limited to fish, was a good man to have in her corner.

Amy had little knowledge of these goings-on; her whole being was concentrated on the task at hand, getting to the next landing, place getting the right fuel, getting a little sleep. When she reached Bandar Abbas on the Persian Gulf, she couldn't find the airfield. Circling the place, she found a flat, clear area: no airfield, but large enough to land on. She landed fast, as usual – and, like most light aircraft of the era, the Moth had no brakes. Her left wing scraped the ground, breaking a strut. Despairingly, Amy studied it, close to tears. How would she find a replacement in this godforsaken place? She soon found out. A white man met her, and explained apologetically that the "aerodrome" was no longer in regular use. He had "an excellent man called David," however, who looked after the family car and would do everything he could for her aircraft. The man turned out to be the British consul; what's more, David was able to find a replacement for the broken bolt in his extensive collection of spare parts. The Johnson luck was holding.

She reached India, landing at Karachi's Drigh Road aerodrome, having beaten the previous London-to-Karachi record by a whopping two days. She immediately examined the engine, which had been misfiring all the way from the Persian Gulf. Finding the problem didn't take long: one of the spark plugs had been shorting out because of the engine cowling touching its terminal. When the plug had been installed, the old washer had not been replaced, making the plug too long and bringing it in contact with the metal cowling.

By now, the London papers had made Amy a celebrity. Imperial Airways took over the servicing of *Jason* so that she could rest. She had been travelling for a week. Fatigue weighed upon her like a crushing physical burden, slowing her movements, blurring her thoughts.

It was a measure of her enhanced celebrity that when she left Karachi, she was escorted by a Moth flown by the local de Havilland agent and an aircraft of the RAF. She was aiming for Allahabad, some nine hundred miles away. But vigorous headwinds slowed her progress and she landed at a place called Jhansi, some two hundred miles short of her destination. Worse, her lack of brakes led her to run into a post, damaging the leading edge of her wing. Again, Dame Fortune did her stuff. Amy had landed on the parade ground of the 3rd and 8th Punjab Regiment, touching down between rows of barracks. The troops immediately swung into action, arranging for the village carpenter to repair the wing and the tailor to patch the torn fabric.

When she landed at Calcutta, she was greeted by a large crowd. She was famous now, her picture splashed across every newspaper.

But fame did nothing to ease the exhausting business of flying the tiny, ill-equipped Moth over some of the world's least hospitable terrain. Fatigue was playing tricks on her. May 13, her ninth day of the journey, found her circling Rangoon, searching for the race-track – which had to serve as the municipal airport since the city had no airfield of its own. She couldn't find the track, so she landed on a soccer field in a downpour – only to run into a ditch. With a sickening crunch, the port lower wing collapsed and the undercarriage sagged, badly damaged. Unhurt but aghast, with persistent rain still falling, drenching her, Amy gazed at the wreckage. No doubt about it, this was the end. She had to face reality, to think about creeping back to England an abject failure, having accomplished practically nothing, except wasting the money donated by so many generous people who had believed in her.

But again her incredible luck came into play. She discovered that the soccer field belonged to a Burmese engineering school, full of helpful students eager to repair the wing ribs and the landing gear struts. A local pharmacist mixed a concoction which, he declared, would act like dope to shrink and tighten the fabric, which was actually material for men's shirts manufactured during the war. While this work was being done, Amy supervised the installation of her spare propeller and the repairs to the landing gear. That done, the Moth was towed a dozen miles to the Rangoon racecourse. Incredibly, she was still in the running. She took off in good order, the hope of reaching Australia still alive.

The days became a blur, memories of one place becoming entangled with those of another. At Bangkok, she had to service the Moth by flashlight, with the eager – though not always efficient – help of scores of smiling Siamese. She took off, only to discover that the engine cowling had not been securely fastened. She had to turn around and return to Don Muang airfield to have the necessary adjustments made.

At Singapore, several light planes came out to escort her to the RAF airfield, Seletar. Here, a stylish crowd resplendent in pith helmets and parasols met her, looking as if they had arrived for a garden party. As Amy clambered out of the Moth, her face oil-stained, her hands raw, the well-dressed colonials applauded politely as if she had struck a jolly good volley to win a tennis match. A reporter wrote, "Miss Johnson smiled through the oil on her face, looking more like an Indian than an Englishwoman. She was wearing a man's khaki shorts, men's stockings, much oil-stained heavy brogue shoes, and a drill jacket, under which her long-sleeved purple blouse was pinned at the throat by her mother's swastika brooch [a symbol of good luck not yet tainted by the Nazis]. She had a pepper-and-salt topee, and her face and hands were burnt almost brick red."[1]

By now her fame had spread far and wide. British and Australian papers were outdoing one another with offers and counter-offers for the rights to her story; in England, Will Johnson handled the deals, with the assistance of James Martin, the affable Irish designer who had, in a way, set the whole crazy business in motion. To the big London dailies, she had become "the British girl Lindbergh." Australian papers were urging her not to terminate her flight at Darwin but to press on to Sydney. A tour of Australia was suggested. Big sums were bandied about. A lifetime of luxury and prosperity seemed to be within her grasp.

But only if she succeeded. The press had little interest in failure. At Seletar, air force mechanics serviced *Jason*, even fitting a new wing when the original proved to have a cracked rear spar, no doubt the result of one of her spirited landings. "I was so tired by this time that my sole thought was to reach Australia so that I could sleep for as long as I wanted," she declared.[2]

She ran into ferocious weather over the Java Sea, but she battled on, flying through darkening skies with heavy rain pelting down, splashing into the cockpit, drenching her. Grimly, she wondered what would happen if she experienced engine trouble. The sea below was alive with sharks. Best not to think about it. Conditions improved a little over the coast of the Dutch East Indies (now Indonesia). Amy brought *Jason* down on a field which turned out to be sodden enough to drag the Moth to a halt without tipping over. Sharp bamboo stakes ripped the fabric of the lower wings but did no structural damage. She found she had landed at Tjomal, on the northern coast of Java, some 250 miles from Surabaya. The next morning, she repaired the torn fabric of the lower wings and filtered motor fuel through a chamois cloth.

Australia was now tantalizingly close, beyond the Timor Sea, but she had trouble finding the landing field at Semarang – and to compound the problem, darkness was gathering rapidly, as it always did in the East. At last she glimpsed a stretch of open land. Down she went, touching the earth with a clatter. When the Moth came to a halt, she found to her astonishment that she had landed among a vast assemblage of anthills, some of them as high as six feet. Miraculously – and unknowingly – she had threaded her way through them without hitting one. Incredibly, fortune still beamed down on the indomitable Yorkshire lass. A group of locals surrounded the Moth, brandishing knives. But there was no cause for alarm. What appeared to be the leader approached the aircraft, touching it. Smiling, he motioned for her to get out of her cockpit. She did so. He led her to a small log cabin. She entered, sank to the floor, and fell asleep, utterly exhausted.

She awoke to find a priest beside her. He was Portuguese but spoke some French. They were able to communicate, after a fashion. Amy had some cheese and wine. She slept again. In England, the papers were reporting her missing. Nothing had been heard of her since she had flown over Bima. The wiseacres said they had known it all along. No mere slip of a girl could expect to tackle a trip halfway around the world; she didn't have the skill; she didn't have the experience. The remarkable thing was that she had gone as far as she did. A shame, but there it was. . . . The Dutch East Indies authorities announced that they were organizing a search for her. They didn't have to. Word came through that she was safe. In a village called Haliloeli.

The biggest problem was getting out of the place. She managed to explain to the priest that the anthills would have to be removed. He told the locals and, with much grinning and chuckling, they set to work. While they did so, Amy filtered two cans of gasoline through a chamois. Then she paced the takeoff strip. She reckoned it was long enough. *Just.* She wanted to organize a flying start, with everyone holding the Moth back while she ran up the engine, letting go simultaneously on her signal. But how to explain such a complicated procedure? The locals were willing enough, but they had probably never seen an aircraft, let alone pondered its takeoff problems.

They held *Jason* while she swung the propeller. The familiar drone was reassuring. Oil pressure good. Magnetos good. *Jason* quivered as if eager to be away. Amy turned and waved at the goggle-eyed spectators. She advanced the throttle, signalling for the last eager hand to let go. *Jason* bumped over the remains of the anthills, gathering speed. Ahead, the end of the makeshift strip was a forbidding wall of tangled plants. It grew as she approached, ready to engulf her. The temptation to haul the stick back was almost irresistible. No, keep her on the ground until the last instant, accumulating precious, irreplaceable speed. Speed was insurance. Speed was safety.

The ground slipped away. She felt her wheels brush the trees. Then . . . she was clear! A quick rock of the wings to the people below, an aerial thank you. The strip vanished from view as if the omnivorous jungle had consumed it. Amy settled back in the familiar seat, preparing for the last lap of her journey: a brief stop at Atamboea for refuelling and servicing, then it would be off across the Timor Sea, that unpredictable stretch of ocean separating the Dutch East Indies from Australia. On Saturday, May 24, the twentieth day of her journey, she clambered aboard the weatherbeaten *Jason* with her strips of adhesive tape still adorning her wings where the bamboo stakes had ripped it: "With a little prayer to my guardian angel I opened up and just managed to pull the machine off in time to clear the boundary trees. In about fifteen minutes I was over the coast and there before stretched five hundred miles of shark-infested sea which I must cross to reach Australia. . . ."[3]

She suffered a few heart palpitations an hour or so later when her engine started to splutter. Amy knew what to do: pull back the throttle, then open it quickly. It worked, blowing the carburetor free of whatever was blocking it. The engine resumed its purr. The sea seemed endless. And empty, until the Shell tanker *Phorus* hove into view; she had been told that it would be stationed midway between Atamboea and the Australian coast. She waved to the tanker's sailors lined along the rail; they waved in reply. It boosted her spirits. Now it was only a matter of pushing on – that had been the story of the flight ever since she left Croydon . . . how many

years ago? But now she felt much more secure, with the tanker just
behind her and all of Australia dead ahead.

"Then I saw a dark cloud on the horizon. . . . The cloud slowly
assumed shape and after half an hour's flying I made out an island,
which I knew to be Melville Island and I was sure of my exact
whereabouts. In another half an hour my wheels were touching
Australian soil."[4] She had done it! After all the dangers and disappointments, her odyssey was over. No more brain-sapping weari-
ness, no more heart-stopping frights.

She knew that the world's newspapers – and particularly those
in the British Empire – had been agog with her story for the past
few days, but she was amazed at the size of the welcome at Darwin.
It looked as if the entire population of the city had come to greet
her. She was amused – and embarrassed – to find that a song had
been written about her: "Johnnie's in Town" (Johnnie was the
nickname by which she was known by her flying club friends). It
was all very flattering and exciting, and soon there were messages
of congratulation from the King and Queen, from Charles and
Anne Lindbergh, Louis Blériot, and many other notables – as well
as sackfuls of mail from ordinary citizens. She was the celebrity of
the moment, news about her pushed all other events off the front
pages. Soon she would become Amy Johnson, Commander of the
Order of the British Empire. And to think that only a matter of
weeks earlier life seemed to offer nothing but failure and frustration. Now she had the world at her feet.

Amy spent six weeks in Australia. Hectic weeks. The days collided, merged into one another, creating a rosy blur in her mind –
with nasty days of tears and stomach upheavals to punctuate the
glow. There were speeches galore. Endless eulogies that never
seemed to have any connection to her; and why could no one say

anything in half a dozen words? The speakers seemed to think that the length of the speech was proportional to its importance. She was tempted to say goodbye and catch the next ship home. But her life was now controlled by contracts. She had become a property, a commodity, to be exploited, to be used to the benefit of goodness knows who. There were reporters waiting everywhere, with open notebooks and pencils poised, eyes roving her features as if trying to commit every detail to memory. She gave speeches and interviews, sat before threatening-looking microphones in radio stations, uttering the same words over and over again until she wondered if everyone in Australia hadn't heard everything she had said a dozen times. Gifts – or promises of gifts – kept flowing in. A car, a new Moth, fur coats, jewellery, even a baby kangaroo. It was great fun, but it was hard on her nervous strength – never robust at the best of times. She rarely had a moment to herself. She lost weight and was often physically sick. At Brisbane's Eagle Farm airport, she landed too fast and, having no brakes, went careering through a fence into a field of millet and flipped end over end. Amy, securely strapped in, was shaken but unhurt. The crowd cheered her as she scrambled from the wreckage of *Jason*, apparently unperturbed by the near thing, waving cheerfully as if to say it was all a little show for the spectators.

After that, she travelled courtesy of Australian National Airways, the airline founded by Charles Kingsford Smith and Charles Ulm, which, sadly, had only two months left before bankruptcy brought it to premature dissolution. Ulm himself was her captain; the co-pilot was a transplanted Scot, a cocky fellow with a lofty opinion of himself and his flying ability. His name was Jim Mollison. Two years later, he would become Amy's husband.

Early in July, Amy sailed for England aboard the P&O liner *Naldera*. Her passage had been provided free of charge by the shipping line's chairman, Lord Inchcape, whose daughter, Elsie Mackay, had died in an attempt to fly the Atlantic two years before. Amy transferred to Imperial Airways at Cairo and flew the last leg of the trip aboard one of the company's boxy Argosy airliners.

Her arrival at Croydon was in marked contrast to her inconspicuous departure three months earlier. The place was packed with people eager for a glimpse of the girl who had become Britain's favourite heroine. The bevy of notables greeting her included Louis Blériot, Sir A.V. Roe, Beverley Nichols, J.B. Priestley, Noël Coward, Alfred Hitchcock, and Ivor Novello. At lunch they were served such delicacies as "Oeufs pochés Port Darwin," "Délice de Sole Jason," and "Coeur de Romaine Amy Johnson."

Amy's journey into London was a royal procession, watched by endless lines of her adoring subjects. Spectators clutched copies of the *Mail*, which had printed a map of the route Amy would be taking. Amy and her family were staying at the posh Grosvenor House Hotel in Park Lane, courtesy of the *Mail*. Following the London revels, she was due to embark on a three-month tour of Britain. Receptions and speeches were scheduled at nearly forty locations. She had to go; it was the price of success, with signed contracts and endless clauses to prove it. Wherever she went she heard the song "Amy, Wonderful Amy." A book about her had been rushed into print; her name was on everyone's lips. A rather shy individual, she hated the endless personal appearances, but they were a great success. She had an unpretentious way about her that captured the public fancy and convinced everyone that she never thought herself superior in any way; she was just another typist from the City who happened to like flying. She always managed to say the right thing, with absolute sincerity and attractive simplicity. "I want to show by my flying how much I love England and its people, how glad I am to be back home, how proud I am to be a member of our own great Empire, and how deep is my gratitude to you all."[5] Intense applause. It never failed.

Her life should have been tranquil from now on. She wanted to continue her long-distance flying, but she couldn't settle on a specific goal. It was a problem faced by many flyers at this period; the significant flights – the Atlantic, Australia, South Africa, the Pacific – were now history. Where next to apply one's courage and endurance? She made a semi-exploratory flight to Siberia in a Moth given her by readers of the *Sketch* and *Graphic* newspapers, but it ended in a potato field with some damage to the aircraft, although none to herself. She had a second aircraft, a Puss Moth cabin monoplane, a gift from de Havilland, and formulated plans for a flight to Tokyo with Jack Humphreys, who had been her mentor in the early days at the London Aeroplane Club. They flew across the Soviet Union, where, to their surprise, oil and fuel were supplied free of charge at airfields, although facilities were primitive in the extreme. They arrived successfully in Tokyo, welcomed by the president of the Imperial Aviation Society, General Nagaoka, who claimed to possess the longest, whitest whiskers in the world. Unfortunately, several other long-distance flights were taking place at the same time – the Americans Clyde Pangborn and Hugh Herndon, Charles and Anne Lindbergh, Francis Chichester – and suddenly the world's newspapers were more interested in economic woes than aviation.

Around Christmas 1931, she went into hospital for an operation – probably a hysterectomy, although it was reported as an appendectomy – after which she spent a few days in a convalescent home near Colchester. She loathed the place and left for a cruise to South Africa, travelling aboard the *Winchester Castle*. During the voyage she heard a news report about a solo flight from England to Cape Town by a certain Jim Mollison.

CHAPTER ELEVEN | *The*
Mollisons

Jim Mollison undertook a solo flight from London to Cape Town, arriving on March 28, 1932, in a state of utter exhaustion. In the four-day, seventeen-hour trip, he had found time for less than a dozen hours of sleep. Dizzy, disoriented (and probably suffering from the effects of too much brandy, his favourite aerial stimulant), he found his vision deceiving him and decided not to attempt a landing at the airport. Evening was gathering. The lights confused him, he later said.

He flew to the beach at nearby Milnerton and got the Puss Moth safely down. But the beach sloped more severely than he realized. He swerved, ran into the sea and turned over. Water poured into the tiny cabin. Soaked to the skin, Mollison struggled to the beach and took a taxi for the last half dozen miles to the airport. One of the first familiar faces he saw among the crowd was Amy Johnson's. They had met once before, aboard the ANA airliner during Amy's triumphal tour of Australia in 1930. At the time,

Mollison had been earning a living as a co-pilot with ANA, a job that bored him to tears. The following year, he had earned a place in the record books for completing the fastest flight from Australia to England, losing his way over Malaya (now Malaysia), mislaying his goggles over India, running out of fuel over France and, typically, having no funds to buy more. (The Imperial Airways representative at Le Bourget had to guarantee payment.)

Mollison, a Scot, was twenty-seven – two years younger than Amy – a compact man, with pleasant features, a winning way with the ladies, and a weakness for alcohol. This was a pity, for he became belligerent when drunk. Although he cultivated a somewhat languid manner, complete with a phony southern English accent, he was by no means effete, being a capable boxer. At the time of the Cape Town meeting with Amy, he was said to be engaged to Lady Diana Wellesley, the attractive, eighteen-year-old half-sister of the Earl of Cowley, although he denied the stories.

Amy had her own troubles. Her health had still not been fully restored. She avoided public appearances – for which she was chastised by the press. But by now she had experience of life in the public eye and she ignored the barbs. The vacation in South Africa seemed to do her good. When she arrived back in England aboard the *Winchester Castle*, she was in fine spirits – and soon they would be even better. She and Mollison renewed their friendship early in May. He invited her to lunch at fashionable Quaglino's restaurant – where he popped the question. For a few weeks the Mollisons were the most famous couple in England – the "flying sweethearts," the popular press persisted in calling them. The couple flew to Glasgow, where Amy met Jim's mother and stepfather. It was not the easiest of meetings; Amy found Jim's relatives "well-meaning but dull." She was no longer the shy, wide-eyed young girl from the provinces. She was world-famous and she had discovered the satisfaction of crafting her life to her taste. She lived in London's finest hotels, the Dorchester and later the Grosvenor House, still able to afford such luxuries thanks to the lucrative Australian flight. During the evening of July 28, while Mollison was planning a solo transatlantic flight, a telegram arrived at the Johnson family's home in Bridlington, Yorkshire, where they had recently moved: "Jim and I are getting married tomorrow morning at ten o'clock but we are trying to keep it as quiet as possible. We should have much liked your presence but in the circumstances of Jim's approaching flight have decided to keep it an absolutely private affair between ourselves. Much love, Amy."

It was a remarkably cool communication by any standard. It stunned Amy's family. At the time, none of the family had even met Mollison, and the little they knew about him was garnered from newspaper stories. There were plenty of those. Mr. and Mrs. Johnson and Amy's two sisters immediately packed a few essentials and set out to drive south, a journey of some two hundred miles on slow roads in wet weather. They drove through the night, not stopping for refreshment, hoping to get to the church in time for the ceremony. They didn't make it. Neither did they exchange a single word with Amy or Jim. So they turned around and drove back to Yorkshire. Amy's mother later described her daughter's behaviour as "cruel and heartless," although she later blamed it on the fact that she was "in a different sphere now." All was soon forgiven.

Mollison had for some time been planning a *solo* transatlantic flight from east to west. (The Germans von Huenefeld and Koehl, together with the Irishman Fitzmaurice, had made the first ever east-to-west crossing in 1928.) He set off on August 18 in his small Puss Moth cabin monoplane, named *Heart's Content*, the name of the Newfoundland village where he planned to make his landfall. He squeezed himself into his tiny cabin with a supply of brandy within easy reach. Sidney Cotton, a good friend, remarked, "Jim's long-distance flights differed from those of others in that others came down when they ran out of petrol, but Jim's ended when he ran out of brandy."[1] Fellow airmen marvelled at how well he could fly when intoxicated – and at how he managed to survive in spite of it all.

He landed in Newfoundland thirty-one hours and twenty minutes after takeoff, having completed the first solo crossing of the Atlantic from east to west. For a day or two the papers sang his praises, but the story soon faded from the front pages. The golden age of record-breaking flights was winding down. With the Great Depression tightening its grip on every aspect of life, unemployed citizens could hardly be expected to thrill to the antics of rich playboys and playgirls in their airplanes. Jim, who had originally thought of returning to England in the Puss Moth from New York, decided against it. A lingering spell of bad weather was one reason; Amy's impassioned pleas by telephone were another. Lack of financial support may well have been a third. With the economies of the western world apparently teetering on the brink of collapse, the papers were no longer offering fat fees for exclusive stories of long-distance flights.

It says much for the power of Amy's name that she had a useful offer from Britain's *Sunday Dispatch*, which wanted to run her life story to coincide with her next major flight: England to Cape Town and return. She made it safely to Cape Town, beating Jim's time by ten hours but battling ferocious weather en route. She had received some instruction in blind flying at the Air Service Training School at Hamble, but she was never comfortable relying totally on a flickering needle. She lost control in thick cloud and was lucky to emerge intact. The flight received excellent newspaper coverage, in spite of the grim economic times. Amy won the

Segrave Trophy for 1932, having accomplished "the most out-standing demonstration of the possibilities of transport by land, air or water." The year ended on a positive note: Amy and Jim went off to St. Moritz for a holiday. It was probably the happiest period of the marriage for Amy. She was fit. Mollison was behaving himself. They shared chuckles with celebrities, including Harold Lloyd and Clara Bow. Chanel gave Amy an evening dress, further offering to dress her "at cost," an offer she refused, saying that she had all the clothes she needed.

Jim flew *Heart's Content* across the South Atlantic to Brazil, winning the Royal Aero Club's Britannia Trophy for his flight. During 1933, the world's only husband-and-wife long-distance flight team acquired a new de Havilland Dragon, named *Seafarer*, a biplane transport that was a good-looking and successful design, but dated in concept compared with the Boeing and Douglas aircraft being produced in the United States. The Mollisons' bold plan was to capture the world's long-distance record, flying first to New York, then, after a day's rest, speeding to Baghdad, after which they would return to London. Three large aluminum fuel tanks, each holding two hundred gallons, took up most of the *Seafarer*'s cabin space. The tanks were suspended from the roof inside the aircraft by steel cables and were separated by rubber pads, leaving a mere eighteen inches for Jim and Amy to squeeze through on their way to and from the cockpit. The difficulties of escape in an emergency were something best not contemplated. With reason, Jim called the aircraft "the flying coffin," adding that "it only needed brass handles to make it look like the real thing."[2]

Early on the morning of June 8, they went to Croydon and clambered into the jet-black Dragon. Jim opened the throttles. The aircraft eased forward, straining under its huge load of fuel. It picked up speed, but not enough. Dashing across the grass and beyond, the Dragon seemed about to take to the air when, with a loud crack, the landing gear collapsed and the aircraft slithered to a halt on its belly. Incredibly, the fuel did not ignite. Amy and Mollison climbed out, tight-lipped but unhurt. It took a few weeks to repair the *Seafarer*. The flyers decided they needed a larger field for their departure. After inspecting a number of sites, they picked Pendine, Wales, with its expanse of firm, sandy beach. This time the Dragon got away in good order; it was a little lighter than on the previous, unsuccessful takeoff because it was carrying less gasoline – which would have unhappy consequences later in the flight. They headed for New York on the first leg of their triangular trip.

As they neared the North American coast, they became concerned about their fuel; the gauge was reading close to empty. They had been in the air for about twenty-four hours when Amy spotted land – a tiny fragment of Newfoundland's coast. Much relieved, they flew on. She wanted to land at Boston and refuel while there was still a little daylight. Jim disagreed; he was determined to make New York non-stop. They weren't far away. A stone's throw . . . a mere fifty miles. Bridgeport was immediately below, just visible in the fading light. Which was when the engines coughed into silence. Exhausted, possibly feeling the effects of too much brandy, Mollison tried to land downwind and crashed into the marshes on the airfield border. The long-suffering *Seafarer* flipped onto her back. When the rescuers arrived, they found Mollison unconscious, his face bleeding. Amy was bruised and cut on the arm and one leg. Both, improbably, were alive.

Mollison returned to England, but Amy remained in America; she liked the country and its friendly inhabitants, and they seemed to be equally fond of her. She had lunch with the Roosevelts at Hyde Park. She was soon on the best of terms with Amelia Earhart, two women with a great deal in common.

After Amy had returned to England, she and Jim spent six weeks in Bermuda. It should have been a perfect holiday, but Jim's persistent drinking spoiled the trip for Amy. A few months later, the couple flew a speedy de Havilland Comet in the England-to-Australia race. They led in the early stages, then had to withdraw with technical problems. It was yet another frustration.

Not only the flying was disappointing. The marriage was a disappointment too. Jim was flagrantly unfaithful, sometimes even bringing his latest girlfriends back to the Grosvenor. He had always had trouble with the concept of marital fidelity. "Mollison was woman-mad," commented a friend, "and a great many women were Mollison-mad."[3] Amy herself was not without her admirers. One, François Dupré, was notably persistent, though Amy was never attracted to him. Some fifteen years Amy's senior, the affluent Dupré had an international reputation as a hotelier and racehorse owner. He took an interest in an idea of Amy's, a company to be known as Air Cruises, essentially a service to transport well-heeled holidaymakers by air to glamour spots around the world. Amy, who intended to be the chief pilot, believed the idea could be highly successful. Dupré believed so too, but he was concerned about the world political situation – the Nazis had just reoccupied the Rhineland, and the signs seemed ominous.

Amy wanted to improve on her London-to-Cape Town performance. For the attempt, she borrowed a Beechcraft 17, better known as the Staggerwing, but landing after her first flight in the powerful aircraft, she smashed the landing gear. Landings were still her *bête noir*. She then talked to the Percival company. The small company was only too anxious to be associated with such a luminary as Amy Johnson, offering to lend her a Gull monoplane with long-range tanks. There was little interest from the press, however. All Amy could do was hope that when the flight started, things

would improve. She took off from Gravesend airport wearing a
Schiaparelli suit, to show the world that in modern aircraft it wasn't
necessary to be garbed in leather and fleece. The first lap went
well. But the next stop, the Algerian town of Colomb Bechar, was
her undoing. She had refuelled and was on her takeoff run when
a stone jammed itself into the metal fairing over the wheel. The
gear collapsed.

Again Amy was lucky; the Gull didn't burn. Her steely determination came to the fore. She immediately organized repairs, and
at the end of the month she was ready to try again. Jim chose that
moment to arrive from Australia. Amy was ecstatic. Jim wanted to
effect a reconciliation. Life was good again. She took off in the
Gull and broke records for the return trip and the round trip. The
papers could hardly contain themselves, full of praise for "Our
Amy." It was like old times, with the *Daily Express* and *Paris-Soir*
paying handsomely for exclusive stories. With Jim back, Amy lost
interest in Air Cruises and in Dupré.

Unhappily, Mollison soon slipped back to his old ways, apparently unable to resist any attractive woman who came within
reach, and in September 1936, Amy started divorce proceedings.
Jim raised no objections. He moved to the Hyde Park Hotel, then
began preparations for yet another Atlantic flight, this time in an
American Bellanca 28-70 low-wing monoplane named *Miss
Dorothy* after revue actress Dorothy Ward, with whom he was currently involved.

Amy had a job for a while with Portsmouth, Southsea, and Isle
of Wight Aviation Ltd., for whom she flew planeloads of passengers on sightseeing flights around the south coast of England. As
talk of war became more prevalent, she tried to join the Civil Air
Guard but was turned down. Six months after the outbreak of
war, she joined the Air Transport Auxiliary to fly service aircraft

around the country, principally on delivery from factories. Here, she encountered another ATA pilot, none other than Jim Mollison. Relations were cordial enough, according to fellow pilots, but there was no rekindling of their old romance.

CHAPTER TWELVE | *Bill*
and
Chubbie

S ometimes the realization of an ambition comes at a fearful price. A case in point: Bill Lancaster. Born in Birmingham in 1898, he emigrated to Australia as a youth. On the outbreak of the First World War, he enlisted in the Australian army and saw service in the Middle East and France before transferring to the Australian Flying Corps. He proved to be an excellent pilot, highly regarded by his superiors. After the war he returned to England and married. He was in the reserve for a spell before joining the Royal Air Force. He liked the RAF, and he would have been happy to make the service his career, but after five years on the active list, his time was up. The RAF was cutting back. Like it or not, he had to make a living in the civilian world. He hoped to do it in aviation – no easy task in the mid-twenties. But he was lucky. An acquaintance told him of a job going begging at the famous aircraft firm of Avro. The company had a new light plane, the Avian, a biplane to compete with the successful de Havilland Moth. Lancaster applied and was hired to fly the Avian on a long-distance proving flight to Australia; no doubt his knowledge of Australia made him a favoured candidate. He was the man to demonstrate the efficiency and reliability of the aircraft and its eighty-horsepower Cirrus engine. Lancaster signed on without a moment's hesitation and began making his plans for the flight.

Fate stepped in. A few weeks before his scheduled departure, he met Mrs. Keith Miller at a party. She was the wife of an Australian journalist. Everyone called her Chubbie. A remarkable character, Chubbie – not outstandingly beautiful, but possessed of a singularly powerful personality – was a born salesperson. Anything, no matter how outlandish, seemed possible when she talked about it. When Lancaster told her he was planning a flight to Australia, she wanted to go along. Impossible, he said. She said she would help pay for the flight. Still impossible, he declared, no doubt thinking of his wife and what would be said. The two of them, in a small, two-seat biplane . . . *quite* impossible. Or was it? After an earnest discussion with Chubbie, Bill found himself thinking that perhaps it wasn't such an impossible idea after all. Lancaster, a conventional, conservative young man, had never met anyone like Chubbie. She had a way of looking at things that was quite original, quite captivating. Anything was possible, if you just approached it the right way. Chubbie's way. It was like being caught in a tidal wave: like it or not, he found himself agreeing to the idea – and somehow he managed to sell it to his wife.

On October 14, 1927, Bill Lancaster took off from the grass at Croydon, at the controls of a brand-new Avro Avian named *Red Rose*, with the pert young woman named Chubbie in the front cockpit. A group of well-wishers waved them off; they included

Lady Ryrie, wife of the Australian High Commissioner, as well as Bill's parents, his wife, and his two young daughters. What was said about Chubbie's presence in the Avian is not recorded.

The flight started well. But technical troubles and bad weather held them up. Then a crash landing on an island off Sumatra slowed progress even more. Week followed week while repairs were made. Not until March 1928 did the weatherbeaten Avian finally touch down at Port Darwin – more than five months after takeoff. Predictably, the relationship between Bill and Chubbie had matured during the long flight with its repeated delays and doubts. They had fallen in love. The question was, what should be done about it? Lancaster didn't know. By this time he was totally devoted to Chubbie; he could not imagine life without her. Somehow the mess had to be sorted out.

Bill worked for some months in Australia. He had been hired to demonstrate Cirrus engines, a job which involved much travel around the country. No doubt Lancaster suffered agonies of guilt when he thought of his wife and daughters. He should have returned to them; he knew that, but good intentions are no match for sexual attraction. Lancaster, totally infatuated, kept maintaining the pretense day after day, hating himself for what he was doing, yet powerless to change anything.

In March 1929, events took control. The company told Lancaster to go to the United States to demonstrate the Cirrus engine. He was perfectly content to do so as long as Chubbie came along. But there was a sizable snag: Bill's wife wanted to go to America with him. He immediately wrote to her, explaining how impractical the idea was. He would be travelling endlessly, he said, staying in ramshackle towns, eating in unsavoury diners – not the sort of life for a wife and children. She accepted the argument, although reluctantly, and no doubt suspiciously. Bill was relieved. He had won a little time. He remained in the United States, moving in with Chubbie in the small house she had rented in Miami.

In America, Bill felt reasonably confident about his ability to find freelance flying work. For a time this confidence was justified, and he sent money to England to support the family. As the weeks rolled on, this new life assumed a kind of normality. Perhaps things could be sorted out to everyone's satisfaction. Bill had no wish to hurt his wife – but she had to realize that divorce was the only solution. They had grown apart, he said. Eventually she would have to come around and agree to a divorce. And so the weeks dragged on. Then something quite unexpected occurred, something that changed everything. In October the stock market crashed. Soon unemployment soared. Almost overnight, the enthusiasm for aviation – sparked by Lindbergh's 1927 flight – faded like a Wasp starved of fuel. Bill completed the jobs he had, but there were precious few lining up for the future. The good times were over – although everyone said they would soon be back. Blue skies were just around the corner, according to the popular songs. But what corner? Bill's career, once so promising, was coming apart at the seams. The months dragged on. Chubbie's divorce became final in 1931 – a solitary bright spot in a depressing period. For her part, Bill's wife still refused to consider divorce. What made the situation even more difficult was the time taken for letters to cross the Atlantic by ship, prolonging the torture, stretching out the misery, day by day. It had its effect on the relationship. Chubbie's feelings seemed to harden. She still claimed to hold Bill in the highest regard, but living with him meant scratching out a precarious existence, worrying about finding five dollars for groceries or the rent, week after dreary week, with the oppressive heat and humidity building up in the tiny, cramped dwelling.

There's no telling how long the unhappy situation might have dragged on, but for a call from a man named Haden Clarke early in 1932. Bill was away at the time, working on a flying job, earning a few much-needed dollars. Clarke said he was an author; he wanted to "ghost" Chubbie's life story. It had all the elements, he said, to make it a success. Who wouldn't be flattered? Chubbie was. She told Bill about it when he telephoned, which he did nightly, from various landing fields in the southern States. He was less enthusiastic, no doubt thinking of the time it would take Clarke to research and write the book then peddle the manuscript among umpteen publishers. It might be years before anyone saw a cent. But Chubbie wanted it, so he agreed, as he always did. He soon regretted his decision, for Haden Clarke took up residence in the Miller-Lancaster home in order to get on with the book. The situation was explosive, but Bill, apparently an extraordinarily trusting soul, raised no objection.

Life plodded on. Clarke claimed to be making good progress on the manuscript describing Chubbie's adventurous life, but no one saw any completed pages. In March 1932, Bill obtained work that required him to spend a lot of time away from Miami. He followed his practice of calling every evening from wherever he happened to be, but his conversations with Chubbie were not reassuring. Was it his imagination or had a certain curtness found its way into her voice? Was there a hint of impatience with his questions about Clarke and the book? Bill suffered agonies of suspicion. What was going on in Miami? He soon found out, receiving a letter from Chubbie that said she had fallen in love with Haden Clarke and intended to marry him. A second letter followed, this one from Clarke saying essentially the same thing.

Bill's response by wire must have floored them: "Congratulations to you both, but wait until I return so that I can be best man."

It might have been written by Noël Coward. Lancaster had always been the perfect English gentleman; even in this moment of crisis he couldn't step out of character and reveal his true feelings. But while in St. Louis, he bought a gun.

On April 13, Bill arrived back in Miami. He had been away five weeks. Five agonizing weeks. He was in low spirits, trying to grapple with the fact that he had probably lost Chubbie forever. How on earth was he going to face life without her? The simple act of entering the house must have been an ordeal. In fact, it turned out to be easier than he anticipated. It was as if he had walked in on strangers. Conventional words of greeting filled the void, sparing everyone the need for saying anything meaningful. For a surreal hour or two, the unlikely trio talked about everything except what was on their minds. They ate a meal together. It loosened their tongues. Voices were raised. Tempers flared. Bill accused Clarke of betraying the confidence he had placed in him. Clarke accused Bill of running off and not caring for Chubbie. Chubbie sobbed as the harsh words flew. Then Clarke, in his erratic way, was suddenly remorseful. He agreed that he had betrayed Bill. He felt terrible.

The party broke up. In view of the situation, the sleeping arrangements were bizarre. Chubbie slept in the bedroom; the two men made up single beds on the verandah. They talked briefly. Then darkness enfolded the small house and its occupants.

During the night, Chubbie awoke to a pounding on her door. Alarmed, she turned the key. Bill stood there, distraught. Something terrible had happened, he managed to say. Clarke had shot himself. Bill sent for a doctor, and the physician declared Clarke dead. The revolver that Bill had bought in St. Louis was beside Clarke's body. Nobody touched anything. The police arrived. They found two notes, both typewritten, both signed by Clarke. One was addressed to Clarke's mother, the other to Chubbie. "I can't stand the economic pressure," it said. "Will you help sustain my mother in her deep grief?"

A week later, to no one's surprise, the police charged Lancaster with Clarke's murder. A handwriting expert declared that the signatures on the suicide notes were forgeries. It was murder in the first degree. If convicted, Bill would probably get the electric chair.

Chubbie stood by him. She told the papers that Haden Clarke had committed suicide. She was sure of it. Bill would be fully and honourably exonerated. Others wondered. The police had found Lancaster's diary in which he had poured out his heart during his long assignment out of town. "My mental agony is hell," he wrote. "I am determined to have it out with Clarke when I get back." Even Bill's attorney, James Carson, was dubious about his client's chances; he had initially refused the case when first approached by Lancaster's father. He changed his mind after he met the pilot, impressed by his demeanour and his matter-of-fact way of telling his story. Bill claimed that he and Clarke had retired at about one in the morning after chatting "amicably" for some time. Later the sound of a shot awakened Lancaster. He sat up and saw Clarke lying on the edge of his bed, a smoking pistol in his hand. He rushed into the bungalow to wake Chubbie. At that moment, he declared, he realized that his recently purchased gun was missing. Alarmed at the thought that suspicion might fall on him, he had typed the suicide note. But Clarke, in his weakened state, had been unable to sign them. So Bill signed them himself. Lancaster's attorney must have shuddered. The story had holes big enough to drive a truck through. What would the prosecution do with it?

During the investigation, interesting facts emerged about Haden Clarke. His proposal of marriage to Chubbie was meaningless; he was already married – and, in addition, had entered into a bigamous marriage with another woman. He was a drug addict and suffered from a venereal disease, reported as "a recurring disease" in the press. He had never written any books. As the pathetic truth dribbled out, things began to look a little brighter for Bill Lancaster. Clarke, it was reported, had spoken of suicide before. Perhaps he had finally plucked up sufficient courage to carry out his threat. The defence caused a sensation when, in the middle of the trial, they introduced the dead man's skull. Appalled, the court watched as the members of the jury passed the skull around. It looked particularly gruesome with its gaping holes where the bullet had smashed through the bone. The defence made much of the fact that the gun had been fired at very close range: proof, they claimed, that the wound was self-inflicted. A criminologist, Arthur H. Hamilton, stated that there was not a "scintilla of evidence to show that Clarke was murdered."

The jury liked Lancaster. He was a victim of circumstance, a thoroughly fine fellow who had simply fallen into the clutches of an unscrupulous woman and a thoroughly unprincipled man. Carson couldn't have arranged things better himself. Bill began to feel more confident. Perhaps there would be a way out of this nightmare after all.

There was. After deliberating for four hours and forty-eight minutes, the jury returned a verdict of Not Guilty. The decision was greeted with "shrieks of joy" by the many women in the courtroom – Lancaster, with his dignified manner and good looks, had made quite an impression. The *New York Times* reported that "Fashionably gowned women wept and shrieked. . . . One portly matron who had been an interested front row spectator since the start of the hearing, moaned with delight."

Chubbie was not in the courtroom to hear the verdict. Later, she expressed satisfaction and commented, "I knew Old Bill would come through."

Lancaster was a free man. But a more or less unemployable one. Everyone in the U.S. aviation scene knew of him and of the scandalous goings-on in Florida. If finding flying work was difficult before the trial, it would be impossible now. He had no alternative but to return to Britain. His parents, who had financed his defence, offered him a home and some money to help him re-establish himself in the British aviation industry. They asked only that he make every effort to effect a reconciliation with his wife. Bill agreed; he really had little choice, although his feelings for Chubbie were unchanged.

Lancaster found that flying opportunities in Britain were just as bad, if not worse, than in the States. He rapidly came to the conclusion that there was only one thing to do: complete a record-breaking flight. It was the magic formula. Success would re-establish him. He would be a Someone again. His would be a name to be reckoned with. He decided to break Amy Johnson's record time to Cape Town.

Lancaster's parents weren't rich, but they were remarkably generous. His father agreed to finance the new record attempt. Amy Johnson had flown to Cape Town in four days, six hours and fifty-four minutes. Lancaster had an opportunity to purchase the Avro Avian named *Southern Cross Minor* once owned by Sir Charles Kingsford Smith. He knew the Avian well and had great confidence in it. It carried 115 gallons of fuel and had an endurance of some fourteen hours. The one big problem with the Avian was that it was almost twenty mph slower than Amy's Puss Moth. Lancaster had to fly an exceptionally accurate course and cut his ground time to an absolute minimum. He studied the charts. He would fly almost due south to Oran (now Wahran) in Algeria, then across the Sahara, refuelling at Reggan some six hundred miles south of Oran.

On April 11, 1933, Lancaster journeyed to Lympne airfield, where the *Southern Cross Minor* was waiting, full of fuel, ready to go. His parents were there to see him off. So was Chubbie. "I owe this chance to come back to my father and mother," Lancaster declared. "My father has committed himself to heavy expenses so that I can make an attempt on the record, and for their sake alone I hope to win through."[1] He added that he was attempting the flight at his own risk and he expected no efforts to be made to find him if he went missing. Privately, he had told a friend that if this last-ditch attempt to re-establish himself in British aviation failed, he didn't wish to come back. There would be no reason to.

Dawn was beginning to lighten the sky as Lancaster climbed into the Avian. His mother handed him a packet of chicken sandwiches and a religious poem she had composed. Farewells were brief. Bill ran up the Avian's engine, then waved. The Avian rolled forward. It was 5:38 a.m.

The fates were against him from the start. Although he crossed to France without difficulty, he encountered strong headwinds at Toulouse. Precious time slipped away like sand in an hourglass. Wasted. Lost for ever. And there was nothing he could do about it. When he landed at Oran he was more than four hours behind schedule. He would have to make up the time later. Somehow. Making it all worse, the personnel at Oran took six hours to prepare the Avian for the next leg – Amy Johnson had done it in four. Frustration bubbled up within him like a volcano. He needed luck, lots of it, to make up the time already lost. He got away from Oran at three o'clock in the morning, crossing the Atlas Mountains in darkness – a nerve-racking business, because a small error in navigation could have meant the end of everything. It was one thing wending your way through a series of visible dangers, quite another when you couldn't see them. His cockpit was not equipped with lighting; he had to strike matches every few minutes to check the compass. Daylight came. Now the bleak landscape lay ahead, clearly visible. He landed at Adrar, taking off again little more than half an hour later, already aching with fatigue. The Trans-Saharan motor track lay ahead, but a sandstorm reduced visibility. He wandered east, landing at Aoulef. Although he wasted no time there, high winds played havoc. In more than three hours' flying he had covered a mere hundred miles.

When he landed at Reggan he was exhausted and depressed. It was all going wrong. Time slipping away. Irreplaceable time. What was the point of going on? What hope was there of making up the lost time? God knows what would become of him. He was a failure. But he had to keep going. *Had to*. At four that afternoon he was ready to take off, but the winds were as strong as ever. The head of the Trans-Saharan post at Reggan advised him to wait. With this wind, he said, the beacons on the motor track would be invisible. Later in the afternoon the wind eased a little. Lancaster decided to press on to Gao, some seven hundred miles almost due south. He estimated an arrival there at two-thirty in the morning. The Trans-Saharan man shrugged; he promised to send a search party if he had heard nothing from Lancaster in twenty-four hours.

Lancaster took off, in an uncharacteristically sloppy, slapdash manner, according to eyewitnesses. Normally a stylish pilot, he seemed unable to coordinate the controls. He was exhausted, everyone said; he should have rested for hours before tackling the desert. The diminutive Avian became a dot in the fading light, then vanished entirely.

Hours went by without word. At first there was no general alarm; he might have come down to check his position, or make some minor repair, or wait for better conditions. A sandstorm perhaps. For a little while fears were calmed. No need to panic. These people were always getting lost and found. Lancaster's parents – and Chubbie – believed it fervently. He would show up. He always did.

Bill Lancaster had indeed come down in the desert. His engine had begun giving trouble about an hour and a half after takeoff. It coughed. Then cut out entirely. In the darkness – the intense, almost palpable darkness of a desert night – Bill had groped his way to the ground, peering out, seeing nothing, having only the vaguest idea of his height and speed. Suddenly, shockingly, he hit the ground hard, his head slamming against the windshield. The Avian came to rest upside down, Lancaster was unconscious, soaked in fuel – which by some miracle did not burn.

Several hours elapsed before Bill regained consciousness. It was still dark. And cold. The dawn revealed the arid landscape. A sea of sand. No sign of life. No sound but for the mournful whisper of the wind. He tried to move. Everything ached. He had lost a lot of blood from his facial injuries. Already he craved water. He thought of trying to walk to the Trans-Saharan track but quickly abandoned the notion. Far better to stay with the plane. Everyone said so. Rescuers were far more likely to find a plane than a solitary figure in the desert. He ripped strips of fabric from the wings and fuse-lage; when night fell, he would soak them in fuel and light them, to signal his location.

He'd had no food since departing from Lympne two and a half days earlier. He tried to eat one of the chicken sandwiches his mother had made, but it was as hard as a rock. He swallowed a few drops of spirits of ammonia mixed with water, then managed to get a piece of chocolate down. It cheered him: a tiny sign of hope. Somehow he would get out of this mess.

It was bitingly cold. Bill got into all his flying clothes, but still he shivered. During the night, he lit several of his homemade flares. They burned with an encouraging brightness, then died. The desert night closed in again.

It went on for eight days. Eight days of agonizing thirst and delirium; eight days of flickering hopes and precipitous plunges into despair. In his lucid moments he scribbled notes, describing what had happened, and personal messages to his parents and to Chubbie. His homemade flares had achieved nothing. The world had forgotten about him. Bill still clung to life, day after frightful day. Then at last Bill Lancaster's agony was over.

In the days that followed, the newspaper stories shrank steadily, as if they were a measure of the hope still left for him. Finally they disappeared. Bill Lancaster became a name out of the past, soon forgotten.

Until February 1962. A French Army motorized patrol from Reggan came across the wreckage of the Avian and the mummified remains of Bill Lancaster, looking eerily like a marble statue. Long after death he continued to clutch at his throat. He had crashed nearly two hundred miles south of Reggan in an area of the Sahara known to the Bedouin tribes as the "land of thirst."

In his last hours, Bill Lancaster managed to jot down a record of his final days. Curiously, he made no mention in any of his writings to the events in Miami. Some say this was proof of his innocence. Will the truth ever be known? It seems unlikely.

CHAPTER THIRTEEN | *A*
Costly
Contest

Isaac Schlesinger had a good deal to be grateful for. When he
first journeyed from his native United States to South Africa,
he had to travel by steerage. Never again. On his way to becoming
one of the early twentieth century's most successful businessmen,
he acquired wealth with the effortless efficiency of a shark feasting
on a school of sardines. He soon became a multi-millionaire, con-
trolling banks, newspapers, theatres, as well as the African Broadcasting Company. By the mid-thirties, he had a new interest: air
communications within the British Empire. To promote the cause,
he decided to sponsor an air race from Britain to South Africa. It
was a route that had long intrigued airmen – and several had died
attempting it, including Bill Lancaster. Schlesinger wanted to
make this an all-Empire race; he limited the entries to British
Commonwealth pilots with a minimum of one hundred hours'
solo flying to their credit – little enough considering the difficulties
of the route. And they had to fly British aircraft powered by British

engines. The prize was ten thousand pounds. Although the event was billed as the "London-to-Johannesburg" race, the actual starting point was Portsmouth airfield, on England's south coast, close to the Isle of Wight. *The Aeroplane* magazine commented, "A thoroughly good event is promised." Unhappily, the promise wasn't realized.

Schlesinger was disappointed by the response to the announcement of the race. At first, not a single entry was received. And, to make matters even worse, one pilot who had stated his intention of participating, the well-known racer Tom Campbell Black, met with an unfortunate accident. He had flown his Percival Mew Gull to Liverpool for the double purpose of showing his backers what their contributions had purchased and to attend the official christening of the aircraft as *Miss Liverpool*. He was taxiing across the grass airfield when he collided with a Hawker Hart light bomber of the RAF's 611 Squadron. Black was killed, an event that cast a pall over the entire proceedings. Some said the race should be cancelled or at least postponed. It wasn't. But the starting line on September 25 was considerably skimpier than Mr. Schlesinger had anticipated. Nine entrants assembled at Portsmouth. Four of them were Percival aircraft: two of the pretty but diminutive Mew Gull single-seaters, and two Vega Gulls designed for four, although rear seats were replaced by fuel tanks to extend the range. Two of the entrants were Miles racing aircraft: a Sparrowhawk (the only open-cockpit entry) and a Hawk Speed Six. Two twin-engine aircraft were entered: the BA (British Aircraft Manufacturing) Double Eagle flown by Tommy Rose, and the Airspeed Envoy with Max Findlay and Ken Waller, two Brooklands instructors, at the controls, accompanied by a passenger, C.D. Peachey. Another BA product, the handsome single-engine Eagle flown by C.G.M. Alington, carried two passengers.

The Aeroplane criticized the "rich Mr. Schlesinger" for insisting on the all-British rule: "Because there is nobody with whom to compete except ourselves, few people have bothered to enter and nobody has built anything special for it. Consequently, as an encouragement to improve the design of British aeroplanes, the race is unfortunately a flop." The magazine had a point.

First lap of the race was Portsmouth to Belgrade (1,073 miles); the second, Belgrade to Cairo (1,160 miles); followed by Cairo to Khartoum (1,020 miles); Khartoum to Entebbe (1,070 miles); Entebbe to Broken Hill (1,045 miles); and the final lap, Broken Hill to Johannesburg (840 miles). For those who preferred an alternative final segment, the option was to fly from Khartoum to Kisumu (1,130 miles), then to Mpika (870 miles), finally to Johannesburg (1,050 miles). Even the finish of the race stirred up controversy. Schlesinger had wanted to use the field at Greater Baragwanath, home of the light plane club of Johannesburg, and the South African headquarters of de Havilland. The airfield had excellent facilities, including a clubhouse, hangars, and a refuelling station; unfortunately it lacked floodlighting. In the end, Germiston, the official airport for the Rand, was selected.

The first aircraft away was the Airspeed Envoy *Gabrielle*, the only radio-equipped aircraft in the race. Next off was the Percival Mew Gull, piloted by Stanley Halse, a tough and highly experienced instructor at the Johannesburg Aero Club. Tommy Rose, a well-known British pilot, took off in the BA Double Eagle, accompanied by John Bagshaw, a qualified ground engineer. Then came the BA Eagle *Frobisher*, piloted by C.G.M. Alington, with his brother as a passenger and P.A. Booth as co-pilot. Next, ex-fighter pilot Flight Lieutenant A.E. Clouston, a New Zealander, took to the air in his Miles Hawk Speed Six. He displayed an impish sense of humour by placing an "L" plate in the cabin window – a sign used on British roads to warn other drivers of a "learner" at the wheel. The Percival Vega Gull of Charles Hughesdon and David Llewellyn got away next, followed by the tiny Mew Gull *The Golden City* flown by Allister Miller, the founder of Union Airways. Then came the other Vega Gull, flown by Charles Scott, winner of the 1934 MacRobertson race, and Giles Guthrie. Victor Smith in his blue Miles Sparrowhawk experienced a delayed start due to engine trouble. The Sparrowhawk was in fact the only one to encounter a problem, so organizers could congratulate themselves on a highly satisfactory beginning for the race.

The problems soon began, however. At Nuremburg, the BA single-engine Eagle stopped to refuel, and part of its engine cowling came loose; then a bumpy landing at Regensburg caused the landing gear to retract. The Eagle was out of the running. It wouldn't be the last casualty.

The Mew Gull of Allister Miller was making excellent time until it approached Belgrade. At that point Miller had to withdraw with instrument trouble. The next casualty was the BA Double Eagle of Tommy Rose. An airlock forced him down at Linz, Austria. He refuelled at Vienna and flew on to Cairo, where the starboard undercarriage leg gave way, shattering the propeller. The pretty Sparrowhawk flown by Victor Smith experienced an oil pressure problem at Skopje. After repairs, Smith took off again and reached Cairo, but he was by now hopelessly behind. He retired. The Percival Vega Gull of Llewellyn and Hughesdon was making fine time when a fuel-tank leak brought the aircraft down on the shore of Lake Tanganyika. The Gull was a write-off, although the crew survived uninjured.

Not so fortunate was the crew aboard the Airspeed Envoy *Gabrielle*. The twin-engine aircraft landed at Kareima because of higher-than-expected fuel consumption. The delay cost a day, after which the crew pushed on, heading for Broken Hill. Still they were consuming too much fuel, so they decided to land at Abercorn, Southern Rhodesia (now Zimbabwe). After repairs, the Envoy began its takeoff run. The strip was about 1,000 feet long – but the altitude was 5,500 feet above sea level. This, combined with the tropical heat, created a lethal situation. The air simply couldn't provide the necessary lift. With engines roaring at full power, the Envoy crashed headlong into the trees at the end of the field, killing two of the four men aboard: Findlay, one of the two pilots, and Morgan, one of the two passengers. Schlesinger's race was becoming a disaster.

Stanley Halse in his Mew Gull was at this stage in the lead. He reached Kisumu successfully, but he was exhausted and airsick after a violently bumpy flight. Nevertheless, he pushed on, stopping briefly at Mbeya. Approaching Salisbury, darkness was falling. There were bushfires burning all around, and he became confused. Low on fuel, he decided to land in a nearby field. Unfortunately it was ploughed. As soon as he touched down, the wheel spats became clogged with wet earth and the Mew Gull overturned. Halse was knocked out but was otherwise unhurt. When he woke up in hospital, he was told that he had crashed only a few miles north of Salisbury (now Harare), close to the finishing post.

Engine trouble plagued Flight Lieutenant A.E. Clouston in his Hawk Speed Six and he crashed at Gwelo, 130 miles southwest of Salisbury. He wrote off the aircraft but survived.

Spectators at Johannesburg airport expected a stream of competitors fighting for a first-place finish. They were disappointed. A single aircraft appeared, the Vega Gull of Charles Scott and Giles Guthrie, wobbling in a brisk wind, the last aircraft still flying. To everyone's relief, it landed safely, having flown the route in fifty-two hours, fifty-six minutes. The "rich Mr. Schlesinger" organized no more air races.

||||

The lure of long-distance flying captivated many unlikely characters, none more so than the Russian dictator, Josef Stalin. He saw it as a means of promoting the Soviet system, glorifying its achievements and its people. Thus, on June 18, 1937, the huge ANT-25 *Stalinskiy marshrut*, took off from Moscow and headed for the North Pole. Designed by Andrei Tupolev, the aircraft might be considered a type of powered glider. It was equipped with a single 950-horsepower engine yet sported a wingspan of 112 feet. The crew numbered three: pilot Valeriy Chkalov, co-pilot Georgiy Baidukov, and navigator/radio operator Alexander Belyakov. The pilots worked on a strict routine of eight hours on, eight hours off, during the three-day flight. Although a heating system was installed, it proved totally inadequate: at times, the temperature dropped to as low as -6 degrees Celsius in the cabin. Over the Polar Sea, dense clouds and icing conditions forced the crew to climb to nearly twenty thousand feet and thus use more oxygen than they had planned on. They turned west, hoping to find better conditions. In vain. By now the two pilots were exhausted and suffering from anoxia. As the oxygen supply dwindled, they were forced to descend, with Baidukov in particularly bad condition. Chkalov landed the aircraft at a U.S. Army airfield. The crew received a warm welcome in the United States. They obeyed the instructions they had received before departure and repeated the party line, telling Americans not to be fooled by stories of purges and primitive conditions. Judge us by feats such as this, they said. Over and over again. When they returned home, they were made Heroes of the Soviet Union.

Encouraged by this first venture and anxious to prove that it was no fluke, the Soviets did it again a month later, using another of the giant ANT-25s. Commanded by Mikhail Gromov, the aircraft reached San Diego, California, but had to land at San Jacinto because of fog. They had flown 6,295 miles. Warming to the business of record-breaking, the Soviets then sent a four-engine DB-A transport to perform more feats of Soviet airmanship. The aircraft vanished without a trace; thereafter, Soviet enthusiasm for long-distance flights waned.

In Japan, the management of the newspaper *Asahi Shimbun* decided to commemorate the coronation of King George VI with a flight from Tokyo to London. On April 5, 1937, pilot Masaaki Iinuma and navigator/mechanic Kenji Tsukagoshi took off in a prototype of the new Mitsubishi 97, a neat single-engine two-seat aircraft, later widely used in military form. The crew had never flown outside Japan before, yet they found their way to Croydon aerodrome without difficulty in a flight time of fifty-one hours at an average speed of almost two hundred miles per hour. Britain's *The Aeroplane* magazine was extraordinarily mean-spirited about the flight, describing Iinuma's touchdown at Croydon as a "brick-like landing with the bounceless plop of a mashed potato." The writer was notably condescending about Japanese aviators in general. The fact that Iinuma had completed a difficult and challenging flight seemed to prove that the pilot was only "partly Japanese." At the time, professionalism in aviation was believed to be the preserve of Europeans or Americans. Other races' efforts were a joke. In *The Aeroplane*'s "expert" opinion, Tsukagoshi looked "more like an Iberian from Wales or Southern Ireland, or possibly a Malay-Portuguese mixture. Iinuma is not the typical Japanese either, but is more so than his partner." The writer went on to explain in his imperious way that Japanese pilots, when confronted with the unexpected, "are apt to let go of everything, put their hands to their heads and ask – 'What does the book say?'" Such racist opinions were common at the time, and apparently no one on the editorial staff of *The Aeroplane* thought them offensive.

Actually, the Japanese proved to be highly capable long-distance aviators. In 1940, the non-stop flight of a specially built twin-engine aircraft, the Tachikawa A-26, was planned between Tokyo and New York. The war put a stop to the plans, but in 1944, the A-26 set a remarkable – though unofficial – distance record of 10,212 miles over a closed circuit in Manchuria.

CHAPTER FOURTEEN | *Pacific Tragedy*

*B*y the mid-thirties, Amelia Earhart had become the world's most famous aviatrix. She was an icon, a role model for countless young women who admired her courage and skill – and her progressive views about women's place in a male-dominated world. Her marriage to George Putnam seemed to be working; the couple were on affectionate terms, although some acquaintances felt their relationship was more about business than romance. Certainly GP, as the urbane Putnam was widely known, spent a major part of his time promoting his wife's career, tirelessly arranging publicity opportunities, personal appearances, business deals, photo sessions by the dozen, as well as endorsements for everything from Lucky Strike cigarettes and Beech-Nut gum to the Franklin automobile. She was a commodity to be marketed with all the not-inconsiderable vigour and imagination at his command. He crafted every aspect of her life, telling her what clothes to wear, what to say, and how to say it.

In 1932, Amelia had proposed a solo Atlantic flight. GP was enthusiastic. Here was a way to achieve two "firsts": the first woman to fly the ocean solo, and the first person to fly it twice. Such a venture had been on Amelia's mind ever since she had crossed the ocean as a passenger on the *Friendship*. GP lost no time in recruiting the Norwegian airman Bernt Balchen as technical adviser. Amelia had a Lockheed Vega, a single-engine monoplane (500 horsepower Wasp) of splendid lines and excellent performance, though a demanding aircraft to fly. She took off from Harbour Grace, Newfoundland, and enjoyed good weather for the first few hours – after which several problems materialized almost simultaneously. The altimeter failed (the first such failure in Amelia's dozen years of flying), a weld in the exhaust burned through, setting off an alarming vibration, and she picked up ice in the turbulent clouds. With daylight, she found herself between two layers of murk; the wind was blowing from the northwest. When she reached up to turn on the reserve tank, the tap broke. It would have been a catastrophe half an hour earlier; but now Amelia found she was over land, a blanket of lush green fields lay below. She searched for an airfield and, finding none, landed instead in a pasture owned by one James Gallagher on the outskirts of Londonderry, Northern Ireland. She had flown for fourteen hours and fifty-six minutes after takeoff, the first woman to make the flight solo.

Amelia received a wild welcome in Ireland and later in England, meeting the Prince of Wales and dancing away most of one night with him. She also met Amy Johnson and her then-fiancé, Jim Mollison. At Cherbourg, she was reunited with GP, but she refused to embrace him for the cameramen. She was repelled by the phony sentimentality hawked by papers all over the world. She tried to avoid the ceremonies in New York, but Mayor Jimmy Walker used all his legendary charm on her and she gave in. More ceremonies followed with bewildering rapidity. Then it was off to Washington and more hoopla, including dinner with President Hoover (who was noticeably cool to GP – hardly surprising, since Putnam had just published a book intensely critical of his administration). More of the same in Cleveland and Chicago and other cities. It was tiresome but essential, according to GP.

The following year, in August, Amelia flew her Vega across the continent in a record time of nineteen hours and five minutes. At the same time she set a women's record for distance, flying 2,447 miles. GP took every advantage of the news she was making, arranging more lectures, more public appearances. She was becoming better at handling them, despite her continued dislike – even fear – of crowds. Next, she set her sights on the Pacific. She and GP disposed of their house in Rye, New York, and moved to California. Amelia sold her Vega to the Franklin Institute in Philadelphia and bought a new model with improved navigational equipment. This aircraft was secured to the deck of the SS *Lurline* when she sailed from Los Angeles to Honolulu in December 1934. Aboard the ship were Amelia, GP, and Paul Mantz, a well-known Hollywood stunt pilot who was acting as a technical and navigation adviser. A group of Hawaiian businessmen was offering ten thousand dollars for a flight from Hawaii to California. Amelia and GP, perpetually in financial straits because of the crippling cost of long-distance flying, were understandably keen on winning the prize. But mainland newspapers claimed that Amelia was being manipulated by business interests determined to persuade Congress to reduce tariffs on Hawaiian sugar. Dismayed by the uproar, Amelia's sponsors began to have second thoughts; perhaps it would be best if she forgot the whole thing and went home. Angrily, Amelia told them that she intended to fly to California with or without their support. At that, the sponsors decided to leave things as they were.

On January 11, 1935, she was ready to take off. But the weather turned against her. A tropical downpour hit the Honolulu area, making the grass-covered Wheeler Field a semi-quagmire. Amelia cursed her luck. If she didn't get away now, she might be delayed up to ten days by other storms brewing in the central Pacific; but if she *did* leave, there was a strong possibility of better weather along her projected route. Typically, she made up her mind at once. It was now or never. She clambered aboard the Vega and waved to her team. She was off, come what may. She taxied off the concrete apron and the wheels sank into the mud. She opened the throttle. The heavily loaded airplane groaned as it rolled into motion, the mud grabbing at the tires. Amelia was acutely conscious of the weight she was hauling: some three tons with a load of more than five hundred gallons of fuel. Ahead, she could just make out the checkered flag, the last-chance point on the takeoff run. If she wasn't airborne by the time she passed the flag, she had to cut the throttle and slam on the brakes. Soldiers stood beside the strip, each man with a portable fire extinguisher at the ready.

The Vega picked up speed . . . slowly, excruciatingly slowly. The entire structure quivered with apparent frustration, the engine roaring. As the checkered flag whisked by, she felt the wings take the weight. The ground dropped away. She was off, airborne in some three thousand feet, with another three thousand to spare.

The takeoff proved to be the toughest part of the entire trip. The weather cleared soon after her departure from Wheeler, and the aircraft performed superbly. Eighteen and a quarter hours after takeoff, she landed at Oakland, watched by a crowd estimated at ten thousand. The Earhart legend was growing, although the Oakland *Tribune* criticized her Honolulu-to-California flight as a "publicity stunt" and a potential danger to aviators and sailors who might have to search for her "if she encounters stormy weather or loses her course." Three months later she flew to Mexico City, then pushed on to New York. The journey to New York (actually, Newark, New Jersey) was climaxed by a hysterical welcome. The police had to be called to escort her through the throngs of adoring spectators. Her reputation soared.

In June 1935, Amelia accepted an appointment as aeronautics adviser at Indiana's Purdue University. It was a happy period for her; she was idolized by the students, a living symbol of modern womanhood, the perfect role model. She in turn was stimulated by the students' intense interest in every aspect of her life. The icing on the cake was the university's decision to establish a fund for aeronautical research; at the time, Amelia was contemplating another record-breaking flight, a trip that would be the pinnacle of her career – a circuit of the globe at the equator. Amelia had told her husband that she had "one last big flight" in her and this was going to be it. Funding for the costly venture was now assured, thanks to the Purdue grant. Amelia purchased a new twin-engine Lockheed 10E Electra, which she liked to refer to as a "flying laboratory." It cost $36,089.70, and that was before the multitude of modifications necessary to ready the aircraft for a round-the-world flight. There had been round-the-world flights before, but they had not circled the globe at its circumference; they had found their way around in the northern hemisphere, considerably reducing the distance to be flown. Amelia envisaged a flight of a little over twenty-five thousand miles, by far the longest ever attempted by anyone of either sex.

While preparing for the big flight, Earhart and Helen Richey (formerly one of the first women airline pilots until the all-male pilot's union forced her to quit) flew the Electra in the 1936 Bendix race. They had trouble with the plane's fuel lines and a hatch that wouldn't stay shut, and came in a disappointing fifth. Nevertheless, the male-dominated race was won by two women, Louise Thaden and Blanche Noyes, in a stock Beechcraft 17.

Early in 1937, GP and Amelia released news of the forthcoming round-the-world flight. A flood of photographs appeared in the papers, stock photo-op stuff in the main: Amelia beaming through the ring made by the Bendix direction-finder; Amelia with a small suitcase and the clothes she planned to take; Amelia with Harry Manning, the navigator; Amelia with Kelly Johnson, Lockheed's project engineer; Amelia in the Electra, gazing at fuel tanks, standing beneath the Electra's nose, touching the two propeller tips, checking out the emergency raft, standing on a wing, purportedly talking with a representative of Western Electric. She hated having to pose for such pictures, but GP kept reminding her how important they were. Publicity was vital if they were to pay for the vastly expensive enterprise. So she obediently smiled (as usual taking care to keep her mouth closed as much as possible lest the gap in her front teeth be revealed) and did as the photographers asked, standing here, sitting there, holding this, reading that. Or pretending to.

On March 17, 1937, the Electra took off from Oakland, California, and headed for Honolulu. Aboard were Amelia and her crew, consisting of Paul Mantz, co-pilot, and two navigators, Harry Manning and Fred Noonan. The plan was for Mantz to have a final check of the aircraft during the trip to Honolulu, after which the others would continue without him. Manning, on leave from the American President Lines, was to be chief navigator as far as Australia, with Noonan assisting on the Honolulu-to-Howland leg. Amelia planned to fly on alone after they had crossed the Pacific. She said, "I hope this flight will yield some valuable knowledge about human reactions and mechanical performance at high altitudes and high temperatures for long intervals. I am racing nobody but I do have a time schedule which I shall endeavour to follow. I am not interested in setting any records; I hope the data we shall bring back on fuel consumption and other mechanical details, as well as airport facilities and conditions, may hasten and encourage world-wide civilian plane travel. The flight has been carefully plotted to cover the maximum distance with the minimum number of stops. We expect to log about twenty-seven thousand miles from Oakland back to Oakland."[1]

It all sounded appropriately technical and infinitely worthy, but the truth was that the flight had been conceived solely to boost her reputation and her marketability. The "stunts" of the long-distance flyers had been becoming increasingly challenging ever since the faltering flights of Zeppelin and Blériot. They had to be. If the public didn't raise eyebrows and thrill at the dangers the aviators were facing, it was all in vain. Like trapeze artists, the long-distance flyers had to come up with ever-more-demanding tricks to capture the public fancy.

The flight to Honolulu took a little less than sixteen hours. As arranged, Manning left the crew in Hawaii, having used up his leave from American President. Fred Noonan, an ex-Pan Am pilot and a highly competent navigator, was now the sole occupant of the tiny office aft. A wry individual, recently married, he had only one shortcoming as far as Amelia was concerned: a reported weakness for alcohol. Amelia seemed fated to encounter alcoholics in every phase of her life. She was concerned, but Noonan said he had sworn off the stuff for the duration of the flight. Amelia believed him and kept him in her crew. Noonan, on his part, wrote to his bride that Amelia was the only female pilot with whom he would fly on such a trip, "Because in addition to being a fine companion and pilot, she can take hardship as well as a man – and work like one."[2] Noonan, in the navigation station, was able to communicate with Amelia only by means of scribbled messages attached to a bamboo fishing pole hung from the roof of the aircraft.

The weather was poor. The flyers waited a day, and when conditions improved, Amelia ordered an immediate start. On the morning of March 19 she opened the throttles and the Electra, carrying 590 gallons of fuel, gathered speed as it roared along the paved runway at Luke Field (now Ford Island). It looked as if the heavily laden Electra would get away splendidly. But just before liftoff, the right wing seemed to sag and sparks were seen flying from beneath the fuselage. Amid an eruption of dust and dirt, the aircraft whirled into a ground loop. The gear collapsed and the Electra slammed down on the runway, fortunately without catching fire. It was a sorry sight. Landing gear sheared off. Starboard wing crumpled. Right engine nacelle bent. Both propeller blades twisted. Amelia was close to tears as she surveyed the mess. GP at once sent a radiogram from Oakland: "So long as you and the boys are okay, the rest doesn't matter. Whether you want to call it a day or keep going is equally Jake with me."[3]

Amelia told reporters that she had no intention of abandoning the flight, but secretly she wondered if the exchequer would stand the cost of the repairs, for which Lockheed quoted a formidable $14,000. But GP's publicity paid off. Contributions came in from dozens of people, most of whom Amelia had never met. Bernard Baruch, the financier and statesman, sent her a cheque for $2,500, "Because I like your everlasting guts!" Jacqueline Cochran and Admiral Byrd were other contributors. The mechanics at Lockheed voted to work an entire Sunday without pay. By late May, Earhart could send a wire to President Elliott of Purdue: "Our second attempt is assured. We are solvent. Future is mortgaged, but what else are futures for?"[4]

What had caused the crash? Everyone had a different theory.

Amelia herself thought it was due to the collapse of a shock absorber; others blamed a burst tire; others pointed to the sloshing of the huge weight of fuel; Paul Mantz, the flight's technical adviser, was of the opinion that Amelia may have unwittingly done it herself by choosing to "jockey" the throttles to keep the Electra on its path along the runway and using the rudders only minimally, a habit of hers.

The crash at Luke literally turned the flight around. Weather patterns, particularly those over the Caribbean and Africa, no longer favoured the original flight plan. Now the flyers intended to fly east instead of west. The formidable Pacific would be the last leg of the trip rather than the first. The route would take them from Oakland to Miami then on to San Juan, Puerto Rico, and Caripito before crossing the Atlantic, Natal to Dakar. From there Amelia planned to travel to Karachi, Calcutta, Bangkok, Singapore, and Darwin, striking out across the Pacific to Howland Island and Honolulu on the way back to Oakland. It was a formidable trip by any standard. Paul Mantz had equipped the Electra with the very latest navigational equipment, transmitter and receiver designed for operation on the standard aviation frequencies as well as on the long-range five-hundred-kilocycle international emergency wavelength.

On May 21, Amelia and Fred Noonan left Oakland in the Electra, now fully repaired. The trip was described as a shakedown flight, but in fact it was the first leg of their eastward trip. On June 1, the Electra left Miami bound for Puerto Rico. From there it was all very familiar to Noonan, because it was the Pan Am route: down the coast of South America to Natal, crossing the equator for the first time on this trip. Amelia crossed it again on the way to Dakar – and once more demonstrated her stubbornness when she ignored a note from Noonan telling her that she was drifting north. The result was that she landed at St. Louis, Senegal, rather than Dakar.

She dismissed the error as unimportant; after all, she had the entire African continent before her. Noonan didn't comment. They pushed on, following the equator across Africa, to India and Burma, crossing the equator for the third time in the East Indies.

Thirty days later, on June 30, Amelia and Noonan landed at Lae, New Guinea, touching down on a three-thousand-foot runway hacked out of the jungle. Both flyers were exhausted. Amelia was suffering from intermittent stomach cramps and she looked thin and nervous, and older than her thirty-eight years. She and Noonan had travelled some twenty-two thousand miles and had about seven thousand to go. They spent the night in a hotel in the town.

They had hoped to get away the next morning in an effort to make it back to the U.S. by July 4. But bad weather held them up. There was another hitch too: because of radio problems, Noonan was unable to calibrate his chronometers. Amelia had the utmost faith in Noonan; he had been totally abstemious, not touching a drink from the first takeoff. She left the navigation problem to him while she busied herself going through the Electra and discarding any item not absolutely essential. She telephoned GP daily and continued to send reports on the progress of the flight (which became a series of articles for the New York *Herald Tribune* and later the book *Last Flight*, edited by GP).

The next leg of the trip was the most critical. The end of the odyssey was almost in sight – but first there was a tiny fragment of real estate to find. Their target was Howland Island, a sliver of land in the vast ocean, two miles long, half a mile wide, its maximum elevation just twenty feet. It had been discovered by Captain George E. Netcher of New Bedford, Massachusetts, only in 1842 and was occasionally visited for the guano, a form of fertilizer endemic to the place. In order to reach it, Amelia had to fly some 2,250 miles over water. They loaded the Electra with more than a thousand gallons (U.S.) of gasoline and took off at 10:30 a.m. on July 2. Amelia seemed confident enough as she gunned the Electra across the field. She held the Electra down until she had used up almost the entire length. Then she climbed, confidently, exhibiting her usual skill and verve. She rocked her wings in farewell as she climbed away. At 5:20 p.m., she reported her position as 795 miles from Lae. She was on course. Everything appeared to be going well. But back in California, Paul Mantz was deeply concerned when he heard that the flight was proceeding without the trailing antenna that was vital to bring in the homing signals from Howland Island. It was jeopardizing the whole enterprise. Why was he hired as a technical adviser if his advice was not accepted? At Miami, Amelia had ordered the removal of the 250-foot trailing antenna because it slowed the aircraft imperceptibly – and, probably of more importance, it was a chore to play out and reel in. But its elimination sharply reduced the range of the five-hundred-kilocycle radio transmissions and the ability of ground stations and ships at sea to get a fix on the Electra. In the early stages of the flight, the absence of the antenna had made little difference. It was about to become all-important.

The Coast Guard cutter *Itasca* had been ordered to cruise in the vicinity of Howland Island to transmit homing signals. Aboard the *Itasca*, one group of radiomen had the responsibility of operating the ship's low-frequency direction finder. Amelia was to transmit her call signal, plus important flight information, at quarter to and quarter past the hour. The *Itasca* would call the Electra by voice signal on the hour and half-hour, tapping the Morse code letter A to provide a homing beam.

5:20 p.m. New Guinea time: a message from Amelia to Lae. She was past the Solomons and dead on course.

2:45 a.m. Amelia reported cloudy weather.

3:45 a.m. Amelia came on the air again, her voice stronger, advising the Coast Guard that she would be tuned in on the agreed-upon frequency.

4:15 a.m. Another message – but it was drowned out by static.

Two hours later, shortly before she was due to arrive at Howland, Amelia requested a radio bearing, saying that she would whistle into the microphone to enable the *Itasca* to get a fix. Unfortunately, the brief whistle was barely distinguishable through the audio clutter.

The *Itasca* requested a longer transmission, preferably on the five-hundred-kilocycle emergency wavelength. Amelia didn't reply.

Amelia's estimated time of arrival at Howland Island, came and went. Aboard the ship, concern was growing. Why didn't Amelia broadcast on five hundred kilocycles, using her long antenna? The Coast Guard men didn't know that the antenna was lying on the floor of a hangar at Miami.

6:45 a.m. Amelia's voice came through loud and clear. "Please take bearing on us and report in half-hour. I will make noise in microphone. About 100 miles out."

Again, frustratingly, she was on the air too briefly for the Coast Guard to get a good fix. She was out there somewhere. But where? It was now that the lack of the trailing antenna was felt. Tragically, it was compounded by Amelia's remarkable lack of radio know-how, and neither she nor Noonan could send or receive Morse code.

At 8:45 a.m., Amelia's voice was heard again: "We are on the line of position 157-337." The voice was faint, but there was no mistaking the note of despair.

The *Itasca* began to search for the Electra and its occupants at 10:40 a.m., although no one knew exactly where to look. The garbled, uncertain messages from the Electra had been of little help. Nevertheless, the U.S. Navy initiated a massive search of about a quarter of a million square miles of ocean. The carrier *Lexington* was at Santa Barbara, California, in preparation for a July 4 reception, but now the big ship immediately weighed anchor and headed out to sea. Three destroyers, *Drayton, Lamson,* and *Cushing,* soon followed. The group arrived in the Howland area on July 13 and launched sixty aircraft to assist in the search.

George Putnam was stunned by the news of Amelia's disappearance, although he did his best to appear confident about her survival. He contacted Jacqueline Cochran, the noted woman pilot with a reputation for "finding" lost aviators. Jackie declared that she "saw" Amelia floating. She even provided the position. GP immediately radioed the information to the *Itasca.* Although the ship sailed to the location without delay, nothing was found. The ghouls soon emerged. A former seaman had found one of Amelia's scarves in the hangar at Wheeler Field, Hawaii, left there after the takeoff accident. The man demanded five thousand dollars as his price for revealing where Amelia was being held by smugglers. His story soon fell apart. GP didn't prosecute him; in fact, he gave him fifty dollars for the scarf. A piece of driftwood was found bearing the inscribed message: "To my husband – I have crashed 250 miles from Hawaii – NW. Our motors went into flames – sharks about me. A.E." It was of course another hoax, providing God knows what satisfaction to some twisted someone.

| *Breaking*
More
Records

Howard Hughes rose early on the morning of July 7, 1946. He wolfed down a slice of banana cream pie with a scoop of vanilla ice cream, then, clad in khaki pants and a white shirt, he walked out to a waiting aircraft, the twin-engine XF-11. Hughes clambered aboard the sleek photo-reconnaissance machine – the latest product of Hughes Aircraft – and settled himself in the pilot's seat. He spent much of the morning in taxiing trials and brief hops to test the aircraft's controls. During the afternoon he took off from Culver City airfield and spent some time circling over the city. The new aircraft performed flawlessly; the only problem was a malfunctioning landing-gear light, a minor item in a new plane, particularly one as advanced as the XF-11. But then Hughes felt the aircraft pull to the right. Hard. Instinctively, his eyes scanned the instrument panel. No sign of problems there. He reduced power to the starboard engine. Still the asymmetrical thrust persisted. By now he was down to little more than a thousand feet, almost skimming the immaculate roofs of Beverly Hills. The aircraft rapidly became uncontrollable. Hughes could do nothing but put his feet on the instrument panel and prepare for the impact.

It came soon enough. The XF-11 hit the home of dentist Jules Zimmerman at 803 North Linden Drive, a moment later slamming into actress Rosemary De Camp's house, demolishing the garage, and then the home of Lieutenant Colonel Charles Meyer, whereupon it burst into flames. One of the aircraft's engines spun sixty feet into the air before crashing into a house owned by Swedish industrialist Gosta B. Guston. A Marine sergeant, William Durkin, happened to be staying at the Guston home. He ran to the burning XF-11 just as Hughes emerged from the remains of the cockpit and fell to the ground. Durkin rolled Hughes away from the flames. The multi-millionaire woke up in the Good Samaritan Hospital in Los Angeles. He had a punctured lung, broken ribs, broken left shoulder, broken nose, plus third-degree burns. The papers said Hughes had a "fifty-fifty chance." Somehow it seemed typical of this enigmatic individual that he would be fighting for his life while receiving visits from such glamorous Hollywood stars as Lana Turner, Linda Darnell, Ava Gardner, Jane Russell, and Jean Peters. But would he survive? If not, a fabulous chapter in aviation history would be over.

His was the classic silver-spoon story. He had been born rich – and with practically no effort on his part, he kept getting richer. The source of his wealth was an oil drill-bit invented by his father. Howard himself had little interest in oil. Aviation captured his imagination. As did the movies. He hurled himself into both more or less simultaneously. He learned to fly in 1927, when he was twenty-one, quickly demonstrating unusual aptitude – a "natural" by any measure. Determined also to become a movie producer, he initially tried to buy such studios as Universal, Paramount, and

Warner Brothers, but discovered to his considerable displeasure that they weren't for sale. Unfazed, he became an independent producer, bringing little more than enthusiasm and a fat cheque book. His first production was a film called *Swell Hogan*. On viewing it, he rated it so awful that he ordered the negative destroyed. He had invested an impressive eighty thousand dollars in the production, but he considered it money well-spent. He had learned a lot. Next he made a rather more successful production called *Two Arabian Nights*, after which he plunged into production of the First World War epic *Hell's Angels*. Spending lavishly, he acquired more than eighty wartime aircraft for the production and modified others to look the part. He shot some of the best aeronautical footage seen to that date, using an airfield called Mines Field, which later became better known as Los Angeles International Airport. During the shooting, Hughes crashed a Thomas Morse scout biplane and was lucky to emerge from the wreck with nothing worse than minor facial injuries.

Howard Hughes's stars in *Hell's Angels* were Ben Lyon and James Hall, with a Norwegian actress named Greta Nissen providing the romantic interest. When production was almost complete, a shockwave hit Hollywood – sound. Hughes had already invested some two million dollars in *Hell's Angels*. He immediately sank another million to reshoot all the dramatic scenes with hastily written dialogue. Greta Nissen had to go. She was an attractive girl, but she had a strong accent. Hughes decided to avoid incurring the price tag of an established star; presumably the cost of the project was beginning to concern even him. His production manager, Joe Engel, produced a pretty newcomer named Harlean Carpenter, who sported what was then called "albino blonde hair." Hughes renamed it "platinum blonde" and told Miss Carpenter that her name was now Jean Harlow. She turned out to be just as big an attraction as the flying scenes. And she was a bargain, earning a mere $1,500 on a production that eventually cost some four million dollars, making it the most expensive film that had ever been made. Hollywood wiseacres told Hughes that his movie would be a financial disaster, but in spite of their dire predictions, and the Wall Street crash of 1929, the movie was a smash, one of the most successful films of the period. Hughes was twenty-four. He went on to produce several more movies, but only *The Outlaw*, made in the early forties, attracted the same sort of attention as *Hell's Angels* – and that was largely due to the physical attractions of another statuesque star, Jane Russell.

Hughes next set out to create the fastest plane in the world. Although he had no engineering training, he had a lot of sound ideas and an unerring eye for good design. He hired a recent graduate of the California Institute of Technology, Richard W. Palmer, and set him to work on the new aircraft. The result was a lean and lovely airplane called the Hughes H-1, popularly known as the Racer. Powered by a neatly cowled Pratt & Whitney Twin Wasp, the H-1 had stubby wings spanning a mere twenty-five feet. The landing gear retracted into the underside of the wings, to be sealed by tight-fitting doors. Even the tail skid retracted, an advanced feature for the day. Hughes's bank account enabled him to get just about the best airplane skin available: aluminum alloy sheets butted together with rivet heads meticulously shaved so that they didn't interfere with the airflow. The glasslike finish was achieved by stretching finely woven fabric over the structure and sealing it with many coats of dope, paint, and wax. Elegantly curved fillets smoothed the airflow between wing and fuselage, preventing the creation of turbulence that could buffet the tail.[1] The plane cost Hughes in excess of one hundred thousand dollars. He tested it in August 1935, then broke the world's airspeed record by flying it at

352.388 miles per hour. Later, equipped with a larger wing, the Racer broke the transcontinental record, flying from Burbank to Newark in a little over seven hours.

Next, Hughes decided to beat the record for an around-the-world flight. He originally wanted to use his Sikorsky amphibian for the flight, but he eventually decided on the successor to the Lockheed Electra, the Lockheed 14 (the military version of which soon became famous in service with the British as the Hudson reconnaissance bomber). He had its interior stripped and equipped with the latest in navigational equipment, extra fuel tanks, three radio systems, and a self-contained oxygen system. Hughes named the aircraft *New York World's Fair 1939*. On July 10, 1938, he travelled to Floyd Bennett Field in company with his current girl-friend, movie actress Katharine Hepburn, in her Lincoln limousine driven by her driver, Charles Newhill. En route to the airport, the police stopped them for speeding, but didn't recognize the famous couple in the rear. Clutching his traffic ticket, Newhill drove to Hangar No. 7 at the airport and stopped to let his passengers out. To Hughes's dismay, he found that a large crowd of onlookers and press photographers had gathered to see him off. Normally obsessive about avoiding people, he surprised everyone by waving and grinning in an uncharacteristically friendly way. A microphone was placed before him and he said a few words in his oddly high-pitched voice: "We hope that our flight may prove a contribution to the cause of friendship between nations and that through their outstanding flyers, for whom the common bond of aviation transcends national boundaries, this cause may be furthered."[2]

Hughes stepped into the Lockheed, followed by his crew, consisting of Tommy Thurlow, co-pilot and navigator, Harry Connor, second navigator, Richard Stoddard, radio engineer, and Edward

Lund, flight engineer. Hughes had organized a network of reporting stations to provide up-to-the-minute weather information at
every stop along the way. Radio-equipped ships and ground stations were required to stay in touch with the aircraft, and emergency landing sites were stocked with spares. It was a perfect
example of how to carry out a globe-girdling flight – for someone possessing a bottomless bank account. But money could do
nothing to help Hughes get the Lockheed into the air. Groaning
under the weight of 1,500 gallons of fuel and 150 gallons of oil, the
aircraft began its takeoff run at an agonizingly leisurely pace.
Onlookers held their breath. Would the round-the-world journey
end right here?

The Lockheed's tail was only just off the ground when the aircraft hit the end of the runway, and bumped on to an area of dirt
and grass. With an eruption of dust and debris, engines howling,
the silver aircraft eased into the air. There was a huge sigh of relief
from the assembled throng, many of whom must have been anticipating a funeral pyre to match that of Rene Fonck's Sikorsky
twelve years earlier.

The Lockheed was airborne. The big flight was actually
happening.

Hughes turned east and headed into the gathering dusk. Over
the Atlantic, Hughes encountered unexpected headwinds. While
the radio man, Stoddard, exchanged greetings with ocean liners, the
turbulence gradually diminished. Hughes put the Lockheed down
at Le Bourget, Paris, after a flight of just over sixteen hours – about
half the time Lindbergh had taken eleven years earlier. Hughes was
pleased – he had calculated that this part of the trip would take
about twenty hours – but then less pleased when he discovered that
a strut had been damaged during his takeoff from New York. The

ground staff looked after it without delay, and Hughes was on his way to Germany by midnight. With the international situation in a decidedly delicate state, Hughes had agreed to fly over the country at twelve thousand feet, well above the altitude at which any spying could be done. Nevertheless, the Luftwaffe monitored the flight all the way.

The Lockheed landed at Moscow to a friendly reception from the Soviets, who supplied the flyers with food – including caviar, a gift from Stalin himself. Next it was on to Omsk, where heavy rains had turned the airfield into a quagmire and where the Lockheed slid on the muddy surface, fortunately without incurring any damage. They now flew over some of the most desolate terrain in the world. Shortly after leaving Yakutsk, with Hughes still at the controls, the *World's Fair* came close to hitting a Siberian mountain. Hughes was flying at 7,000 feet, and according to the charts, the mountains were only 6,500 feet, yet there it was, a wall of granite dead ahead. Hughes responded instantly. Pouring on full power, he managed to pull the aircraft out of danger. Stoddard later said he could count the pebbles on the mountain top as the Lockheed passed over. Had he not been delayed in Paris, Hughes would undoubtedly have flown straight into the mountain in the darkness. The reason for the near-disaster was simple. The crew's charts were metric, with the mountain height expressed in metres, not feet. No one had noticed.

Hughes was becoming utterly exhausted, yet he would not relinquish the controls for more than a few minutes at a time. Harry Connor kept asking him questions to test his alertness. In a way, the very efficiency of the flight was a problem, because nothing happened to jerk the crew out of their lethargy. The engines, those superb Wright Cyclones, kept humming contentedly. Below, the toy world of miniature trees and ant-like people slid by like an image in an endless cyclorama. The checkpoints passed, one after the other, smoothly, effortlessly. Hughes was demonstrating how a long-distance flight should be handled, how technology and planning – aided by limitless funds – could defeat mileage.

In mid-afternoon on July 13, Hughes landed at Fairbanks, Alaska. There, he met Mae Post, the widow of the man whose 1933 record he was busy shattering. With tears running down her cheeks, Mae wished Hughes Godspeed. He was off again. A scheduled stop at Winnipeg had to be abandoned due to a sudden storm. Instead, Hughes went to Minneapolis, where a lone radio reporter got the scoop of his life when the plane the world was watching landed without fanfare. Thirty-four minutes later, Hughes took off on the last lap of his global odyssey.

The roads around Floyd Bennett Field became jammed as thousands of cars streamed into the area to greet the flyers. Mayor Fiorello La Guardia was there with Grover Whalen, the president of the World's Fair and New York's "official greeter." Whalen was becoming increasingly concerned about the numbers of people flooding into the airfield. He had arranged for one thousand policemen to be there to control the crowds. Now it looked as if thousands more would be needed.

Hughes was over Pennsylvania. With throttles wide open, he headed for New York, knowing that, barring last-minute problems, his flight had been a triumph, both of technology and planning. As Floyd Bennett Field slid into view, the airmen stared in amazement at the people swarming over the runways and grass areas below. Characteristically, Hughes ignored the instructions from the control tower and landed on a remote part of the field, far from the throng.

But that solved nothing, for the barriers that had been put up to keep the crowd under control hardly slowed them. Police ran in every direction, yelling, gesticulating, only adding to the confusion. La Guardia and Whalen were left on the welcoming stand, looking bewildered.

Hughes landed and taxied with extreme care lest he hit someone with his propellers. At last the Lockheed came to a halt. The odyssey was over. Crowds swarmed around the aircraft, with police vainly trying to restore order. One by one the weary crew emerged, rubbing unshaven chins and tugging at wrinkled shirts. Hughes was the last to appear, obviously exhausted, far from happy to be surrounded by shrieking, adoring people. Microphones were thrust at him and he mumbled a few impatient words before being whisked away by Grover Whalen's committee to the Hampshire House Hotel. During interviews, Hughes excused himself and said he wanted a clean shirt. He promptly disappeared into a Yellow cab and hurried away for a rendezvous with Katharine Hepburn. The next day, rested and groomed, he participated in the traditional tickertape parade – but only after insisting that his crew and ground staff also take part. The *New York Times* mused that Hughes had "the face of a poet and the shyness of a schoolboy." Hepburn probably had other words to describe him when she discovered that Hughes's affections had abruptly been transferred to actress Bette Davis. One has to wonder how he kept track.

IIII

A matter of days after the successful conclusion of Hughes's round-the-world flight, a young man named Douglas Corrigan set off from Floyd Bennett, the same field that Hughes had used – but there the similarity ended. Hughes had unlimited funds; Corrigan had almost none. Hughes flew a brand-new aircraft; Corrigan flew an elderly Curtiss Robin, a high-wing monoplane dating from

1928. Hughes had the most up-to-date servicing facilities money could buy; Corrigan had to fasten his cabin door with a piece of wire, since the latch had broken. Corrigan had been a worker at the Ryan plant in San Diego during the construction of Lindbergh's *Spirit of St. Louis*. One morning, Lindy had greeted Corrigan and exchanged a few words – and for the young man it was a moment never to be forgotten. As far as Douglas Corrigan was concerned, Lindbergh was the greatest man ever. "Even greater than Lincoln," he claimed.[3]

Corrigan drifted about America, taking a job here and there, never settling. In 1933, he found himself in New York. He had accumulated a little money and purchased a second-hand Robin for $325. Accompanied by a friend, he flew to California, taking up the occasional passenger to help with the expenses. At San Diego, he landed another job with Ryan, but he still yearned to emulate his hero, Lindy. He acquired a used Wright J6-5 engine developed from the excellent Whirlwind and installed it on the Robin, together with extra fuel tanks. The Department of Commerce would license the aircraft for cross-country flights, nothing else. It was probably then that Corrigan conceived the notion of an "accidental Atlantic flight."

The superannuated Robin took to the air at Long Beach, California, on July 8, 1938, just two days before Hughes's departure from Floyd Bennett. Corrigan landed at Roosevelt Field – and no one took the slightest notice. He was just another young guy with a beat-up airplane. On the evening of July 16 Corrigan transferred his Robin to Floyd Bennett Field in Brooklyn. In the early hours of July 17, with a supply of figs, chocolate, and water, and his cabin door secured with a fresh length of wire, he took off, having told officials that he was heading for California. But he headed east, not west. No one noticed. The Atlantic stretched out before him, immense and intimidating. After a few hours, Corrigan's feet became chilly. He looked down and found that gasoline was leaking from a connection and dripping on his shoes. As it evaporated, it chilled his feet. Fuel sloshed around on the floor of the cabin. Corrigan patched up the leak as well as he could and continued on his way. Hours passed. It seemed at times as if he were suspended in space, making no headway, just hanging in a noisy, swaying world that stank of gasoline.

Mist blanketed the ocean. Corrigan felt the leaden weight of uneasiness in his gut. He could drift an awfully long way off course in these conditions . . . Then the mist parted a little, revealing green fields. Land! He grinned, relieved. His grin soon widened when he came across an airfield with the name Baldonnel painted on the roof of a building. He landed and taxied up to a hangar. A man looked enquiringly at him. "I'm Douglas Corrigan," he told the man. "I just got in from New York. Where am I? I intended to fly to California, but I got mixed up in the clouds and must have flown the wrong way."[4]

No one believed that he had flown the Atlantic by accident, but everyone thought it a great joke. The American Legation in Dublin sent a car for him, and Corrigan found himself the guest of the U.S. ambassador, John Cudahy. He told his story again and again, about flying a reciprocal course, over mist-covered seas, about mistaking Boston for Baltimore. He became an honorary member of the Ananias Club, named after an early Christian struck dead for lying. He flew to London to meet ambassador Joseph Kennedy. Someone pointed out that he had broken Irish law by failing to get permission to land on Irish soil. But it seemed to be of little concern to anyone. Corrigan was an amiable young man, and he had succeeded where so many had failed. Dennis Mulligan, director of the Bureau of Air Commerce, remarked, "It was a great day for the Irish,"[5] and most people seemed to agree. The only fear was that others would attempt to do the same. And there was good reason to think so, for in short order Corrigan's exploit netted him a cool seventy-five thousand dollars, the fruits of his autobiography, *That's My Story*, and a brief movie career in which he played himself in something called *The Flying Irishman*.

Another "shoestring" pilot of the era was twenty-seven-year-old Carl Bachman, a native of Sweden, now residing in Chicago. He had been a professional pilot in Sweden but in America had to make a living as a painter and decorator. No doubt inspired by Corrigan's example, he scraped up the cash to buy a tiny Monocoupe cabin aircraft, intending to fly it to his native land. Knowing that he would never get permission for such a flight from the Department of Commerce, he got a friend in Sweden to agree to purchase the Monocoupe. Then Bachman set off to deliver it, taking off from Botwood, Newfoundland, on May 16, 1939. No trace of him or his aircraft was ever found.

Only a matter of a couple of weeks later, Thomas H. Smith took off from Old Orchard Beach, Maine, turned in the direction of Europe, and vanished for all time. A pair of young men from Brooklyn left Nova Scotia in an old Ryan monoplane named *Shalom*. It was their second attempt; in July they had tried but succeeded only in bursting a tire. Officialdom did its best to ground the pair but they managed to get to Canada. They took to the air on August 11, 1939, and vanished somewhere over the ocean, two more casualties of what was still a hazardous business.

||||

Benito Mussolini, the leader of the Italian National Fascist Party, saw great propaganda value in long-distance flights – "for the glory of Fascist Italy." In 1927, he had ordered a spectacular South Atlantic flight commanded by the Marchese de Pinedo. He insisted that the aircraft – a twin-hulled Savoia-Marchetti flying boat with twin engines in tandem – be named the *Santa Maria* after Christopher Columbus's ship. The Marchese de Pinedo had previously flown from Rome to Melbourne and Tokyo. His co-pilot was Carlo del Prete. A mechanic was carried, but no radio. The *Santa Maria* took to the air from Sardinia on February 13, 1927, droning steadily to Morocco, following the coastline to Dakar, then striking out over the ocean and arriving at Pernambuco, Brazil, on February 24. The Italians received an ecstatic reception in Brazil. They toured the country, basking in the adoration of huge crowds. They were the heroes of the moment. When they were reported overdue during a flight over the endless jungle, the news sent shock waves throughout Brazil. Despair turned to joy when the flyers turned up, unhurt. De Pinedo waved casually to the throng when he boarded the faithful Savoia-Marchetti and headed north to the West Indies and Cuba and eventually to New Orleans. Americans – particularly those of Italian descent – greeted the *Santa Maria* crew as rapturously as had the Brazilians. A tour was arranged, utilizing lakes and reservoirs, since the aircraft could operate only from water.

On April 25, in Arizona, the *Santa Maria* was at the Roosevelt Dam, warming up for a flight to San Diego, California, when someone noticed gasoline spreading on the reservoir's surface. A moment later, with a breathy roar, it ignited. The crew scrambled for their lives. They could do nothing for the aircraft, which burst into an uncontrollable blaze and was soon reduced to blackened fragments floating on the water. In Italy, the papers could barely contain their anger, hinting at anti-Fascist sabotage and international jealousy over Italy's achievements. For a few days, the situation seemed dangerous, then the culprit owned up: a seventeen-year-old had been scuffling with a companion in their boat and his lighted cigarette had fallen overboard, setting off the fire.

The U.S. Navy flew the de Pinedo crew to San Diego to await a second Savoia-Marchetti sent by Mussolini to his favourite pilot. *Santa Maria II* arrived at New York protected by an armed Fascist guard – the Italian dictator wasn't taking any chances. De Pinedo and his crew completed their North American tour aboard the new aircraft, winding up at Trepassey Bay, Newfoundland. From there, the *Santa Maria II* took off for the Azores and home. Like Harriet Quimby in 1912, de Pinedo couldn't have picked a worse day. Charles Lindbergh had just landed at Le Bourget, and the world's newspapers had little space to devote to the Italians. To make matters worse, de Pinedo encountered fierce headwinds and had to land some three hundred miles short of the Azores. The ocean was calm and the doughty flying boat was still afloat the next day, when a schooner arrived on the scene. Towed to Horta, the *Santa Maria II* flew on to Rome and received an enthusiastic welcome – despite Lindy.

Sadly, de Pinedo didn't have long to enjoy his fame. When another great Italian air armada was being organized, de Pinedo wasn't included. He had been deposed as Mussolini's favourite airman in favour of Italo Balbo. Seething, de Pinedo planned a solo flight from Rome to Baghdad in an effort to capture the world's non-stop long-distance record and restore his lost prestige. He obtained a Bellanca, which he named the *Santa Lucia*. In May 1933, he prepared to depart from Floyd Bennett Field, New York. He didn't even get airborne, swerving off the strip and coming to a sudden halt. Onlookers saw him tumbling out of the cabin. They heaved sighs of relief when he scrambled to his feet. He was safe. Or was he? He reached into the cabin of the Bellanca, probably intending to turn off the ignition. At that instant the aircraft exploded in flame. De Pinedo was engulfed, dying almost instantly.

The second great Italian flight, with Italo Balbo as commander, was a grand formation of no less than twenty-five aircraft making their way across the Atlantic, the kind of grandiose project that appealed to Mussolini. Balbo, a former journalist who had made his mark both in aviation and in politics, was an ambitious man of thirty-seven, a general in Mussolini's air force. He had already acquired a good deal of experience in leading formations for long distances. In January 1931, he had led a flight of fourteen Savoia-Marchetti flying boats from Rome to Natal, Brazil. Only eleven of the aircraft made it all the way. Two went down over Africa in fatal nighttime crashes; a third was forced down over the ocean, the crew being rescued by one of the Italian naval vessels sent to keep a benignant eye out for the flyers. The mission was in effect an elaborate delivery flight, for the aircraft were sold to the Brazilian government and the crewmen went home by sea. After the trip, Balbo declared that he would rather fly the ocean three times alone than do it again in formation. But Mussolini knew a great propaganda stunt when he saw one. In 1933, he commanded Balbo to lead a formation flight to the Chicago World's Fair, or, to give it its full title, the Century of Progress International Exposition. Whatever Balbo thought of the idea, he agreed without hesitation. He had little choice. Il Duce had spoken. Balbo decided to use the twin-hulled Savoia-Marchetti S55X, flying boats similar to the aircraft that had already served him so well: "This is the most perfect combination of material: Italian hydroplanes, Italian motors, Italian instruments for navigation, the whole animated by the inflexible will to risk and to succeed, which today constitutes the essence of the new soul of Fascist Italy which, in the glorious tradition of Rome of the Caesars, conquered its place in the world in the name of the Soldier King under the auspices of the Duce." So gushed the "official logbook" of the flight.

Balbo organized the event meticulously, setting up bases and weather stations at Amsterdam, Londonderry, Reykjavik, Cartwright in Labrador, Shediac, New Brunswick, Montreal, and Chicago – with an additional base at Julianehaab, Greenland, in case weather forced the flight to that area. A yacht, *Alice*, was despatched to Labrador to serve as a floating hotel for the aircraft crews.

The crews were selected a year in advance of the flight. Each aircraft would carry four men: commander-pilot, second pilot, radio operator, and engineer-mechanic. The pilots sat in a so-called control cabin in the centre section of the wing; the others occupied positions in the twin hulls.

Balbo trained his men well. For months, they practised formation flying, operating in flights of three aircraft. The flights sported markings of various colours, as well as bearing registration letters consisting of "I" for Italy, plus the first four letters of the pilot's name; thus Balbo's aircraft was coded "I-BALB." The three-aircraft teams flew one behind the other, with the leader occupying the highest position. Balbo could look back and survey his entire formation, forming what looked like giant steps in the sky.

On July 1, 1933, the aerial armada took off, with Balbo leading. It was a wonderfully impressive sight, and the Italian newspapers could hardly contain themselves, striving to outdo each other as they extolled the wonders of the Fascist system that had made all this possible. But there were problems ahead for the Italian flyers. At Amsterdam, one of the aircraft flipped over, killing a crewman and injuring two others. The twenty-four remaining aircraft continued in good order, flying through fog over the Irish Sea and Iceland, with even worse conditions south of Greenland. The fog was so thick that none of the flyers caught a glimpse of the mountainous coastline. Balbo's rigorous training paid off, however. He contacted each plane by radio, ordering the pilots to fly in "spread" formation to minimize the danger of collision, maintaining a propeller speed of 1,600 rpm. Although they had to grope their way through the murk, rarely seeing their comrades, the aircraft arrived safely at Cartwright on the eastern tip of Labrador, twelve hours after taking off from Iceland. Airmen of every nation applauded the brilliant performance. Reports from home spoke of an exultant *Duce*. Balbo had every reason to feel pleased with himself and his crews.

They flew to Shediac, New Brunswick, and on to Montreal and a tumultuous welcome from huge crowds on both banks of the St. Lawrence. But not everything went quite according to plan. A radio announcer, seeing Balbo declaiming vigorously, thought that the general had started his speech – and thrust a microphone at him. In fact, Balbo was energetically cursing a number of motorboats that were darting across the water, directly in the path of the aircraft still on their approach. To his embarrassment, Balbo discovered that his vituperative remarks were being broadcast. Hastily the radio people switched off, muttering something about "technical difficulties." Meanwhile the rest of Balbo's flying boats managed to avoid the motorboats and all landed safely.

En route to Chicago, the Italian formation flew headlong into a storm. Balbo ordered a change of course, but not all his aircraft received the order. The formation broke up. Balbo's training paid off once more, however, and the individual aircraft were able to join forces with their comrades over Detroit. The sighs of relief were felt clear across the Atlantic. As Balbo's flying boats arrived, forty-two Air Corps fighters from Selfridge Field, Michigan, came zooming overhead, arranging themselves so that they spelled out "Italia" across the sky. Ah, if only *Il Duce* could have been there to witness the glorious sight for himself! The next morning, Balbo and his men marched to Chicago's Holy Name Cathedral to attend a Mass of Thanksgiving for their safe arrival, and on July 15, all of Illinois celebrated Italo Balbo Day, with a Chicago street being named in his honour. Then it was off to New York and a parade up Broadway through a blizzard of tickertape. Balbo had lunch with President Roosevelt, who presented the flyer with a gold commemorative medal.

The flight home had its problems. The aircraft left New York on July 25, heading for Shediac. Two of the formation had to land at Portland, Maine, for fuel. The following day, another had to land with water pump trouble. Balbo, concerned about the possibility of bad weather – particularly fog – along the Great Circle route, elected to go via the Azores and Portugal. The next day, tragedy struck. One of the S55Xs flipped over on its takeoff run, killing one crewman and injuring three. Balbo didn't let the loss deter him. On August 12, he brought the remains of his formation back to Rome, touching down near the mouth of the Tiber River. The reception was rapturous – and included a personal welcome by Mussolini in the Roman Forum, a moment which, according to Balbo's flowery autobiography, was one never to be forgotten:

> The first person to greet me as I stepped ashore was the *Duce*. Neither of us spoke for quite a long while, but the look in his eyes and the warmth of his handclasp were eloquent of tense emotion. Then in a tone of camaraderie he congratulated me and my men on the successful conclusion of our task in a few simple and sincere words, which rang in my ears like anthems of victory. He added that he had arranged the details of a triumph for us such as greeted the return of the Roman legions in ancient days. The route of the procession would be under the arch of Constantine and along the Imperial Way.

Afterwards, we were to go to the Palatine. "It is a tribute that your country owes you, Balbo," he concluded with a kindly smile. . . . When the whole squadron was drawn up on the wharf, I called out in a loud tone:

"Attention!"

There was a sharp click of heels as they stood at the salute.

"God save the *Duce!*" I shouted.

"God save the *Duce!*" they repeated with one voice, fixing their eyes proudly on their chief.

Their words had hardly died away when the crowd redoubled their thunderous applause and clapped their hands in a frenzy of enthusiasm, while the last rays of the sun were reflected in the waters, and the shadows of our first night in Italy began to descend. . . . The motor-cars drew up in front of us, one for the crew of each flying-boat. I asked the *Duce* to take the first in the line but he refused, and with a gesture that brooked no gainsay, ordered the crews of the Atlantic squadron to start for Rome. . . . Meanwhile the *Duce* leaped onto the little terrace, kissed my wife's hand, and took my little fair-haired baby boy, Paolo, in his arms – a charming gesture which was a testimony to his kindness of heart.[6]

IIII

One of the most unusual – and luckiest – families of the era was the Hutchinsons of Baltimore, Maryland. Father George had started out as a golf caddy, but in recent times he had made something of a name for himself by taking his entire family on his travels, usually accompanied by a lion cub, à la Roscoe Turner.

The Flying Hutchinsons had already achieved a measure of fame by visiting all the state capitals by air. Their pictures were often in the papers, George, his wife, Blanche, and their two daughters, Blanche Kathryn, six, and Janet Lee, eight, all decked out in a kind of uniform of camel's hair sport coats, tan polo shirts, tan riding breeches, and berets – tan of course. In August 1932, they set off on their most ambitious venture to date: flying to London via the Arctic. In addition to the Hutchinsons there were four crew members: Peter Redpath, navigator; Joseph Ruff, mechanic; Gerald Altissish, radio operator; and, very necessary, a cameraman, Norman Alley. A twin-engine Sikorsky S-38 named *City of Richmond* was the aircraft to be used; it, and indeed the entire trip, was financed by a broadcasting company in return for exclusive bulletins about the adventure. George had an undeniable knack for making advantageous deals. This one, conjured up in the depth of the Great Depression, had to be considered a remarkable achievement.

The *City of Richmond* left Floyd Bennett Field on August 23, adults and children packed into the narrow cabin of the Sikorsky, a total of eight individuals plus a substantial load of fuel. It was with some relief that onlookers saw the amphibian heave its burden into the air and disappear to the northeast. The Sikorsky flew up the Labrador coast, already becoming cold in late August, crossing Davis Strait to Godthaab, the capital of Greenland. The Danish authorities had refused George permission to land in Greenland, but he went anyway, paying a thousand kroner fine slapped on him by local authorities – who surprisingly agreed to help him get to Angmagssalik on the eastern coast. Under no circumstances, however, was he to fly across the ice cap. Navigation had officially ended for the season, and there was the danger of being ice-locked there. Hutchinson agreed and flew to Julianehaab (now Qaqortoq) in the south of Greenland. Icebergs were already starting to form. On September 11, he took off for Angmagssalik and ran into thick fog. Hutchinson sent out a distress call on his radio. He got no reply. At home, the papers discovered the story and, in their inimitable way, suggested that the worst had probably already happened. Editorials crackled with righteous indignation about parents who would subject their children to such dangers.

A British trawler, *Lord Talbot*, happened to be in the vicinity and steamed at once to the position broadcasted. There was no sign of the missing aircraft. The trawler continued to search, and was joined by a Danish naval aircraft and a British motorboat. Two days later, a member of the crew of the *Lord Talbot* saw a flare dart into the sky. Investigating, the ship found the Hutchinsons and their crew-mates safe and sound, though chilly. Incredibly, none of them had thought to bring Arctic clothing. Hutchinson had landed the Sikorsky in the water and had taxied in the fog to the shore. He hit the rocks hard; everyone scrambled out safely, but the Sikorsky was soon battered into debris by heavy seas. The Hutchinsons found shelter with a group of Eskimo hunters.

Now that the story was big news all over the world, a London newspaper chartered the *Lord Talbot* to take the rescued aviators to Scotland. Soon they were in London and coping with the same criticism they had endured in America. George received an offer from a Brooklyn theatre for the family to appear in a vaudeville act entitled "The Flying Hutchinsons." The plans fell afoul of the Brooklyn Children's Society and the City of New York, who refused to issue the necessary permits, bringing to a climax heated criticism of the way the Hutchinson children's lives had been put at risk. George responded, "I did not subject my family to any more hazards than if we were travelling in an automobile. We are depending on the younger generation to carry aviation on in the future, so why should they object to my taking my children?" But no one listened. The Flying Hutchinsons were grounded.

| | | |

Although the craze for long-distance flights was definitely on the wane, a young New Zealander set out to make her name in the air. She was Jean Batten, a dentist's daughter, a seventeen-year-old who looked like an angel yet had the tenacity of a bull mastiff. Talented as well as beautiful, she had at one time entertained thoughts of becoming a concert pianist. But upon hearing about Charles Kingsford Smith's exploits, she abandoned all thoughts of music and decided that her destiny lay in the air. She would become a record-breaking pilot and be world-famous and adored. Countless thousands of hopefuls must have toyed with similar notions, soon forgetting them and settling for more mundane lives. Jean didn't forget. A career in flying became her *raison d'être*. She talked to her father (her parents had separated) about taking flying lessons. He refused. Too dangerous and too bloody expensive, he declared. Jean promptly sold her piano and set off for England with her mother, her faithful ally and confidante, ostensibly to study music, actually to embark on a career in aviation.

She enrolled at the London Aeroplane Club and was soon spending all her time – and money – there. Funds were a constant, nagging worry. Her father sent a few pounds every month, still believing that his daughter was training as a pianist in London. It helped, but she always needed more. Flying was indeed bloody expensive. She and her mother were living in a tiny flat near the "aerodrome," eating frugally and seldom venturing out for anything but the basics. Life had become uncommonly dreary for both of them, but Jean never wavered. She intended to become a famous

flyer and nothing was going to stand in her way. Curiously, it seems
that neither Jean nor her mother ever seriously considered employ-
ment to help with their financial difficulties. Both apparently felt
that genteel penury was preferable to any type of work.

Jean had one asset that saved the day: her striking good looks.
The London Aeroplane Club had among its members a number of
well-heeled young men. Drawn irresistibly to this exotic – and
absolutely stunning – creature from Down Under, they were soon
competing with one another in their efforts to seduce her. In this
they were probably unsuccessful – in spite of lending her not only
their aircraft but various sums of money which, as far as can be
determined, she never paid back. She seemed to accept these
favours as her due, a proper tribute to her beauty and promise. She
had already decided to attempt a solo flight to Australia as the first
step in what she *knew* would be a brilliant career. Without a
glimmer of embarrassment she would ask anyone for a loan, more
or less on the theory that if you ask a sufficiently large number of
people there's a good chance of eventually finding someone who
will say yes. One who did say yes was a New Zealand pilot in the
RAF, Fred Truman. Thoroughly smitten, he turned over his entire
gratuity of five hundred pounds to her when he left the service. It
was a sizable sum in the early thirties, sufficient to purchase a comfortable house. Although the money was supposed to be a loan to
enable her to secure her "B" licence, Jean kept Truman waiting for
four years before paying him back – and even then it is believed she
repaid only a portion of the debt. Debts never seemed to trouble
her. Great, prosperous days were just ahead, therefore she should
not be troubled by such trifling problems as a few pounds of other
people's money.

Jean was developing a remarkably arrogant attitude. After
obtaining her "A" licence, she was criticized by club officials for

flying in dangerous weather conditions. Curtly, she responded, "I'll do what I want when I want."[7] Like most of the long-distance flyers of the period, she had enormous confidence in her own ability, and she did in fact become one of the most skilled aviators of either sex. But it took time. In common with many of her contemporaries, she had her troubles with landings; the "tail draggers" of the period were forever trying to ground-loop and bite their own tails. She had one minor landing accident; she wasn't hurt, but her pride took a nasty rap, soon forgotten in the excitement of gaining her "B" (commercial) licence early in 1932. She immediately applied for a job with the highly successful "flying circus" then being run by the recently knighted Sir Alan Cobham – the first time in her life she had ever attempted to find work. To her chagrin, Cobham turned her down, telling her to "go away and get married."[8]

Fred Truman's funds were soon exhausted, so Jean found another benefactor, Victor Dorée, the son of a prosperous linen merchant. Victor fell hard for Jean. His family occupied a splendid residence close to Stag Lane airfield, where Victor, a licensed pilot, kept his private Gipsy Moth. In 1932, at the time of his meeting with Jean, he was thirty, she was twenty-three. Victor immediately began assisting Jean with the fees for her flying time – two pounds ten shillings per hour for dual instruction, and one pound ten shillings per hour for solo time. (Today that seems absurdly low, but at the time an hour's dual instruction was the equivalent of a week's wages for a family breadwinner, if he was lucky enough to have a job.) Victor made a practice of lending her his Gipsy Moth, which she promptly wrecked, characteristically leaving him with the bills for the repair work. She was quite candid about her intention of flying to Australia, less candid about her involvement with Victor while still supposedly engaged to Fred Truman. Early in

1933, Victor purchased a second Gipsy Moth and registered it jointly in the names of Jean Batten and V.H. Doree. The aircraft, which had previously belonged to the Prince of Wales, had been modified for long-distance flight with the installation of two extra fuel tanks and the elimination of the front cockpit, just as Amy Johnson's *Jason* had been three years earlier. Thus it was tailor-made for Jean.

The great day arrived at last. On a chilly April morning in 1933, Jean took off from Lympne shortly after 6 a.m. Her mother and the generous Victor saw her off. Weather conditions were good, and the flight began well. She flew to Marseille, then crossed the Mediterranean and landed at Rome's Littorio airport. There, she encountered an unforeseen difficulty. It was Sunday; fuel could not be obtained. She took off and headed down the coast to Naples, but it was the same story there. She would have to wait until Monday morning to obtain fuel. The Italians took their weekends seriously.

She left Naples the next day, arriving at Athens, then pushing on for Syria. Her navigation was excellent and she had no cause to worry about where she was, but she ran into violent weather in the lee of the Taurus Mountains. To her intense relief – and faint surprise – the little aircraft came through the ordeal in good order. Near the Turkish–Syrian border, she had to climb to 12,500 feet to clear the cloud that hugged the mountains, a dark, evil-looking mass that seemed to be waiting to ensnare her. Light-headed from lack of oxygen and numb with cold, she crossed the mountains and began the perilous descent on the other side in thick cloud. "Down, down, down I glided," she wrote later, "my eyes glued to the instrument board until the altimeter read 1,000 feet and still no sight of the ground. Lower still to 700 feet – 500 feet, and then suddenly, to my relief, I saw green fields and half an hour later landed on the French military airdrome at Aleppo, after a flight of nine hours from Athens."[9]

Now she ran into a terrifying series of violent sandstorms. Surviving one, she immediately encountered another. At one point the Moth snapped into a spin – a dangerous condition given the aircraft's complete lack of blind-flying instrumentation – but she was able to see enough to get safely on the ground.

She waited out the weather and took off, but daylight was ebbing away; she had to land again in semi-darkness in the desert. A few hours' sleep beside the Moth ended when she awoke to find herself surrounded by Arabs, who examined the aircraft and regarded her with expressions alternately lustful and larcenous. Unable to converse with them, she took cigarettes from her luggage and handed them over. They worked wonders. With good relations restored, she took off, heading for Karachi. She didn't get there. Another sandstorm brought her down in the wilds of Afghanistan – and her wheels sank into glutinous mud the moment she touched down, tipping the little biplane onto its nose, fracturing the wooden propeller. Although she obtained a new propeller at Karachi, she suffered a connecting rod failure which brought her first long-distance flight to an ignominious end, upside down in the sand, the wings buckled and twisted, the undercarriage torn away from the fuselage. Jean was shaken but unhurt – but she was broke, in debt, and didn't have the money to pay for transportation back to England.

Fate had a pleasant surprise in store. The Wakefield Oil representative in Karachi called to say that his boss, Lord Wakefield, had heard of her bad luck and was prepared to pay for her and the badly damaged Moth to return to England by sea. It was a remarkably generous gesture, and Jean disembarked in England confident that she would soon be taking off on another long-distance flight. She was to be disappointed, however. The next few months turned out to be the bleakest in her life – as they were for millions at that economically depressed time. Even the prosperous Doree family was having difficulties. There was no spare cash available for the flying pleasure of pretty girls, so Jean promptly terminated her relationship with Victor. He said later that there "were sides to her character he did not admire."[10]

Chronically hard up, Jean did not step into an airplane for five months; her membership in the London Aeroplane Club lapsed, and there were no admirers in sight with the means to help her. In her memoirs she said she had not a penny in the world; she and her mother often had nothing but a cup of tea for dinner. But work was still out of the question.

It says much for her extraordinary self-confidence that at this nadir in her fortunes she still expected to be flying to Australia in the near future. And she succeeded in getting Lord Wakefield – who had paid for her return to England – to help with her next flight. His assistance amounted to 400 pounds, not sufficient to finance the entire enterprise, but a good start. She paid 260 pounds for a second-hand Moth and took it to Brooklands, north of London. She and her mother had moved into rented accommodations nearby. As she had done at Stag Lane, Jean captured the hearts of several young men, and early in 1934, she became engaged to one of them. Edward Walter was a former officer in the Indian Army, now a stockbroker. His family had connections with *The Times* newspaper. He was enchanted with Jean and – inevitably – his enchantment was causing him to dig deep in his pockets.

In April 1934, she set off again. Her departure from Lympne was not major news, but she was beginning to become known. Some papers referred to her as the "Try-Again Girl." She reached Marseille in good order, but there the weather turned foul and the airfield was sodden from heavy rain. Determined as ever, Jean took off. The weather deteriorated, and near Rome she was flying almost blind as rain continued to pound down upon her. She came close to hitting a tall radio mast – then a row of trees materialized out of the murk. In trying to turn the Moth, Jean stalled and crash-landed in the Italian Navy's San Paolo radio station, near the basilica of St. Paul's. The Moth was badly damaged, but Jean escaped with cuts and bruises.

The incident did nothing to deter her; she immediately set to work to ready the Moth to continue the flight. Fortune beamed down on her and, incredibly, she found a derelict Moth in a hangar at the airport. An Italian airline pilot named Savelli owned the aircraft. He agreed that she could borrow the wings for one month, provided she paid two-thirds of the cost of reconditioning them. Jean agreed at once. After all, what was one debt more? She cabled Ted Walter and asked him to remove the propeller from his Moth and send it to her in Rome by air freight. Later she had him send her the lower wings of his aircraft so that she might return those belonging to Signor Savelli. Who owed what to whom is uncertain, but it was a matter of little importance to Jean.

She had probably forgotten about Signor Savelli when on May 8, 1934, Jean took off on her third attempt to fly to Australia. She made good time, the only untoward incident being at Nicosia, Cyprus, where she had to drop a smoke bomb because the windsock was not in operation; the locals thought that she was attacking the field. She pushed on, passing Karachi to Calcutta. She had four thousand miles to go to reach Darwin – and she had to weather a vast wall of thunderstorms to get there. She was tempted to turn back, "But the thought of failing a third time was too terrible."[11] Pride overcame fear. Stubborn courage sent her headlong into the vast cauldron of churning air and stygian gloom. Her instrument panel was only inches in front of her, but as it wasn't equipped with electric lighting she couldn't read it. The Moth lurched through the sky, staggering as if hit by gigantic fists. There would be brief respites from the terrifying conditions, then there was more, and still more. At times it seemed that the small biplane would break up in the sky. She could hear the structure crying out as if in pain at the intolerable treatment. But, in spite of it all, the stalwart little Moth held together.

On the twelfth day, Jean arrived at Singapore. She was two days ahead of Amy Johnson's time – and the world's press was at last taking an interest. Her picture – just as pretty as any film star, everyone said – adorned newspapers from New York to New South Wales.

Now she faced the last lap, the Timor Sea and its 560 miles of shark-infested water. It was by no means a sure thing, for Jean had no life jacket or inflatable dinghy. Engine failure would surely be the end. In London, in the newsroom of the *Daily Express*, Jean's mother told her story to eager reporters, making no mention of Lord Wakefield, Fred Truman, Victor Doree, or any of the others who had helped her daughter realize her ambitions. Both Jean and her mother seemed to feel that to acknowledge anyone else's help was somehow to diminish their own accomplishments.

On May 23, at 1:30 p.m., she arrived at Darwin, setting off a frenzy of publicity all over the world. In Britain, her story dominated the front pages. "JEANIUS" proclaimed the *Star*. The *Express* delighted in the fact that the first thing she asked for on clambering out of the Moth was a cup of tea. In Auckland, the papers called her "New Zealand's Amy"; she had beaten Johnson's time by an impressive four days. Cables of congratulation flooded in from all over the world, including such luminaries as Amy Johnson and Amelia Earhart. She had realized her ambition. She was famous. She was admired. Important people like Lord Wakefield called her by her first name. Soon her pretty features would be adorning advertisements for engine oil and other products. At Sydney, a boisterous crowd of some five thousand greeted her, many clinging to rooftops and hanging precariously from windows. She had to listen to orotund speeches from local politicians. She smiled through it all and made the appropriate comments about hoping that her flight would strengthen the bonds that bound the British Empire. Everyone loved her, so gallant, so attractive, so utterly *perfect*. Within hours, she had been outfitted in suitable style, in a lace gown, fur coat, and white silk shoes – all courtesy of the government of New South Wales. She attended countless banquets, dinners and receptions, with huge crowds cheering her wherever she went. Jean's world had undergone a metamorphosis; it was no longer the grim, cheerless place where there was never enough money and the newspapers seemed to talk of nothing but an ever-worsening economy – now it was a sunny, sublime kingdom where whatever she needed was magically hers, just for the asking. She stayed at the Hotel Australia without paying a penny. It was the same in Melbourne, and Canberra, and later in Brisbane, where she could hear the huge crowd cheering even as she glided in to land. She revelled in the adoration; yet, according to some, out of sight of the adoring public she tended to be cold and self-centred, a very lonely person and difficult to know. She sailed for New Zealand, where she was received with even greater warmth and enthusiasm than in Australia. "My sudden popularity surprised me," she wrote with a not very convincing attempt at modesty, "for I really did not expect it."[12] When answering questions about how she raised the money for the flight, she didn't mention Lord Wakefield or Fred Truman, Edward Walter, or Victor Doree; according to her, she and her mother had done it all, by diligently saving and scrimping.

Fan letters poured in every day, and with the aid of a secretary supplied for her use, she replied to every one, although she used "form" letters in most cases. As her fame and popularity grew, so did her opinion of herself. She became more and more demanding, more and more impatient if anything was not exactly in accordance with her wishes.

In April 1935, Jean flew her Gipsy Moth from Australia to England (in seventeen days, sixteen hours, fifteen minutes), becoming the first woman to make the round trip. Later that year, in a Percival Gull Six, she flew from Lympne to Natal in two days, thirteen hours, fifteen minutes, then she flew the South Atlantic from Senegal to Brazil. The following year, in the same Gull Six, she broke more records, flying 14,224 miles in eleven days and forty-five minutes. In October 1937, she broke the solo record for the return flight to Britain from Australia. It was the end of her career in aviation. She had realized her ambition: she had become one of the finest female pilots in the world, yet she is not remembered with the affection inspired by so many of her contemporaries.

CHAPTER SIXTEEN | *Incredible Journey*

A lex Henshaw and Howard Hughes had something in common: plenty of money and a total dedication to aviation. The son of a wealthy British businessman, Henshaw learned to fly in 1932, acquiring a succession of light aircraft, starting with a Gipsy Moth and progressing to a Comper Swift, a Leopard Moth, an Arrow Active, and eventually two Percival products: a Vega Gull and a single-seat Mew Gull. He achieved considerable success as a racing pilot and won many events, including the King's Cup. At the same time he developed his navigational skills and blind-flying ability, becoming a highly professional aviator.

In the late thirties, Henshaw decided to attempt a solo, there-and-back flight from England to South Africa in the diminutive Mew Gull. He wanted to beat the record set by Arthur Clouston and Betty Kirby-Green of five days, seventeen hours, and twenty-nine minutes in the Comet *Burberry*. First, however, he and his father surveyed the route together in their four-seat Vega Gull to determine whether the journey was feasible in the tiny Mew Gull.

They set off in March of 1938 and made their way from a wintry England to the arid heat of the Sahara, then followed a track cut into the sand – not always that easy, because frequent sandstorms obliterated every mark. Every ten kilometres, the French had placed *balises*, small concrete structures to assist the traveller, but the Henshaws soon found the system unreliable; in many locations, sandstorms had completely buried the markers. They flew on. For some time they had no clue as to their precise location – a daunting experience in that area. Then they spotted a truck belonging to the Compagnie Transaharienne heading for Colomb Bechar.

They followed the vehicle's tracks until declining oil pressure forced them down near Niamey, Nigeria, at nightfall. They needed more oil – and were fortunate to be able to make use of a ten-gallon drum sent out for Amy Johnson for her attempt on the Cape record in April 1936. The next morning saw rain of incredible intensity but mercifully brief duration. They gave the engine a fifty-hour check, a chore made utterly miserable by the swarms of insects that invaded the place. Soon thereafter, near Swakopmund, wild dogs were the problem; fortunately, they kept their distance. In Europe, Hitler had just taken over Austria, and the German population of Southwest Africa seemed convinced that in a matter of days the German fleet would be sailing in to reclaim the old pre-war colonies.

As the return journey began, Alex Henshaw felt the aching, sweating onset of a fever. He knew that it was malaria but insisted on continuing the flight, despite his father's pleas. Alex was only partially aware of what was going on as he flew the Gull north. At RAF Khartoum a medical officer examined him and promptly sent him to the nearest hospital, where he stayed for four days until he had recovered. The next stop was Cairo. From there they flew to

Tunis, then home after a stop at Lyon. And this was merely a survey flight; the solo trip was still to come.

During the Henshaws' absence, Jack Cross, of the highly innovative firm of Essex Aero in Gravesend, embarked on a series of modifications to the Mew Gull in preparation for the Cape flight. He made various adjustments to streamline the plane, enlarged the fuel tank, installed a constant speed de Havilland propeller, replaced the Gipsy Six R engine with a Series 11 engine, increased the oil capacity and cooling capability, and replaced the pilot's seat with a sponge rubber pad. In addition, he made various modifications to facilitate carrying nourishment, medical supplies, a 6.35 mm automatic, and other essential equipment. In its modified form, the Mew Gull, G-AEXF, had a sea-level top speed of 247 mph, a cruising speed at seven thousand feet of 235 mph, and a range of approximately two thousand miles. The aircraft was tailor-made to Alex Henshaw's dimensions, fitting him like a superbly streamlined glove. He had hoped to complete the journey to the Cape in three long stages, taking the eastern route over Africa. First, Cairo, then Khartoum, followed by Kisumu, then Entebbe or Nairobi, all of them subject to murderously high temperatures. "The most misleading aspect to be found in flying from these high and extremely hot airfields," he would write, "was the difficulty in selecting a point at which to abort a takeoff. If the wheels did not leave the ground, then at a critical point, with luck, it was possible to throttle back and bring the machine to a standstill; so often, however, particularly on a rare tarmac runway, I found that some aircraft would become airborne in less than half the length of the airfield but would float along just above the stall on the ground-effect cushion of air, deluding one into expecting a buildup of climbing speed before leaving the aerodrome."[1] He soon realized that he would be lucky to complete the odyssey in four, not three, legs.

Henshaw embarked on a strict regimen of riding and squash to prepare him for the ordeal, and at 3:30 on the chilly morning of February 5, 1939, he clambered into the Mew Gull wearing shorts in anticipation of the hot weather to come – to be greeted by the sight of fog rolling across the field. Henshaw refused to consider postponing his departure. The aircraft was pointing in the right direction. He waved farewell and opened the throttle.

"It may have been the pressing closeness of the fog, the long vortex of petrol vapour streaming over my head from the air vent in the main petrol tank, or the cold air improving the power output of a very well-tuned engine, but the machine appeared to accelerate with astonishing rapidity for the extremely heavy load it was carrying. . . . At all costs the tail of the machine had to be kept well up until ample flying speed had been reached: a takeoff with the tail down meant the probability of being rocketed into the air in a semi-stalled condition which would just invite disaster. The aerodrome was large and there was room to spare, so for a few seconds it was almost like travelling in an express train going through a tunnel, the wheels pattering over the hard ground; out of the corner of my eye the reflection of the exhaust flames against the dull fog produced a sensation of phenomenal speed."[2]

The wheels hit a slight rise in the ground and the aircraft launched itself into the air. In moments England's south coast slipped below; in slightly less than an hour the Mew Gull was over Paris. A quick calculation indicated a ground speed of 227.6 mph from takeoff. The flight was off to a good start. But the moon began to take on a watery aspect. Ice! Henshaw switched to carburetor heat. It meant a loss of power, but he had no choice. He pressed on, reaching Africa in record time and landing at Oran, Algiers. The next scheduled stop was Colomb Bechar, but Henshaw decided to continue to Gao, some 1,300 miles farther south. The desert seemed endless and utterly forbidding, the endless vista of sand broken only by the occasional sight of Arabs with camels and goats.

The Sahara airport at Gao had a Foreign Legion hangar plus a few mud and stone buildings. It was a hazardous field. The landing area was part of the Legion fort. It was not fenced off and Henshaw had seen Arabs with their children and animals strolling across it. In addition, with the dubious aid of a hurricane lamp and a lot of swirling sand, he could see little ahead.

Henshaw touched down on a smooth surface, only to encounter soft sand which caused the Mew Gull to swing violently, almost tipping onto her nose. But supplies of fuel – the correct eighty-seven-octane mixture – and oil were waiting. Henshaw tried to get an hour's sleep before setting off again, but he couldn't relax. Soon he was back on the airfield, shaking hands with the officers of the Foreign Legion and French air force who had been so helpful and hospitable. He strapped himself into the cockpit and prepared for takeoff – at night, with miserably inadequate illumination provided by a few hurricane lamps. The takeoff was nerve-grating, a noisy rushing along a dubious surface with the likelihood of hitting soft sand uppermost in his mind. "Easing the stick very slightly back I could feel the wheels pattering away in an effort to leave the ground; at the same moment I felt the ominous tug of the treacherous soft sand again but this time a quick, gentle pressure on the control column staggered the machine into the air."[3]

Not long after takeoff, Henshaw ran into shockingly violent weather. Rain battered the small aircraft "like so many machine guns"; turbulence hurled it around the sky; rulers, pencils, flashlights, and slide rules went spinning around the tiny cockpit. Henshaw braced himself against the rudder bar and bulkhead, but one period of violence saw his feet forced off the rudder bar, his ankles hitting the bottom of the fuel tank with "a resounding whack." In spite of the tight Sutton harness, his head struck the cabin roof a painful blow. In fact, the frenzied battering left him bruised and bleeding as he fought to maintain some semblance of control.

"At 14,000 feet I began to wonder if I should ever break out over the top of this storm and then I was aware of a noise that I had never before heard in an aircraft in flight, a deep ominous rumble that came over loud and vibrating above the noise of the engine and the rain still beating a hysterical tattoo on the cabin roof – thunder. Seconds after, the sky was rent with a blinding flash of blue and yellow light. We must have been passing between banks of massive cloud because in that flash I glimpsed towering black and grey pinnacles so far above me that I knew there was never any chance of me being able to fly above this storm – those clouds must have been 30,000 feet at least."[4]

All the warnings from the "experts" came back to haunt him. The Mew Gull was totally unsuitable for such a flight. He didn't have the experience or the equipment. Bail out? But where would he land? Jungle? Swamp? Sea? A moment later he ran out of the storm, gasping for air because he had been holding his breath, fiercely, as if preparing to dive into a swimming pool. He found to his intense relief that he was not far from Libreville – but as he began his approach he spotted a gully that had been dug right across his path. A few tense moments followed, requiring the utmost skill to get the little craft down without damage. The place reeked: "A steaming mist rose from among the trees and it did not need any imagination to visualize a bog of rotting wood and foliage at the foot of them. The air was literally putrid; it stank with an almost indescribable odour and was so thick and heavy that one felt one could grasp and squeeze it through one's fingers."[5]

When the time came for takeoff, Henshaw found the Mew Gull swinging badly as it encountered soft earth, an unpleasant lurching as if it was on the point of somersaulting. He had originally intended on a takeoff path that would have avoided the gully; instead he headed straight for it at full throttle, lowering the flaps at the right moment so that the Mew Gull literally leapt over the gully. Heart still thumping, he settled down to fly the next leg, to Mossamedes, just over a thousand miles away. It was a matter of following the western coast of Africa to the desolate little port.

Henshaw approached Mossamedes with the utmost caution. The sun was sinking, causing a confusing glare in the windshield. "It was my practice always when landing XF to open the one and only little side-window and to peer through this, as with any glare or darkness it was impossible to see through the cockpit screen at all. This little window was held back with a steel hook, more or less like a large fishhook with a sharp barb. Closing the throttle, I crossed my left hand over to the right-hand side of the cockpit to hook up the window: at that moment the machine struck a bad gust which jerked my arm, causing this steel barb to pierce my index finger. I immediately pulled, expecting the hook to slip out, but it was held by the barb and only worked deeper into the flesh."[6] By now Henshaw was nearing the ground; the Mew would undershoot unless he opened up the throttle. He tore his hand free, ripping open the flesh, causing blood to spurt freely as he levelled off for a successful landing. Opening the cockpit hood, he was greeted with a blast of superheated air. And crowds of Portuguese officials and natives, many of whom were smoking and had to be told to desist.

Henshaw arrived at Capetown at 18:58 GMT on February 6, 1939. Dirty, unshaven, blood-spattered, he had to endure the ordeal of meeting the mayor and a scrum of reporters armed with note-books at the ready. He tried to eat, but despite the fact that he had not eaten for some forty hours, he found it difficult to swallow the food. Not until the following morning, after a long sleep, was he able to eat. Then he had to depart on the return journey – made more difficult by the presence of coastal fog. He found Mossamedes by means of the fires lit there to aid him. But how to land with all this fog about? "I decided to keep the fires in sight and wait for some improvement. After what felt like years, the fog condensed itself into thick, rolling banks with fairly clear patches in between. By waiting for the right opportunity and manoeuvring for the best approach position, I was able to motor the Mew in a steady glide and eventually touch down with considerable apprehension between two of the large bonfires."[7]

Henshaw was astounded by the enthusiasm of the reception; an American told him that everyone had been up all night waiting for him. When it was time to go, Henshaw found his cockpit crammed with fruit and various gifts – almost all of which he had to give back, because there simply wasn't room for them in the tiny cabin. He left Mossamedes shortly before six in the morning, heading up the coast for Libreville and feeling increasingly confident about the trip. Everything was going well. But not for long. Near Pointe Noire, a wave of sickness assailed him. He attributed it to the intense, enervating heat. It worsened as he approached Libreville; the sweat poured off him and he shivered uncontrollably. Malaria, he thought, his old friend. He took two quinine tablets, hoping they would ward off a serious attack. It didn't help his condition when he flew over a vast area of "steaming, rotting" jungle. At an altitude of eight thousand feet, he could smell the nauseating odour. When he landed, the brakes brought the aircraft to a halt with the nose hanging over the excavations that had nearly brought him to disaster on the way south. He spent little time on the ground in spite of his state of health. The governor of Libreville wanted to meet him, but Henshaw could manage only a brief greeting, then he was back in the Mew Gull, accelerating across the coarse grass and climbing away into the tropical air.

Once safely airborne, Henshaw felt the fever and sickness returning. He stayed low, speeding over the sea while heavy rains battered the aircraft, finding tiny leaks in the cockpit cover and splashing onto him. He tried to concentrate, to focus on the many and varied problems that faced him. It was impossible. He could think only of the cramps that racked his body. He couldn't straighten his limbs, there wasn't room; he had to fight every moment to stay conscious.

Now a new problem faced him. He was lost. He had worked out a time fix to bring him over a large tributary running west from the Niger. But that was before the fever hit. Now he was ten minutes overdue without any sign of a river. Numbly, automatically, he continued to fly. He wondered whether to fly on into darkness until the engine stopped through lack of fuel. It was tempting. It required no effort. But the snag was, he would probably end up in the desert untold miles from a landing ground.

He became aware that the sun was going down. Laboriously, his brain clouded and uncooperative, he reasoned that he had intended to arrive at Gao by sunset, having run up the Niger for three hundred miles or more. Therefore, he reckoned, he was either west or east of his true track. On the way south he had drifted a little to the right, so, assuming similar conditions on the return trip, he had probably drifted to the left. Was that logical? He had to force his mind to work, to reason, to find a way out of this awful mess. He decided to turn ninety degrees to the east . . . and see if anything turned up.

He had become more or less resigned to failure when, to his relief, Henshaw saw a strip of dirty green water, and a landmark that he had previously noted on his chart. The Mew Gull had made good time, but the gallant little plane still had to be brought down safely at Gao:

"I cannot remember how many attempts I had at landing, it may have been two, three or even more. I can only remember rushing over the awful aerodrome at a speed that seemed too fast and saying to myself: I must be careful. Plenty of time. If there is the slightest doubt have another shot . . ."[8]

Henshaw had no recollection of landing or whether he taxied to the hangar or whether the Mew bogged down in the soft sand. He had vague memories of slumping over the controls, completely, utterly spent. Then someone was forcing a "horrid-tasting" liquid to his lips and he drifted into sleep.

He awoke, feeling better, the violent stomach cramps having subsided. He had planned to cross the Sahara at night, landing at Oran about midnight. Could he still do it? He consulted the medical officer at Gao and was given "a large celluloid-looking tablet" to swallow. A meal followed, but Henshaw was again unable to take more than a couple of mouthfuls. He had a few hours' rest, then embarked on the last lap of his remarkable journey.

He reached Oran at dawn, his head throbbing, clouding his thinking and dulling his sight. A worry kept nagging at him – the French officials might detain him, for he had avoided them on the journey south to save time. Now it looked as if his transgression was about to catch up with him. At that very moment, a French official was hurrying toward him, notebook in hand. Henshaw wondered how long the man would detain him; no doubt he would have a detailed list of his earlier offences. It was intolerable! The success of the entire enterprise could be jeopardized by this sweat-streaked wretch and his damned paperwork. Irritably, he turned to the man – only to be asked for an autograph and thanked profusely. Not a word about forms.

But now a new problem loomed. The meteorological office said that fog extended across all of northern France and southern England. Henshaw said he was leaving immediately, fog or no fog. It was an eventful journey. Soon after taking off, he ran into icing conditions. The telltale glare began to appear on the leading edge of the wings, innocuous enough at first glance but deadly if allowed to accumulate. When Henshaw had just come to the conclusion that he could not climb out of trouble, he became aware of a new problem: a warm fluid flowing over his face. Blood! His cuts and scrapes had opened up again. He looked around the cockpit for something to wipe the stuff away. There was nothing; he used his hand.

The Mew Gull emerged from the cloud into clear, calm air – but far below, the dense fog clung to the earth, a grey stratum blocking any sight of the ground: "I looked dully at the large chronometer on the instrument panel and calculated with a bitterness I have rarely felt that there was little over an hour to my destination, Gravesend. Now too tired and completely worn out to worry about the consequences I made up my mind to continue exactly on the compass course I had previously worked out, until my time showed 1345 hours. This was my ETA for Gravesend and at the precise moment I would attempt to get down – how, I did not know."[9]

Head still aching, every limb on fire, he spotted the Eiffel Tower's upper structure peeping through the fog like some metallic creature emerging from its lair. But then a beautiful sight: the fog looked as if it had been cut through with a knife. It was clearing! Beyond it, the Channel . . . and England! Before the ordeal could be over, however, he had to reach the coast and get the Mew Gull down safely. His thighs and buttocks ached from the many hours of flying sitting in the same position. His eyes blurred and went out of focus. The aircraft pitched up: "I groped to regain control and if there had been anything on which I could have put down immediately below I should have gone in for a landing, whatever the consequences."[10] He concentrated every fibre of his being on flying, on getting the Mew Gull across the Channel. Not far. A few more minutes.

He was startled by the abrupt appearance of tall chimneys and white storage tanks along a stretch of water. He knew where he was. Gravesend! The airport was just ahead! "I gently eased round in a shallow left-hand turn, conscious as I did so of an unfamiliar sea of faces on the ground below. I made the last circuit to bring me onto a westerly bearing so that I could use the longest part of the airfield nearest to the southern boundary. I had to make it at the first attempt; if I overshot, I doubted my ability to go through it all again."[11]

He didn't have to. In moments he was safely down. The crowd surged around, gasping when they saw his bloodstained face and shirt. Eager hands reached in and unbuckled his harness. As they eased him out of the cockpit, he drifted into oblivion, his incredible journey now history. He had broken all records, bettering the Clouston/Kirby-Green time by well over a day. Henshaw's official time was an extraordinary four days, ten hours, twenty minutes. His journey – 12,754 miles over desert, jungle, and ocean involving almost eighty hours of *solo* flying in a sadistically cramped cockpit – is still considered among the greatest of solo flights ever.

EPILOGUE

The end of the 1930s brought a unique chapter of aviation history to a close. For a few giddy years, long-distance flying had been the way to achieve fame and, with luck, fortune. Pilots became national heroes, admired and adored. But inevitably, their days of glory soon faded. The overwhelming reason was progress; long-distance flying simply became safer, and soon it became routine. Flights across the Atlantic had become a daily occurrence available to anybody with sufficient cash. Pan American commenced transatlantic mail and passenger service in May 1939 with the Boeing 314 flying boats. The British followed quickly with flights by the Short Empire boats of Imperial Airways, which became the first foreign airline to operate into the United States.

Other portents of the future soon followed. The Germans had already impressed the world with a non-stop flight by a Focke-Wulf Fw 200 Condor transport from Berlin to New York in August 1938. Not long after, the world's first jet-propelled aircraft, the Heinkel 178V1, made its first flight at Marienehe, Germany. Aviation was leaping ahead – and the pace quickened when war broke out. Soon, relatively inexperienced crews were flying military aircraft enormous distances. In October 1946, a Lockheed P2V Neptune of the U.S. Navy – the colourfully named *Truculent Turtle* – flew a remarkable 11,237 miles to establish a new long-distance flight record. But the new record-breakers were, in the main, corporations or countries. The costs had become too gigantic for individuals – although, curiously, the ultimate globe-girdling flight, in December 1986, would be a private venture. Aeronautical engineer Burt Rutan set out to design an aircraft so light and fuel-efficient that it could circumnavigate the world without refuelling. Dubbed *Voyager*, the extraordinary craft was built of low-density, high-strength carbon composites; the airframe weighed a mere 939 pounds, with an all-up empty weight of 2,680 pounds. The *Voyager*'s slender wings span 111 feet; two engines drive pusher and tractor propellers. Like the Wright brothers' original *Flyer*, the *Voyager* has a stabilizer in the front rather than on the tail. For the record-breaking flight, a crew of two was carried, Rutan's brother, Dick, a former fighter pilot, and Jeana Yeager. The unusual aircraft's departure from Edwards Air Force base in California was an unnerving echo of some of the hair-raising takeoffs of the great flights of earlier days. Precisely at 8:00 a.m. on December 14, the aircraft began to roll, the first time it had attempted a takeoff with a full load of fuel. It used up almost all of the fifteen thousand feet of the Edwards runway before lifting off, flexing its slim wings as if testing the air. The spectators breathed again. Nine days, three minutes, and forty-four seconds later, *Voyager* returned, having completed a journey of 26,178 miles at an average speed of 110 mph. One hundred and six pounds of fuel remained in the tank. The world had been well and truly girdled.

SWITCHES OFF

ALCOCK AND BROWN: Jack Alcock didn't have long to enjoy the triumph of his transatlantic flight with Brown. In December 1919, he lost his life in a Vickers Viking amphibian, crashing in fog. Brown died in 1948, having never stepped in another airplane after the famous transatlantic flight.

ITALO BALBO: Balbo's spectacular formation flight earned him an immediate promotion to the rank of air marshal; indeed, many considered him the heir-apparent to the Italian dictator. Mussolini became jealous of the acclaim Balbo received and packed him off to govern the colony of Libya. During the Second World War, he was shot down and killed, apparently by an Italian anti-aircraft battery on the cruiser *San Giorgio.* He was forty-four.

JEAN BATTEN: The beautiful Jean Batten never married. For several years after her flying career, she continued to live with her mother, moving from Jamaica to England, to Spain, to Tenerife, to Majorca. Her mother died in 1966, an event which plunged Jean into a depression that never really left her. Early in 1970, she visited Australia and New Zealand but made no effort to contact any old friends from her flying days. Many acquaintances pointed out the schizoid nature of her personality: one moment the gregarious, amusing individual, the next a reclusive individual, short-tempered, and utterly self-centred. She died in Majorca in November 1982 and was buried in a communal grave, although she was not poor at the time of her death – a curiously fitting end for an enigmatic individual.

LOUIS BLERIOT: Bleriot's *Type Onze* monoplane in which he flew the Channel became the prototype for a series of successful aircraft that won most of the big air races in the early years. With the onset of the Great War, the type was widely used in single-seat and two-seat form. Later in the war, Bleriot bought the Deperdussin company and produced hundreds of excellent Spad scouts, which equipped units of several Allied air forces. After the war, Bleriot's company produced a great number of experimental designs, but none enjoyed much commercial success. Bleriot himself suffered from heart disease in his later years; he died in Paris on August 1, 1937, at the age of sixty-five.

MRS. VICTOR BRUCE: Mrs. Bruce followed up her long-distance flying by running Air Dispatch, carrying light freight to the Continent, as well as operating an air ambulance service. In 1937, a stranger offered to buy her two ambulance aircraft, twin-engine De Havilland Dragons. How much? Mrs. Bruce, not taking the proposal seriously, demanded ten thousand pounds for the pair of them, considerably more than they were worth. To her surprise, the man agreed and said he would be back at dawn the next day with cash. He duly appeared, carrying a black bag from which he produced ten banknotes, each for one thousand pounds, a denomination totally outside Mrs. Bruce's experience. A bank confirmed that the money was genuine. Two pilots arrived by car to take over the Dragons, flying first to France, then on to Spain, where the aircraft were handed over to Franco's forces for use in the Spanish civil war. Their fate is unknown.

ALAN COBHAM: His far-ranging international flights generated a vast amount of publicity for Cobham. In succeeding years, he founded the successful National Aviation Day "flying circus" business with a collection of aircraft which he took around the country, putting on about a thousand performances between 1932 and 1935. Later, he formed Flight Refuelling and conducted experiments on the transferring of fuel between aircraft, a technique now practised by air forces around the world. Cobham died in 1973.

DOUGLAS CORRIGAN: With the proceeds of his adventurous flight to Europe, Corrigan purchased an orange ranch and settled down to a quiet life in the country. He died in 1995 at the age of eighty-eight.

AMELIA EARHART: Sixteen days after Amelia Earhart's disappearance, the U.S. Navy admitted defeat and called off the search. But the drama of her death wouldn't go away. Hollywood concocted a story, *Flight for Freedom,* involving a famous aviatrix who is asked by the U.S. Navy to fake her disappearance during a flight over the South Pacific so that aircraft could photograph Japanese island fortifications while they pretended to search for the flier. It so offended GP that he filed suit against the producers. The case was settled out of court. Since then, the legend has persisted that Amelia was engaged in some clandestine activity which led to her death. Amelia's fame has continued to grow; she is one of the most admired women of the twentieth century. Her death was a tragedy, yet one that spared her what she most dreaded, growing old and infirm.

RUTH ELDER: Following her extraordinarily lucky escape from the Atlantic, Ruth Elder had a moderately successful career in vaudeville. In 1929, she married Walter Camp, Jr., the president of Inspiration Pictures. That marriage was followed by four more. She said that the money from all the lucrative contracts she signed "slipped through my fingers and soon there was nothing." She died in 1977 at the age of seventy-three.

RENE FONCK: Although Fonck planned to make another attempt to fly the Atlantic after the September 1926 crash, it never took place. He died in Paris in June 1953.

HARRY HAWKER: Thirty-year-old Harry Hawker, an Australian by birth, Britain's pre-eminent test pilot, was a national hero after his transatlantic attempt with Mackenzie-Grieve. In 1921, a few days before the Aerial Derby, he was testing the Nieuport Goshawk that he planned to use in the race. He took off from Hendon, climbed steeply, stalled, and crashed, dying instantly. At the inquest into his death, Dr. Gardiner of Weybridge startled those present by revealing that Hawker would have lived only a few weeks anyway had he not crashed. Eighteen months earlier, he had seen a specialist about his painful back. X-rays had revealed a tubercular spine. The injured vertebrae had deteriorated, becoming a shell; it is believed that a haemorrhage occurred while he was flying the Goshawk, paralyzing his legs.

ALEX HENSHAW: After a distinguished career as a racing pilot in the thirties, Alex Henshaw spent the Second World War test-flying the Spitfire fighter with Jeffrey Quill, later becoming chief test-pilot at Supermarine's Castle Bromwich factory. He test flew an estimated 10 per cent of all the Spitfires built and was awarded the MBE for his wartime services. After the war, he embarked on a successful business career.

HOWARD HUGHES: Hughes survived the crash of the XF-11, but his health, both physical and mental, declined steadily. He became increasingly eccentric and dependent on drugs. He lived in hotels surrounded by a staff of sycophants, dying in April 1976 at the age of seventy.

AMY JOHNSON: Early in the Second World War, Amy joined the Air Transport Auxiliary after failing to become a member of the Special Operations Executive, an organization for which she hoped to fly agents in and out of the Continent. Her job with the ATA was more mundane: delivering new and repaired aircraft to bases all over the country, and in all sorts of weather. In January 1941, she set off from Squires Gate,

Blackpool, to deliver a twin-engine Oxford trainer, V3540, to Kidlington, 150 miles away. An Australian ATA pilot, Greg Piddocke, may have been among the last to see Amy alive. After obtaining the latest forecast, he and another pilot, Joe Shoesmith, ran out to Amy's Oxford to warn her about the poor weather, attracting her attention by jiggling the ailerons. Amy said she would go "over the top," meaning she would fly above the weather. She never arrived in Kidlington. Her aircraft crashed into the Thames Estuary. A naval officer, Walter Fletcher, tried to save her but died in the attempt.

CHARLES KINGSFORD SMITH: In 1932, Smithy was knighted for his services to aviation. Three years later, he set off in a Lockheed Altair named *Lady Southern Cross* to set a new England-to-Australia record. He vanished over the Bay of Bengal.

CHARLES LINDBERGH: Undoubtedly the most famous aviator in history, Lindbergh had little taste for fame. He found most aspects of his newfound notoriety distasteful, particularly the requests for him to endorse a variety of products, ranging from cigarettes to cereals, breeches to bread, and personal appearances on the stage or in movies. William Randolph Hearst wanted him to star opposite Marion Davies in a film about flying, a suggestion that probably made perfect sense to Hearst but appalled Lindy. After the glory of the Atlantic flight came many dark days. Although Lindbergh enjoyed a good marriage to Anne, the daughter of the U.S. ambassador to Mexico, their firstborn son was kidnapped and murdered. The Lindberghs moved to Europe and made several visits to Nazi Germany, an unpopular move in America. On his return home, Lindbergh became the leading spokesman for America First, a powerful isolationist movement. During the Second World War, Lindbergh was a test pilot and engaged in combat flying in the Pacific, but he never regained the popularity he had once enjoyed. He died in 1974.

BERYL MARKHAM: Soon after her epic flight across the Atlantic, Beryl Markham gave up aviation and returned to her first love, horses. She lived in Kenya for the rest of her life, dying in 1986.

HARRIET QUIMBY: Little more than two months after her cross-Channel flight, Harriet Quimby flew at the Harvard-Boston aviation meet, piloting a brand-new seventy-horsepower Bleriot monoplane finished in gleaming white. During the meet, she soared over Dorchester Bay with a passenger, William A.P. Dillard, one of the show's organizers. About five thousand spectators watched Harriet's Bleriot bank over the bay and head back for shore. She didn't make it. The culprit appeared to be turbulence. The Bleriot snapped into a dive. Appalled onlookers saw Willard, the passenger, tumble out at 1,500 feet. Moments later, the purple-clad figure of Harriet Quimby followed. A newspaper account described how the bodies turned over and over, "sharply silhouetted against the setting sun, a horrible picture to the spectators who knew what must be the inevitable outcome to the helpless aviatrice and her passenger." Both hit shallow water and died instantly. Relieved of the weight of its two passengers, the Bleriot glided down to a fairly gentle landing with little damage done. Glenn L. Martin, who later became a well-known aircraft manufacturer, witnessed the incident:

> I was watching Miss Quimby's flight and saw the entire unfortunate occurrence. Miss Quimby was returning from the lighthouse at full speed, she had dropped from her previous elevation of 4000 feet with the wind to 1000 feet against the wind in a rather short time. She had crossed the flying field and had made a half circle into the wind, over the bay. ... I was astonished at the speed she was making, with power on, gliding to a landing. On completing the half circle she lowered the elevator quickly, which slanted the machine to a steeper angle and caused a strong pressure on the upper side of the wings. The sudden change of direction, however slight, was enough to unseat both the pilot and passenger and throw both forward and out of the machine, Miss Quimby succeeding manager Willard by a fraction of a second. Her angle was not too great had the power been turned off. Aviators know that any quick movement of the elevator of a fast aeroplane will pitch one out of his seat unless strapped in. ... The weather was good. I

had been flying all afternoon and there was no rough air whatever. Had Miss Quimby and Willard been strapped in, the accident would not have occurred, in my opinion.

Like many early fliers, Harriet had been more troubled about the possibility of becoming trapped in a burning aircraft than being tossed out in mid-air.

CAL RODGERS: A few months after his cross-country odyssey, the irrepressible Cal Rodgers was back at Long Beach, flying over a crowd of several thousand gathered in an amusement park. A large flock of seagulls circled over a shoal of sardines in the water. Rodgers banked away from them, apparently stalled, and plunged into the Pacific. Spectators said the engine broke away and fell on Rodgers, killing him instantly. His widow later married Charles Wiggin, a mechanic and friend of Cal's.

ROSS SMITH: Soon after their highly successful flight to Australia, the Smith brothers began planning another trip, this time around the world. With a nice sense of history, they wanted to complete the flight early in 1922 to commemorate the four hundredth anniversary of the first circumnavigation by one of Ferdinand Magellan's ships. Fate had other ideas. On April 13, Ross Smith was at Brooklands with Jim Bennett who had been one of the crew on the Australian flight. They were there to test a Vickers Viking amphibian; Smith favoured the type for the forthcoming flight. Stan Cockerell, the Vickers test pilot, took Smith for a brief flight to check him out on the aircraft. After landing the Viking, Cockerell got out, leaving Smith to take over the controls. Smith was joined by Bennett (who had clung so tenaciously to the Vimy's rear fuselage at Singapore). They took off, climbing normally to about 1,500 feet. One wing suddenly snapped down. The Viking whirled into a spin and crashed into tall fir trees. Both occupants were killed instantly. Ironically, the Viking was the same type of aircraft in which Jack Alcock had been killed little more than a year before.

FERDINAND VON ZEPPELIN: The old count lived long enough to see his splendid "Zepps" become a dreaded weapon of war. When Germany invaded Belgium in August 1914, she had three commercial airships and six military dirigibles. At war's end, Germany had built eighty-eight airships, the latest being some 750 feet long. It was the size of the ships that seemed to terrify civilians, for the damage they inflicted was relatively insignificant. Besides, few weapons of war were as vulnerable as the huge dirigibles; an unexpected wind could scatter a formation in minutes. The count enjoyed good health until the latter stages of the war, when intestinal problems led to his death from pneumonia on March 8, 1917.

BIBLIOGRAPHY

Archbold, Rick. *Hindenburg*. Toronto: Viking Studio/Madison Press Books, 1994.

Barker, Ralph. *Great Mysteries of the Air*. London: Pan Books Ltd., 1968.

———— *Verdict on a Lost Flyer: The Story of Bill Lancaster*. London: Geo. G. Harrap, 1969.

Bedford, Mary, Duchess of. *The Flying Duchess*. London: Macdonald, 1968.

Berg, A. Scott. *Lindbergh*. New York: Berkley Books, 1998.

Boyne, Walter J. *The Smithsonian Book of Flight*. Washington: The Smithsonian Institution, 1987.

Bruce, the Hon. Mrs. Victor. *Nine Lives Plus*. London: Pelham Books, 1979.

Burke, John. *Winged Legend: The Story of Amelia Earhart*. London: Arthur Barker, 1970.

Cluett, Douglas, Joanna Nash, and Bob Learmonth. *The Great Days: Croydon Airport, 1928–1939*. London: Borough of Sutton Libraries and Arts Services, 1980.

Courtney, Frank T. *The Eighth Sea*. New York: Doubleday, 1972.

Cruddas, Colin. *Cobham: The Flying Years*. Stroud: The Chalford Publishing Company, 1997.

Gwynne-Jones, Terry. *Farther and Faster: Aviation's Adventuring Years*. Washington: The Smithsonian Institution, 1991.

Hack, Richard. *Hughes: The Private Diaries, Memos and Letters*. Beverly Hills: New Millennium Press, 2001.

Hallion, Richard P. *Designers and Test Pilots*. Alexandria, VA: Time-Life Books, 1983.

Henshaw, Alex. *The Flight of the Mew Gull: Record-breaking Flying in the 1930s*. Shrewsbury: Airlife Publishing, 1980.

Hinchliffe, Emilie. *The Return of Captain Hinchliffe*. London: Psychic Press, 1930.

Jackson, A.J. *British Civil Aircraft* (Vols. 1 & 2). London: Putnam, 1959, 1960.

Lindbergh, Charles. *The Spirit of St. Louis*. New York: Charles Scribner's Sons, 1953.

Lovell, Mary S. *Straight On Till Morning: The Biography of Beryl Markham*. New York: St. Martin's Press, 1987.

Luff, David. *Amy Johnson: Enigma in the Sky*. Shrewsbury: Airlife Publishing, 2002.

Mackersey, Ian. *Jean Batten: The Garbo of the Skies*. London: Macdonald & Co.,1990.

Markham, Beryl. *West With the Night*. New York: Houghton Miflin, 1942.

Montague, Richard. *Oceans, Poles and Airmen*. New York: Random House, 1971.

Moolman, Valerie. *Women Aloft*. Alexandria, VA: Time-Life Books, 1981.

Morrissey, Muriel Earhart, and Carol L. Osborne. *Amelia, My Courageous Sister*. Santa Clara: Osborne, 1987.

Nevin, David. *The Pathfinders*. Alexandria, VA: Time-Life Books, 1980.

O'Neil, Paul. *Barnstormers and Speed Kings*. Alexandria, VA: Time-Life Books, 1981.

Penrose, Harald. *British Aviation: The Adventuring Years 1920–1929*. London: Putnam & Co.,1973.

Roseberry, C.R. *The Challenging Skies*. New York: Doubleday, 1966.

Sterling, Brian B., and Frances N. *Forgotten Eagle: Wiley Post, America's Heroic Aviation Pioneer,* New York: Carroll & Graf, 2001.

Stewart, Oliver. *Of Flight and Flyers: An Aerospace Anthology.* London: Newnes, 1964.

Taylor, John W.R., and Kenneth Munson. *History of Aviation.* London: Octopus Books, 1973.

NOTES

CHAPTER ONE: THE EARLIEST BIRDS

1. *Good Housekeeping,* September 1912.
2. *Fly,* January 1912.

CHAPTER TWO: BIGGER CHALLENGES

1. *Current History,* July 1927.
2. *Journal of the Engineers' Club of Philadelphia,* November 1919.
3. Oliver Stewart, ed., *Of Flight and Flyers: An Aerospace Anthology* (London: Newnes, 1964) , p. 76.
4. *Journal of the Engineers' Club of Philadelphia,* November 1919.
5. *American Legion,* December 1969.
6. *Flight,* June 19, 1919.

CHAPTER FOUR: GIRDLING THE GLOBE

1. Harald Penrose, *British Aviation: The Adventuring Years* (London: Putnam, 1973), p. 258.

CHAPTER FIVE: ATLANTIC ANTICS

1. Charles A. Lindbergh, *The Spirit of St. Louis* (London: John Murray, 1953), p. 102.
2. Ibid., p. 138.
3. Ibid., p. 163.
4. *Hamilton Spectator*, May 17, 1927.
5. Lindbergh, *Spirit of St. Louis*, p. 185.
6. Ibid., p. 186,7.
7. Ibid., p. 492.
8. C.R. Roseberry, *The Challenging Skies* (New York: Doubleday, 1966), p. 100.
9. Richard Montague, *Oceans, Poles and Airmen* (New York: Random House, 1971), p. 183.

CHAPTER SEVEN: ENTER THE LADIES

1. Harald Penrose, *British Aviation: The Adventuring Years* (London: Putnam, 1973), p. 131.
2. Mary, Duchess of Bedford, *The Flying Duchess* (London: Macdonald, 1968), p. 96.
3. Ibid., p. 100.
4. Ibid., p. 102.
5. Ibid., p. 104.
6. Ibid., p. 110.
7. Ibid., p. 155.
8. Penrose, *British Aviation*, p. 550.
9. Douglas Cluett, Joanna Nash, and Bob Learmonth, *The Great Days: Croydon Airport, 1928–1939* (London: Borough of Sutton Libraries and Arts Services, 1980), p. 144.
10. Penrose, *British Aviation*, p. 550.
11. Emilie Hinchliffe, *The Return of Captain Hinchliffe* (London: Psychic Press, 1930), p. 109.
12. Hon. Mrs. Victor Bruce, *Nine Lives Plus,* (London: Pelham Books, 1979), p. 106.
13. Ibid., p. 107.
14. Ibid., p. 108.

CHAPTER EIGHT: "IMPENETRABLE MEDIOCRITY"

1. John Burke, *Winged Legend: The Story of Amelia Earhart* (London: Arthur Barker, 1970), p. 78.
2. Muriel Earhart Morrissey and Carol L. Osborne, *Amelia, My Courageous Sister* (Santa Clara: Osborne, 1987), p. 79.
3. Frank T. Courtney, *The Eighth Sea* (New York: Doubleday, 1972), p. 239.
4. Ibid., p.246.
5. Ibid., p. 246,7.

CHAPTER NINE: DISTANT DESTINATIONS

1. Rick Archbold, *Hindenburg* (Toronto: Viking Studio/Madison Press Books, 1994), p. 106.
2. Richard P. Hallion, *Designers and Test Pilots* (Alexandria, VA: Time-Life Books, 1983), p. 46.
3. John W.R. Taylor and Kenneth Munson, *History of Aviation* (London: Octopus Books, 1973), p. 247.
4. Brian B. and Frances N. Sterling, *Forgotten Eagle: Wiley Post, America's Heroic Aviation Pioneer* (New York: Carroll and Graf, 2001), p. 44.
5. David Nevin, *The Pathfinders* (Alexandria, VA: Time-Life Books, 1980), p. 142.
6. Nevin, *Pathfinders*, p. 150.
7. Oliver Stewart, ed., *Of Flight and Flyers: An Aerospace Anthology* (London: Newnes, 1964), p. 92.
8. Mary S. Lovell, *Straight On Till Morning: The Biography of Beryl Markham* (New York: St. Martin's Press, 1987), p. 167.
9. Ibid., p. 173.
10. Valerie Moolman, *Women Aloft* (Alexandria, VA: Time-Life Books, 1981), p. 93.

CHAPTER TEN: AMY, WONDERFUL AMY

1. Constance Babington Smith, *Amy Johnson* (London: Collins, 1967), p. 212.
2. Ibid., p. 216.

3. Ibid., p. 224.
4. Ibid., p. 225.
5. Douglas Cluett, Joanna Nash, and Bob Learmonth, *The Great Days: Croydon Airport 1928–1939* (London: Borough of Sutton Libraries and Arts Services, 1980), p. 162.

CHAPTER ELEVEN: THE MOLLISONS

1. Constance Babington Smith, *Amy Johnson* (London: Collins, 1967), p. 286.
2. David Luff, *Amy Johnson: Enigma in the Sky* (Shrewsbury: Airlife Publishing, 2002), p. 221.
3. Smith, *Amy Johnson,* p. 310.

CHAPTER TWELVE: BILL AND CHUBBIE

1. Ralph Barker, *Great Mysteries of the Air* (London: Pan Books, 1966), p. 200.

CHAPTER FOURTEEN: A COSTLY CONTEST

1. Muriel Earhart Morrissey and Carol L. Osborne, *Amelia, My Courageous Sister* (Santa Clara: Osborne, 1987), p. 190.
2. John Burke, *Winged Legend: The Story of Amelia Earhart* (London: Arthur Barker, 1970), p. 185.
3. Morrissey and Osborne, *Amelia*, p. 207.
4. Ibid., p. 208.

CHAPTER FIFTEEN: BREAKING MORE RECORDS

1. Richard P. Hallion, *Designers and Test Pilots* (Alexandria, VA: Time-Life Books, 1983), p. 57.
2. Richard Hack, *Hughes: The Private Diaries, Memos and Letters* (Beverly Hills: New Millennium Press, 2001), p. 113.
3. C.R. Roseberry, *The Challenging Skies* (New York: Doubleday, 1966), p. 466.
4. Ibid., p. 467.
5. Ibid., p. 468.

6. Oliver Stewart, ed., *Of Flight and Flyers: An Aerospace Anthology* (London: Newnes, 1964), p. 90.

7. Ian Mackersey, *Jean Batten: The Garbo of the Skies* (London: Macdonald & Co., 1990), p. 54.

8. Ibid., p. 67.

9. Ibid., p. 87.

10. Ibid., p. 109.

11. Ibid., p. 143.

12. Ibid., p. 170.

CHAPTER SIXTEEN: INCREDIBLE JOURNEY

1. Alex Henshaw, *The Flight of the Mew Gull,* (Shrewsbury: Airlife Publishing, 1980), p. 164.

2. Ibid., p. 180.

3. Ibid., p. 198.

4. Ibid., p. 201.

5. Ibid., p. 206.

6. Ibid., p. 208.

7. Ibid., p. 219.

8. Ibid., p. 224.

9. Ibid., p. 231.

10. Ibid., p. 232.

11. Ibid., p. 232.

INDEX

Acosta, Bert, 85, 95, 103, 104

Advertiser (London, Ontario), 106

Aerial Derby, 302

Aero and Automobile Exhibition, 72

Aero Club of America, 74

Aerodrome Hotel, Croydon, 198

Aeronautics Branch (U.S. Dept. of Commerce), 112

Aeroplane magazine, 234, 235, 239, 240

African Broadcasting Company, 233

Air Cruises, 217, 218

Air Dispatch, 300

Air King, 113

Air Service Training, 214

Air Taxis, 197

Air Transport Auxiliary (ATA), 218, 302

Alcock, Jack, 2, 25–54, 60, 78, 299, 306

Aleppo airfield, 279

Alington, C.G.M., 234, 235

Allen, Fred, 105

Allen, J.B., 124

Alley, Norman, 273

Alliott, 122

Aloha, 115, 116

Altair, Lockheed, 303

Altissish, Gerald, 273

America, 150

American Banker, 130

America First, 303

American Girl, 126–131

American Legation, Dublin, 264

American Legion, 78

American Newspaper Alliance, 87

American President Lines, 246

America Transoceanic Company, 103

Amerika, 21

Amundsen, Roald, 69

Ananias Club, 264

Ancker, Aage, 128, 129

Andrews, R., 66, 69

Angel of Los Angeles, 113

ANT-25, 239

Antoinette, 9

Anzani (engine), 9, 11

Aquitania, 137

Argonauts Inc., 75

Argosy, Armstrong Whitworth, 209

Armour Co., 16

Armstrong Whitworth, 179

Arregger, Hans, 194

Asahi, 174,176,177, 239

Ash, Thomas, 174

Associated Press, 19

Atlantic, Sopwith, 28, 36

Atwood, Harry, 15

Australian Flying Corps (AFC), 55, 56, 220

Australian National Airways (ANA) 164

Avenue Rapp, 79

Avian, Avro, 134,160, 220–222, 228, 230, 232

Avro 504, 71

Avro Ten, 164

Bachman, Carl, 265

Bagshaw, John, 235

Baidukov, Georgiy, 238

Bailey, Lady, 134

Bailey, Sir Abe, 134

Balbo, Italo, 268–272, 299

Balchen, Bernt, 81, 95, 103, 104, 159, 242

Baldonnel airport, 157, 158

Barendrecht, 131

Barnard, Charles, 122, 123

Baruch Bernard, 248

Batten Jean, 275–284

Beachey, Lincoln, 86

Beaumont, André, 23

Bedford, Duchess of, 121–125

Bedford, Duke of, 121

Beechcraft 17, 191, 217, 246

Bellanca aircraft, 85, 95–103, 176, 267

Bellinger, Pat, 31, 34

Belnap, Reginald K., 147

Belyakov, Alexander, 238

Bendix race, 245

Bennett, Floyd, 81, 159

Bennett, Jim, 56, 59, 60, 62, 305

Bentley, Dick, 134

Berle, Milton, 191

Berlin, 105

Berry, Captain Homer M., 75, 76

Bertaud, Lloyd, 86, 89, 95, 105, 108

Bird of Paradise, 110, 112

Blackburn, Norman, 142

Black Magic, 179

Black, Tom Campbell, 180, 188, 234

Blagoveshchensk, Siberia, 184

Blake, W.T., 63, 64, 68

Bleriot, Louis, 1, 7–14, 21, 22, 208, 209, 247, 300

Bleriot, Alice, 8

Bluebird Blackburn, 141–145

Blue Skies, 102

Boeing 247D, 178

Boeing 314, 297

Boll, Mabel, 136

Booth, P.A., 235

Bow, Clara, 215

Brackley, Major, 28, 43

Brancker, Sefton, 72, 124, 197

Breese, 113, 116

Bremen, 157

Brevoort Hotel, 74

Britannia Trophy, 215
Bromley, Harold, 171–173, 175, 183
Bronte, Emory, 111
Brooklyn Chamber of Commerce, 86
Brooklyn Children's Society, 274
Broome, L.E., 63, 64, 68
Broun, Heywood, 94
Brown, A.W., 2, 27–54, 60, 78, 299
Bruce, Mrs. Victor, 141–145, 300
Bryant, Leland, 113
Buckingham Palace, 41
Buffelen, John, 171, 174
Buhl CA-5, 112, 114
Burberry (Comet), 285
Burrell Tibbs' Flying Circus, 82
Byrd, Richard, 80, 95, 103, 146, 159, 248

C-5, 31,32
Cabral, S., 70
Camp, Walter, 301
Canuck, Curtiss, 182
Cape Cod, 176
Carberry, Baron, 188, 191, 192
Carisi, John, 95,96
Carling Brewery, 106
Carling, Sir John, 106, 108
Carlstrom, Victor, 23
Carmelite House, 47
Carpentier, Georges, 79
Carroll, Madeleine, 193
Carson, James, 226
Carter, Charles, 110,111
Carty, Arthur, 106
Catlin, Hugh, 173
Caudron G4, 56
Caurroy, Mary du, 121
Cedric, 156
Chamberlin, Clarence, 85, 86,
    95–102

Chaplin, Charles, 46
Chavez, George, 14
Chicago, 32
Chicago World's Fair (Century of
    Progress International
    Exposition), 268
Chichester, Francis, 210
Chkalov, Valeriy, 238
Chu Chin Chow, 46
Churchill, Winston, 53
Cirrus (engine), 221
City of Oakland, 110,111
City of Peoria, 113
City of Richmond, 273
City of Tacoma, 172
Civil Air Guard, 218
Clarke, Haden, 224
Clavier, 76, 77
Clifden, 51
Clouston, A.E., 235, 237, 285, 296
Clover Field, 67
Cobham, Alan, 71, 277, 300
Cochran Jaqueline, 180, 193, 248,
    253
Cockerell, Stan, 305
Coli, François, 79, 84
Columbia, 85, 88, 95, 100
Columbia Pictures, 193
Colvin, Charles, 99
Comet, de Havilland, 179, 217
Compagnie Transaharienne, 286
Connor, Harry, 258, 260
Consolidated Press, 94
Coolidge, President Calvin, 69, 133,
    150
Corrigan, Douglas, 262–265, 301
Cosgrove, William, 158
Cotton, Sidney, 214
Courtney, Frank, 152–157
Coutinho, Gago, 70

Covell, Lt., 113
Coward, Noël, 209, 225
Cowley, Earl of, 212
Crissey Field, 110
Cross, Jack, 87
Croydon Airport, 100, 101, 122, 124, 135, 145, 209, 215
Cudahy, John, 264
Culver City airfield, 254
Curtin, Lawrence, 76, 77
Curtiss Field, 77, 85
Curtiss NC flying boats, 128
Cushing, 253
Cyrano, 46

Daily Express, 218, 188, 282,
Daily Mail, 9–25, 42, 47, 209
Daily Mirror, 21, 105
Daily News, 13
Daimler works, 5
Dallas Spirit, 112, 115, 117
Daly's Theatre, 46
Damien, Father, 112
Darnell, Linda, 255
Davies, Marion, 303
Davis, Noel, 78, 112, 116
Davis, Bette, 262
Davis, W, 115
Dawn, 128
DB-A, 239
DC-2, Douglas, 178–180
DeCamp, Rosemary, 255
de Havilland Aeroplane Hire, 72
deHavilland, Geoffrey, 71, 180
del Prete, Carlo, 266
Denison House, 147
Deperdussin Company, 300
de Pinedo, 266–268
Department of Commerce, 263, 265
Deroche, Elise, 20

Dettmann, Professor, 166
DH9 (de Havilland), 57, 63, 64
DH50 (de Havilland), 72
Dillard, William A.P, 304
Dillenz, Lilli, 132
Dodge, Mrs. Robert L, 78
Dole Derby, 110–118, 163
Dole, James D., 109, 110, 116
Don Muang airfield, 203
Doran, Mildred, 112
Dorchester Hotel, 212
Dorée, Victor, 277, 280, 282, 284
Dornier Wal, 69, 71, 152–156
Double Eagle, BA, 234–236
Douglas, Donald, 67
Douglas, R.M., 56
Doumergue, President Gaston, 79
Dove, Sopwith, 56
Doyle, Jack, 193
Doyle, Sir Arthur Conan, 140
Dragon, de Havilland, 215, 216, 300
Drayton, 253
Drigh Road airfield, 201
Drouhin, Maurice, 99, 100
Drouhin, Mme., 99
Drummond-Hay, Lady Grace, 166
Drury Lane Theatre, 46
Ducrocq, Maurice, 26
Dupré, François, 217, 218
Durkin, William, 255
Durr, Ludwig, 165
Duval, General, 89

Eagle (Brooklyn), 118,
Eagle, B.A., 234–236
Eagle Farm airport, 164, 208
Eagle, Rolls-Royce, 26–28, 43, 64
Ealing, London, 46
Earhart, Amelia, 2, 147–152, 193, 216, 241–253, 283, 301

Easterwood, William, 175
Eckener, Hugo, 166–168, 170
Eichwaldt, Alvin, 115, 117
Elder, Ruth, 125–133, 301
El Encanto, 113, 114
Elliott, Mr., 248
Empress, 105
Emsco, 173–175
Endeavour, 137, 138, 140, 141
Engel, Joe, 256
Envoy, Airspeed, 234, 236, 237
Erwin, Bill, 112, 115, 117
Erwin, Constance, 112, 117
Escopette, 11
Essex Aero, 287
Europa, 157
Evening News (Albany), 94
Evening World (New York), 94
Explorer, Lockheed, 171, 172, 187

Fairey IIIC, 63, 70
Farman Company, 1, 14, 99
Felixstowe aircraft, 63
Fields, Charles, 95
Findlay, Max, 234, 237
Fitzmaurice , James, 157–160, 188,
     213
Fletcher, Walter, 303
Flight magazine, 197
Flight for Freedom, 301
Flight Refuelling, 301
Floyd Bennett Field, 176, 186, 258,
     261–263, 267, 273
The Flying Irishman, 265
Focke-Wulf 200 Condor, 297
Fokker aircraft, 80, 103–105, 107,
     110, 111, 120, 122, 146–148, 163,
     164
Fokker Anthony, 81, 103, 106
Fonck, Rene, 75–77, 80, 82, 302

Fontaine, Charles, 12–14
Ford Tri-motor, 159, 175, 176
Fort Worth, 175
Fowler, Robert, 15
Fox, Fairey, 180
Franco, Ramon, 71
Franklin (automobile), 241
Franklin Institute, 243
Fraser, G.H., 57
Friendship, 146, 242
Frobisher, 235
Frontiersman, 65, 66
Frost, John W., 112, 114

Gabrielle, 235, 236
Gallagher, James, 242
Garden City, 87, 88
Garros, Roland, 24
Gates Flying Circus, 176
Gatty, Harold, 173, 175, 183, 185
Gee Bee aircraft, 180
General Aircraft, 124
George V, 53, 160
George VI, 239
Germiston airport, 235
Gilfillan, Frederick, 166
Gilmore, Hugh, 153–157
Gilmour Oil, 178
Gipsy Moth, de Havilland, 121, 125,
     197, 277, 284
Gipsy (engine), 160, 161, 179, 287,
     189
Glendenning's Farm, 36
Glenn Martin aircraft, 145, 304
Goddard, Norman, 113, 114
Goebel, Art, 112, 115
Golden City, 236
Golden Eagle, BA, 112, 114, 116, 117
Goldsborough, Bryce, 128, 129
Good Samaritan Hospital, 255

Gordon, Louis "Slim," 149, 150

Goshawk Nieuport, 303

Gower, Lou, 149

Grace, Dick, 110, 111

Graf Zeppelin, 165–170, 176

Gran, Major, 28

Graphic (London), 210

Grayson, Frances, 128, 129, 148

Greater Baragwanath airfield, 235

Greener, Nick, 175

Grieve, Mackenzie, 28, 36–42, 131, 139, 302

Griffin, Benny, 113, 114

Gromov, Mikhail, 239

Grosvenor House, 180

Grosvenor House Hotel, 209, 213, 217

Guest, Mrs. Frederick, 146, 151

Gull, Percival, 218

Gull Six, Percival, 284

Guston, Gosta B., 255

Guthrie, Giles, 236, 237

Haldeman, George, 126, 129

Haldeman, Virginia, 131

Halford, Frank, 180

Hall, F.C., 183, 186

Hall, James, 256

Halse, Stanley, 235, 237

Hamel, Gustav, 21,22

Hamilton, Arthur H., 227

Hamilton, Leslie, 119, 120

Hampshire House Hotel, 262

Hancock, G. Allan, 163

Handley Page aircraft, 28, 42, 43, 53, 179

Haney, Al, 113

Hart, Hawker, 234

Hartman, Robert, 166

Harvey, A., 67, 68

Hatmaker, Consuelo, 79–80

Hawker, Harry, 28, 36–41, 131, 139, 302

Hawker, Mrs., 107

Hawkins, K.C., 113, 114

Hawk Speed Six, Miles, 234, 235, 237

Hearst company, 168

Hearst, William Randolph, 15, 18, 25,105, 174, 303

Heart's Content, 213, 215

Heath, Lady, 134, 135

Hegenberger, Lt., 110, 111

Heinkel 178VI, 298

Hell's Angels, 178, 256, 257

Henshaw, Alex, 285–296, 302

Hepburn, Katherine, 258, 262

Herald Tribune (New York), 250

Herndon, Hugh, Jr., 176, 210

Heston airfield, 142

Hill, James D., 105

Hinchliffe, Emilie, 140

Hinchliffe, Ray, 102, 136–140

Hindenburg, 170

Hinkler, Bert, 56, 160

Hinton,Walter, 31

His Majesty's theatre, 46

Hitchcock, Alfred, 209

Hoare, Sir Samuel, 137

Hochi Shimbun, 175

Holy Name Cathedral, Chicago, 271

Hoover, Herbert, 243

Hope, Walter, 197

Hosmer, Elwood, 153–157

Hotel Australia, 283

Howard, Edward, 113

Howell, C.E., 57

Hughes, Charles E., 94

Hughes, Howard, 2, 254–302

Hughes, William Morris, 55

Hughes H-I, 257
Hughes XF-II, 254, 255, 302
Hughesdon, Charles, 236
Humming Bird, de Havilland, 72
Humming Bird, Tremaine, 113
Humphreys, Jack, 210
Hutchinson, Blanche, 273
Hutchinson, Blanche Kathryn, 273
Hutchinson, George, 272–275
Hutchinson, Janet Lee, 273
Hyde Park Hotel, 218

Île de France, 145
Imperial Airways, 102, 201, 297
Imperial Aviation Society (Japan),
    175, 210
Inchcape, Lord, 135, 137, 138, 209
Iinuma, Masaaki, 239
Inspiration Pictures, 301
International Aircraft, 113
International Commissionon on
    Aerial Navigation, 178
International Zeppelin Transport
    Company, 167
Irving, Livingston, 113–115
Irwin, John R., 75
Islamov, Jacob, 76,77
Italian National Fascist Party, 265
Itasca, 251–253

Jason, 197, 201–210
Jenny, Curtiss (JN), 182
Jensen, Martin, 115–117
Jensen, Marguerita, 116
Johnson, Amy, 2, 179, 194–219, 228,
    229, 242, 282, 286, 302
Johnson, Kelly, 246
Johnson, Will, 200, 203
Jonas, Grace, 86
Jones, Harold S., 175, 176.

Junkers W33, 157–159
Jupiter engine, 75

Kangaroo, Blackburn, 57
Karklin, 168, 169
Kay, T.D., 56
Kennedy, Joseph, 264
Kennedy, Kathleen, 28, 46
Kerr, Admiral, 28, 43
Keystone Corp., 78
Khartoum (RAF), 286
Kidlington, 303
Kimball, "Doc," 129
Kingsford Smith, Charles, 162, 208,
    228, 303
Kirby-Green, Betty, 285, 296
KLM, 165, 179
Koehl, Hermann, 157–159, 188, 213
Knope, Cy, 112

Lady Southern Cross, 303
Lafayette Hotel, 74
La Guardia, Fiorello, 191, 261, 262
Laine, Mae, 182
Lamson, 253
Lancaster, Bill, 220–233
Lannin, J.J., 126, 127
Last Flight, 250
Latham, Hubert, 9, 11
Lawrance, Charles L., 83
Law, Ruth, 23
Le Bourget airport, 100, 104, 130,
    259, 267
Le Figaro, 13
Legge, General, 55
Legion of Frontiersmen, 65
Le Matin, 12
Leopard Moth, de Havilland, 285
Le Rhone engine, 56
Leslie's magazine, 20

Less Than Dust, 46
Lester's Field, 43
Levasseur PL8, 79
Levine, Charles, 85, 95–103, 136
Levine, Eloise, 86
Levine, Grace, 96
Levine, Isaac, 98
Lexington, 253
Liberty (engine), 31
Libinksky, 129
Lima, 132
Lincoln Abraham, 263
Lincoln, Garland, 112
Lindbergh, Anne, 207, 210, 303
Lindbergh, Charles A., 2, 82, 83,
    89–94, 109, 110, 125, 159, 207,
    210, 263, 267, 303
Lion, Napier, 66, 153
Little America camp, 82
Little, Charles, 32
Little, Robert, 122, 123
Littorio airport, 278
Llewellyn, David, 236
Lloyd George, David, 7
Lloyd, Harold, 215
Locatelli, Antonio, 69
Lockheed 10, 245–253
Lockheed 14 (Hudson), 258
Lockheed P2V Neptune, 298
Lockheed Vega, 112, 114, 183
London Aeroplane Club, 195, 210,
    275, 276, 280
Loraine, Robert, 14
Lord Talbot, 274
Lorraine-Dietrich, 79
Los Angeles, 169
Luke Field (Ford Island), 248
Lund, Richard, 259
Lurline, 243
Lusitania, 70

Lympne airfield, 229, 231, 278, 280
Lyon, Ben, 256
Lyon, Harry W., 163
LZ4, 3–7
LZ127, 165

McIntosh, J.C., 57
Mackay, Elsie, 135–139, 209
MacLaren, Stuart, 66, 67, 69
Macmillan, Norman, 63, 65, 68
MacRobertson race, 236
Maid of the Mountains, 46
Maitland, Lester, 110, 111
Majestic, 139
Malins, Geoffrey, 64, 65
Malloska, Bill, 117
Manhattan, 193
Manning, Harry, 246
Mantz, Paul, 243, 249, 251
Marconi Co., 153
Markham, Beryl, 187–193, 303
Markham, Mansfield, 187
Martin, Major, 67, 68
Martin-Baker, 196
Martin, James, 196, 203
Martinsyde, 28, 40, 57
Mary, 42
Mattern, Jimmy, 175
Matthews, G.C., 56
Mauretania, 28, 97
Maybach engines, 165
Medcalf, James, 106, 107
Men's Air Derby, 183
Messenger, 188, 189, 191
Mew Gull, Percival, 234–237,
    285–296
Mexborough, Earl of, 120
Meyer, Charles, 255
Miller, Allister, 236
Miller, "Chubbie," 221–232

Minchin, Fred, 119, 120
Mines Field, 169, 256
Minnewaska, 156
Miss Doran, 112, 114–117
Miss Dorothy, 218
Miss Liverpool, 234
Miss Veedol, 176, 177
Mitchell Field, 86
Mitscher, Marc, 34
Mitsubishi, 97, 239
Moisant International Aviators, 20
Moll (pilot), 179
Mollison, Jim, 179, 188, 189, 191,
    192, 208, 210–219, 242
Monocoupe, 265
Monospar, 124
Morgan, C.F.W., 28, 36, 39, 40
Mostyn, Most Rev. Francis, 120
Moth, de Havilland, 135, 141, 195,
    201, 202, 210, 221, 279–282, 285
Mount Pearl, 43, 45
Mulligan, Dennis, 264
Murray, Mr., 143
Mussolini, Benito, 95, 102, 265

National Aeronautics Association
    (NAA), 112
Nagaoka, General, 210
Naldera, 208
Napier, 153
National Aviation Day, 300
Navy-Curtiss ("Nancy"), 30
NC-1, 30–36
NC-2, 30–36
NC-3, 30–36
NC-4, 30–36
Netcher, George E., 250.
Nevada Airlines, 183
Newhill, Charles, 258
Newcastle, 28

New York World's Fair 1939, 258, 260
Nichols, Beverley, 209
Nissen, Greta, 256
Noonan, Fred, 246–253
Northcliffe, Lord, 25, 47, 52, 55, 174
Novello, Ivor, 209
Noville, George, 75, 81, 95, 103
Noyes, Blanche, 246
Nungesser, Charles, 78, 84

O'Neil, Dr. 190
Oakland Municipal Airport, 110,
    244
October Field, Moscow, 184
Ogden, Henry M., 69
Oiseau Blanc, 79, 80
Oiseau Bleu, 99
Okamoto, S., 172
Oklahoma, 113, 114
Oklahoma State Industrial
    Commission, 182
Oklahoma State Reformatory, 182
Old Glory, 105, 107, 108
Ontario Provincial Air Service, 106
Orion, Lockheed, 187
Orteig, Raymond, 74
The Outlaw, 257
Oxford Street, 13
Oxford, Airspeed, 303

Pabco Pacific Flyer, 113–115
Pacific, 174
Palmer, Richard W., 257
Pan American Airlines, 297
Pangborn, Clyde, 176, 210
Paramount Pictures, 193, 255
Parer, Ray, 57
Paris-Soir, 218
Paris Peace Conference, 55
Parkhurst, Charles W., 113

Parmentier (pilot), 179

Pasadena Race Course, 19

Paulhan, Louis, 25

Payne, Philip, 105

Peachey, C.D., 234

Peary, Admiral, 23

Pedlar, Augie, 112, 114, 115

Pendine, Wales, 216

Peninsular and Orient Line, 135

Percival, Edgar, 188, 189, 217

Perry, Cdr., 15

Peters, Jean, 255

Phillips, Frank, 113

Phorus, 206

Pickford, Mary, 46

Piddocke, Greg, 303

Pierce, Fred, 153–157

Pioneer Instruments, 99

Plenderleith, J., 66, 69

Ponta Delgada, Azores, 36

Pope Pius XI, 102

Portage Avenue, Edmonton, 185

Portsmouth, Southsea, and Isle of
    Wight Aviation Ltd., 218

Post-Standard (Syracuse), 118

Postjager Pander S-4, 180

Post, Mae, 261

Post, Wiley, 181–187

Poulet, Etienne, 56

Preston, F/L, 124, 125

Pride of Los Angeles, 113

Priestley, J.B., 209

Princess Lowenstein, 119

Punjab Regiment, 201

Pup, Sopwith, 56

Purdue University, 245, 248

Puss Moth, de Havilland, 124, 160,
    210, 211, 213, 228

Putnam, George Palmer, 151,
    241–253

Quaglino's restaurant, 212

Queen Mary, 192

Quill, Jeffrey, 302

Quimby, Harriet, 1, 20–23, 119, 267,
    304

R-34, 31

Rachmaninoff, Sergei, 75

Railey, Hilton H., 147, 151

Raymor, 39, 40

Raynham, Frederick, 28, 36, 39, 40

Read, Albert, 31

Redpath, Peter, 273

Red Rose, 221

Richey, Helen, 245

Richmond, 68, 69

Rich, Pauline, 112

Ritz-Carlton Hotel, 156, 191

Robbins, Reginald, 175, 176

Robertson, Macpherson, 177, 180

Robin, Curtiss, 86, 263

Rodgers, Arthur, 113

Rodgers, Cal, 1, 15–20, 305

Rodgers, Mabel, 16, 17

Roe, A.V., 1, 209

Rogers, Will, 187

Roosevelt Dam, 266

Roosevelt, Eleanor, 130

Roosevelt Field, 76, 89, 95, 126, 128,
    172, 183, 186, 263

Roosevelt, Franklin D., 271

Rosendahl Charles, 169

Rose Tommy, 234–236

Roxy Theater, 80

Royal Aeronautical Society, 197

Royal Air Force (RAF), 220

Royal Flying Corps (RFC), 27, 71

Royal Naval Air Service (RNAS), 26

Royal Windsor, 106, 107

Royce, Charles, 14

Ruff, Joseph, 273
Russell, Lord Herbrand, 121
Russell, Jane, 255, 257
Rutan, Burt, 298
Rutan, Dick, 298
Ryan Co., 82, 89, 90, 93, 111
Ryrie, Lady, 222

S-35, 76, 77
Safari, 193
Saint-Exupéry, Antoine de, 193
San Giorgio, 299
San Paolo (radio station), 281
San Raphael, 120, 121
Santa Lucia, 267
Santa Maria, 266
Santa Maria II, 267
Savelli (airline pilot), 281
Savoia-Marchetti, 266–268
Savoy Hotel, 135
Schiller, Duke, 106
Schlesinger, Isaac, 192, 193, 233–235
Schluter, Paul, 115, 116
Schneider Cup races, 102
Scott, Charles, 180, 236, 237
Scott, Gordon, 114
Seafarer, 215, 216
Segrave Trophy, 215
Seletar (RAF airfield), 203
Selfridge Field, 270
Selfridge's, 13, 42
Semarang, Indonesia, 204
Shalom, 265
Sharpe, Lucien, 72
Sheffield University, 194
Shell Oil, 153
The Sheik, 143
Shiers, Wally, 56, 62
Shoesmith, Joe, 303
Shoulder Arms, 46

Sinclair, Gordon, 137, 139
Sirius, Lockheed, 173
Sketch, 210
Smith, Dean, 86
Smith, Ernie, 110, 111
Smith, Fred, 101, 102
Smith, Keith, 56–62
Smith, Lowell, 68, 69
Smith, Ross, 55–62, 305
Smith, Thomas H., 265
Smith, Victor, 236
Smith, Wesley, 180
Snody, Allan, 76
Southern Cloud, 164
Southern Cross, 165
Southern Cross Junior, 165
Southern Cross Minor, 228, 229
Sparrowhawk, Miles, 234, 236
Spectator (Hamilton), 302
Sperry autopilot, 186
Spider, 122–124
Spindler, Arthur, 157
Spitfire, Vickers, 302
Spirit of St. Louis, 83, 85, 91, 93, 95,
    98, 263
Stag Lane, London, 195, 197
Stalin, Josef, 238, 260
Stalinskiymarshrut, 238
Star (Britain), 282
Star (Johannesburg), 134
Stinson Detroiter, 106, 107, 126, 129,
    130, 137
Stoddard, Richard, 258–260
Stultz, Wilmer, 128, 129, 146,
    148–151
Sun (Baltimore), 94
Sunday Dispatch, 214
Sunstedt, Hugo, 29
Surrey Flying Service, 101
Swell Hogan, 256

Swift, Comper, 285
Swope, Herbert Bayard, 159
Swope Park, 18
Sydney, 61

Tachikawa airfield, 145
Tachikawa A-26, 240
Texas State Fair, 18
Thaden, Louise, 246
That's My Story, 265
The Times, 101, 280
Third Light Horse Regiment, 55
Thomas Morse scout biplane, 256
Thurlow, Tommy, 258
Towers, John, 30
Trans-Saharan Co., 230
TravelAir, 110–112, 114, 116
Tremaine, 113
Tribune (Oakland), 244
Truman, Fred, 276, 282, 284
Tsukagoshi, Kenji, 239
Tully, Terence, 106, 107
Tupolev, Andrei, 238
Turner, Lana, 255
Turner, Roscoe, 178
20 Hrs. 40 Min., 151
Two Arabian Nights, 256

U.S. Air Service, 66, 67
U.S. Army Air Corps, 110
Ulm, Charles T.P., 162–164, 208
Union Airways, 236
Universal Studios, 255

Valentino, Rudolph, 143
Valprato, 156
Van Dyke, Evert, 165
Vedrines, Jules, 24, 56
Vega Gull, Percival, 188, 234, 236, 237, 285

Vega, Lockheed, 171, 173, 175, 176, 186, 242–244
Viceroy, Airspeed, 180
Viking, Vickers, 66, 299, 305, 306
Vimy, Vickers, 26, 42–53, 59–62
Vin Fiz, 16
Virginian-Pilot, 118
von Huenefeld, Baron, 157–188, 213
Voyager, 298
Vulture, Vickers, 66–68

Wade, Leigh, 69, 85
Waggener, Lt., 113
Wakefield, Lord, 197, 280, 282, 284
Walker, Jimmy, 133, 242
Wallaby, Sopwith, 56
Waller, Ken, 234
Walter, Edward, 280, 281, 284
Wanamaker, Rodman, 80, 81
Ward, Dorothy, 218
Warner Brothers, 178, 256
Warner, James, 163
Wellesley, Diana, 212
Western Electric, 246
West with the Night, 193
Whalen, Grover, 261, 262
Wheeler Field, 111, 115, 164, 244, 253
Whirlwind engine, 83, 127, 163
Wiggin, Charles, 305
Wilkins, Sir George H., 57, 163, 168
Wilson, President Woodrow, 23
Winchester Castle, 210, 212
Wings, 110, 178
Winnie Mae, 173, 183–187
Woburn Abbey, 125
Womack, Lyle, 126, 127, 131, 133
Wood, Phil, 106
Wood, J.C.P., 29

Woolaroc, 112, 115, 116
Wooster, Stanton, 78
World Cruiser, Douglas, 68
World Jungle Compound, 178
World (New York), 94, 159
Wright EX, 16
Wright J6-5, 263

Yeager, Jeana, 298
Yoshihara, Seiji, 175

Zeppelin Co., 3–7, 165, 167, 247,
  306
Ziegfeld, Florenz, 133
Zimmerman, Jules, 255